ite
bel

Items should be r
below. Items may
writing or by telepho
number on the barco
items and will include r
or loss of items will be

The Brothers Behan

by

Brian Behan

with

Aubrey Dillon-Malone

ASHFIELD
Press

This book was typeset by
Gough Typesetting Services for
ASHFIELD PRESS
an imprint of Blackhall Publishing
26 Eustace Street
Dublin 2
Ireland

e-mail: blackhall@tinet.ie

ISBN: 1 901658 16 3

A catalogue record for this book is available

from the British Library.

Printed in Ireland by
Betaprint Ltd.

Contents

Acknowledgements

I dedicate this book to Aubrey, whose energy and determination made it all possible.

Brian Behan

I would especially like to thank Paula Furlong for giving me access to many videos, tapes, newspaper articles and general memorabilia associated with Brendan. Also Gus Smith, Ben Kiely, John B Keane and Mick McCarthy for sharing memories and yarns with me. Michael O'Sullivan gave me some very useful contacts and Steven Darcy of RTÉ was helpful in providing footage of Brendan's television appearances. The good folk of the National Library and the Pearse Gilbert Library were, as ever, obliging to a fault in tracking down often arcane source material. To all these and many more, sincere thanks.

Aubrey Dillon-Malone

I remember him riding the air
A mixture of Puck and the gobán saor
With ruffled shirt and hair astray
In Grafton Street on a gusty day
Respectable gents and maiden aunts
Held tightly in their briefs and pants
Lest their bowels might be disturbed
Hearing genius roaring by
Language of love and obscenity
The words he uttered were very simple,
"Your mind is as small as a knacker's thimble,
Scarperer, joxer, fluther, brother,
Hold your hour and have another."

Dominic O'Riordan

Introduction

His real name wasn't Brendan, but Francis. And though he beefed up his working class roots, the reality is that our family back ground was more akin to fallen grandeur. He also liked to tout the notion that his roots were distinctly unliterary, but our father read Thackeray and Dickens to us from an early age. Not only that, but Brendan could read all of Robert Emmet's famous *Speech from the Dock* from the tender age of six. These are just some of the contradictions inherent in a man who spent most of his early years railing against the British presence in Ireland, but whose own presence in Britain kick-started his international reputation.

Brendan highlighted this contradiction when he said, "The British are a wonderful race. First they put me in jail and then they made me rich!"

The point is, if he was dependent on the meagre pickings he earned from The Pike, even playing to sell-out houses, he would never have been able to give up what he called the "retail" business, i.e. his *Irish Press* journalism. It was only when his works were staged across the pond that the big bread started to come in. And I had something of the same experience myself in my own tin-pot way. I would dearly love to have lived my life in Ireland, but at that time it wasn't on for the Irish to put a poor working class lad like myself into university like the English did. That's the hard fact of it.

Max Beerbohm believed that the world was divided into two types of people: guests and hosts. Brendan preferred to think it was divided into patients and nurses – adding rather surprisingly that he saw himself in the latter capacity.

His impersonator and friend Niall Toibin says he went about that unlikely vocation "not with bedpans or enemas or recitals of the Joyful Mysteries" (as if we needed to be told) but rather by spreading hilarity in the most unlikely situations. "His output in this department," says Toibin, "was so unpredictable that many of his finest performances were lost in the prattle of punters at Leopardstown or the market pubs at daybreak". But enough have survived to give books like this one the oxygen they need to bring them to life.

Since Brendan died, a lot of stories have grown up about him, maybe too many. Some of these are true, some have been juiced up and some are mythical. They've been tailored to fit the man the tellers think he was. If you throw a stone in Dublin you'll meet someone who has one of these stories to tell – normally at closing time in some inner-city pub or other. Usually this will be your Dubbalin 'character', a relic of oul' dacency . . . or maybe a bit of a bowsie. Brendan attracted both of these types. Many people will tell you he was both types himself.

I'm open to opinions on that score. From my knowledge of him he was both angel and devil, and you never knew what was coming next. Neither, for that matter, did he. He was a mercurial individual, a victim not only of booze and money, but also the image of him that the media created. Like Narcissus, he fell in love with his reflection.

Brendan was really a throwback to pagan times, to when the Irish were a lot more rollicking and boisterous. The Dublin of the fifties didn't suit him: it was too hypocritical and Church-ridden. In fact I think it drove him to drink.

There were three major dilemmas in his life. The first was political. He was a passionate republican but he saw the movement folding before his eyes. The second was sexual. If we're to believe what we read, he couldn't make up his mind if he loved women or men more. And the third was his ambivalent feelings for Ma and Da. He hated Da and worshipped Ma. I don't know if he lived long enough to work out any of these dilemmas. In fact they probably became more intensified as time went on. Brendan laughed and the world laughed with him, but when he wept he wept alone. "I'm not the enjoying kind," he said in a rare confessional moment, but who could believe him? We didn't want to face up to the truth that he sang his grief like Pagliacci.

He was a man I loved throughout his short life, even though we didn't see one another all that much in his last years. I never liked pushing myself on him after he became famous in case he thought I was trying to cadge drinks, or exploit his celebrity status, but we got on well whenever we met. We shared a love of life and literature, a hatred of cant and an ambition to help the small man wherever possible. We liked to comfort the afflicted and afflict the comfortable. As he said himself, "The fighting poor were my people." And as I said, "My mission in life is to scourge holy people."

He came over to me in England one time when I was organising a strike and he said he admired what I was up to. Those words were music to my ears – a blessing from St Brendan! You had to know him to realise he could have that effect on you. It was like oxygen – even when he was abusing you. Dominic put it like this, "He had such a way with him that would make you go to hell and back and think nothing of it. Then of course he was kind and gentle and above all shy. Whatever he did I imitated, whatever he read I read, whatever he sang, or thought worth singing, I learned."

Many have tried to define the chameleon character that was Brendan Behan, most using clichés like 'rombustious', 'rowdy', 'brawling' or 'boozy', but the real Brendan was as complex as any of us, a unique composite of scallywag and angel. He was gentle and violent, religious and blasphemous, compassionate and cruel, purposeful and wild, iconoclastic and old-fashioned, ambitious and self-destructive . . . and any other contradiction you care to mention.

Brendan always had to be the leader of the pack. More often than not he got the attention he craved. When he didn't he became difficult, but you could never stay mad at him for long. Even – or especially – when he was drunk. He spoke often about himself in typically obscure fashion, but one imagines Brendan would have been as bored by analyses of what made him tick as he was by exegeses on the 'hidden' meanings of his plays. As Ben Kiely suggested, he was "the thing itself", so maybe we should leave it at that. His cup was always overflowing, and not just with Guinness. His life was his monument just as his writings were.

He could be sweet but also prickly, telling perfect strangers what to do with themselves after little or no provocation, drunk or sober. And of course it worked the other way too. Niall Toibin tells a story of Brendan being barred from a pub he had never even been in before, his reputation having preceded him. In a situation like this the temptation is to live down to expectations, to let a self-fulfilling prophecy take root. If you are going to be condemned, you might as well commit the crime – even after the sentence has been imposed.

To the cynics, his talent was all wrapped up in his personality and daredevil exploits; for them, man and showman were one, and as soon as he stopped being controversial, or died, his works would die too. But as I write they're enjoying a renaissance of sorts, and being studied consistently at university level. He will never become the subject of obtuse theses like Joyce or Beckett, nor would he ever have wanted to, but his writings have received enough praise from respected critics to assure us that even if he had never supped a pint, insulted a journalist or fallen into a pothole at the dead of night as the result of imbibing one too many pints of Arthur Guinness' heady brew, he would still be a writer who mattered in the Irish literary pantheon. Posterity, in other words, has given Brendan the respect that often evaded him throughout his all-too-short life, albeit for many of the wrong reasons.

Nothing is worse than pretentious exegeses or attempts to analyse the un-analysable. Brendan was a better writer in his early days, before people put names on him or massaged his ego. Too many people tried to push him in directions he didn't want to go, with the result that he became self-conscious about his talent, which was the worst thing that could have happened to him. He would have been much better off if he had had a bigger body of work behind him before he became a celebrity. Frank McCourt has been able to handle fame because it came to him late in life. When it came to Brendan, he hadn't acquired enough discipline in his work routines. Many writers say it's not the writing that's important, but the re-writing. That was one place he fell down.

He was impatient to get stuff out, to reach the masses by hook or by crook. He may have said a writer's first duty was to let down his country, but he also felt his country let *him* down. He made the grade across the water, let us not forget, before he made it here. When he became a household name in England, Ireland (as is its wont) sat up and wondered if it had missed something. And it seems as if that will always go on.

But back to the book. Frank O'Connor wrote an article shortly after Brendan died in which he said that he would far prefer some young writer to gather up the hundreds of stories circulating about Brendan and put them in a book rather than have to suffer something posthumous from Brendan himself. I take his point. He felt the well was dry, and he didn't look forward to *Brendan Behan's New York*, which, he felt, would neither be Brendan nor New York. And maybe he was right.

Well I'm not a young writer, nor is my co-author, but together we've cobbled together the kind of confection I think O'Connor was suggesting. He felt a book of this nature would tell scholars and critics a hundred years from now much more about what Brendan was about than any number of dry PhDs. Let the reader be the judge of that.

I remember him with his tousled hair and his kiss curl, with the three-quarter smile that could either be taken as bashfulness or arrogance. I remember the buttonless shirt and the trousers more off than on, breaking into song in the middle of a conversation for whatever reason. He was as aggressive as he was emotionally vulnerable – and probably for the same reason.

Earthy insights tripped off his tongue for many years before drink took its toll and he began the lonely trek to Boot Hill while still a relatively young man. People remember him either as a loveable rascal or a pain in the arse – or maybe both – but he followed his own lights, and darknesses, right to the bitter end. What more can we ask of anyone, saint or sinner, than that? All we owe life is a death and Brendan gave it that. Before his time, surely, but with a dignity and resignation that confounded many, myself included.

"A joke never failed him while his lips could move," Ben Kiely said, adding that he had, "a sort of boyish bewilderment at the crazy state he observed the world to be in."

Ma phrased it nicely, "He swung the world by the tail."

The revival of his reputation, in any case, goes on apace. Apart from the projected biopic of his life and the biography by Michael O'Sullivan, in March 1997 the original manuscript of his little-known short story "Christmas Eve in the Graveyard" fetched £5,400 at auction – which isn't bad for an author many felt would have passed out of all favour as soon as he shuffled off this mortal coil. I was actually offered a part in the biopic of him before it got shelved. I hope there was no connection.

Brendan more than any other author in the Celtic literary tradition was responsible for the cult of the writer-as-personality that was to become so much part and parcel of a subsequent era's agitprop agenda. Like his fellow countryman Oscar, he was born to be wild(e). One might have been sartorially dandified whereas the other's idea of dressing up would be putting on a jacket, but both of these tortured souls were noted for their innumerable similarities: the quick wit, the high profile, the imprisonment that cut their literary careers short, etc. etc. Both of them are also as remembered for what they said outside their plays as in them.

"Brendan was as good as a play," Flann O'Brien remarked. Maybe he was even better. O'Brien added, in more piquant vein, "He was a delightful rowdy, a wit, a man of action in many dangerous undertakings where he thought his duty lay, a reckless drinker, a fearsome denouncer of humbug and pretence, and sole proprietor of the biggest heart that has beaten in Ireland for the last 40 years."

A man who could be on all fours in The White Horse Bar one minute and chatting with Albert Camus or Norman Mailer about existentialism the next. He truly was a man for all seasons, somebody who sucked on the pap of life and took no prisoners. The world was his stage – if not his oyster – and though he partook his leave of it prematurely, he left enough anecdotes with the "I Knew Brendan" brigade to fill a book like this ten times over.

This is a book which celebrates his humour, rather than one which delves into his sexuality, pseudo-intellectual innuendoes in his works, or Freudian reasons as to why he alternated his affections between gun, pen and whiskey glass. It doesn't seek to condemn or condone his actions, merely to remember them with the effervescent humour that was his own stock-in-trade. A book that sets out neither to bury nor to praise him, but merely to go down the mine again and relive quotations and anecdotes from his life. I'm grateful to my co-author Aubrey for jogging my memory in this regard, and for trawling the archives in pursuit of his own stories (some of which probably owe more to people's over-active imaginations than anything else). I've heard stories about Brendan told a dozen different ways by a dozen different people. I witnessed some of these circumstances first hand, so I'm in a position to give the true version, which is more than I can say for some of the people who tell the stories.

I'm glad I've had the opportunity to do this book, because it's given me a chance to review Brendan's life from the comfortable hindsight of memory. Time has been good to him, and many of those who said his reputation would die with his body are now themselves dead – along with their reputations.

John Cole, the former political editor of the BBC, wrote recently in *The Guardian*: "A wave of Behanism is haunting Europe." This can't be bad news for any of us. Brendan was like Halley's Comet: a phenomenon that comes into our lives only once.

In one sense, he lived his life backwards. He was able to recite Robert Emmet's *Speech from the Dock* at the age of six, but 35 years later he could hardly mutter his own name without stuttering. Is this the price of fame? Whatever it is, I'm proud to have come from the same womb as he did, and it still breaks my heart to think of him, despite our different perspectives on life.

Brendan was a pampered child running loose in the extended nursery of Irish literature as various minders and handlers ran after him trying to keep a tether on his emotions, while others seemed more intent on accelerating his date with death by inviting him on the kinds of pubcrawls he himself would have initiated in his prime.

He wanted everything yesterday: the quick pint, the quick novel, the quick record-breaking play. His mind was in permanent overdrive, and sometimes it was as if he needed the drink to subdue it, even if it looked the other way round. Drinking took away the shyness he carefully concealed when he was sober, but at a huge price. That was where, as he might have said himself, Aughrim was lost.

Like the aforementioned Wilde, he put his genius into his life and only his talent into his work. He cared more about that work than he admitted, but all too often it seemed to play second fiddle to his Bacchanalian shenanigans in any of the pubs where he held court to the worthies who hung on to every drunken word he uttered, even if they were long in their beds when he really needed them to pick him up out of the gutter afterwards.

He made a ham-fisted attempt to 'go straight' shortly after he married, but the life of the writer combines the maximum of temptation for an alcoholic as well as the maximum of opportunity, so it was never going to be very long before he traded in his sheets of A4 for another gulp of the hard stuff, despite the imprecations of the long-suffering Beatrice, or any of the doctors who told him he was walking a greased tightrope in those last few years.

Towards the end even dedicated friends of yore dreaded him appearing in bars for fear that something might happen – which it usually did. By this stage even the parasites avoided him, but he was far too sick to care. He had also become that thing both loved and hated in almost equal measure in Ireland: A Man Who Spoke Very Loudly To Anyone Who Would Listen About All The Books He Was Never Going To Write But Thought He Would. When he died in March 1964 it was a blessed release for himself and all who cared for him.

They are not long, the days of wine and roses and Brendan had just turned 40 when his health gave out for good. His was perhaps the slowest suicide of all time, and few who knew him were surprised by his early death. The laughing cavalier, in the space of a few short months in 1964, became transmogrified into a pale reflection of his former blustering self, a pathetic ex-rebel clutching at straws of former grandeur as he awaited the premature maw of the tomb. He knew his race was run long before it was, which gave birth to a semi-philosophic Brendan in his last few months. But suddenly the jokes about the hereafter were wearing thin as the spectre of meeting his creator became agonisingly palpable. His last words were reputed to be to a nun, "May you be the mother of a Bishop!" But he had his dark nights of the soul too, which were ill-camouflaged by this, one of his favourite catch-phrases. The gallows humour was Job's consolation for a man who knew he had squandered his talent before it reached its apogee, sold out too often for the twelve pieces of silver and the iconoclastic quip.

In his last months he was like a man in a time warp, a drunk in a midnight choir, as Leonard Cohen might have put it, wandering around the streets of Dublin in search of some elusive past, half-unaware of the fact that his time had already passed him by. A few friends remained, but he hardly recognised them. Instead he seemed to seek out those who would do him no favours, as if he wanted to see his excessive life through to its final masochistic horror. The comic timing was gone by now, as was his memory, and he even slurred his words when sober. He was running out of bars to slink into, or out of, a washed-up, washed-out writer in his own eyes, somebody who had outstayed his welcome on the planet. He knew there was a price to be paid for past misdeeds, and he would pay it; he would bite the bullet of his own destiny.

He had all the wild wilfulness of our mother, but with no chain to bind him. Spoiled from birth by an over-abundance of talk and flattery, he had denied himself nothing in life and by 1964 it was coming back to haunt him. The shadow of a gunman didn't stalk him any more, just his own sick hangovers. The Gospel according to Brendan had become a mere murmur, and a too-often repeated one at that. Put simply, he had lost the plot.

Brendan loved humanity and believed in its causes, but the causes were crumbling like his own life. Fame had driven away his friends, leaving him prey to the detritus left in their wake. His *folie de grandeur* was coming back to haunt him. It was as if Mephistopheles was arriving to collect a debt ten years old. As Dominic said, "Suicide on the instalment plan."

He was harder to get along with too. One night when we were celebrating the opening of *The Hostage* he turned on me and called me a traitorous bastard for leaving the Communist Party – the very party he had refused to join himself.

As well as everything else, he was tired. Tired and bored. Republicanism had failed, his writing had failed, his joy of living was gone. He had also become surrounded by the wrong types of people, toadies and hangers-on. Scumbags who exploited him for his reputation and his wallet, false-faced bastards who praised his every belch as a sign of heavenly inspiration. He feared nothing now, not even death whose sting-a-ling-a-ling he had reached out for so often. In a way it would be a relief for him, a relief from the frustration of stunted hopes.

Like a boxer who had taken too many punches to the head, his speech grew rambling and indistinct, and his anecdotes lacked their old bite – and often even their punch-line. He was on the ropes physically and mentally, in denial over both the decline of his health and his creativity, fanning the flames of his alcoholism with even more booze, in his own preferred version of Russian Roulette. He famously said he would prefer to be dead than to think about death, so he didn't think about it.

The last time I saw him was just a week before he died. He was in a dirty pub, an awful place altogether. He was dying and he knew it. His legs were swinging under him like a rag doll. He was fucked.

Beatrice had been trying to sign him in somewhere for an operation but he told her if she committed him anywhere he'd never forgive her. I remember him sitting on a stool and putting his arms round me. "Hold me tight," he said. He started singing then, he could sing the birds out of the bushes, could our Brendan. But now, for a change, there was no wildness in the singing.

At closing time he stood outside looking so sad and pathetic that it made me cry to look at him. He took my hand and asked me what was wrong, but I couldn't speak. The truth was there in his own eyes, in any case. He was done for and there was nothing he or I or anyone else could do about it. A week later he died and I thought, "Where has he gone, this great bear of a man?" It was even sadder to me than my parents dying years later. They died in bed, but he was dying on his feet.

In Oscar Wilde's words, "He had already lived more lives than one, and more lives than one did die."

We shall not see his like again, but love him or hate him (and with Bengy there's hardly an in between), even his enemies had to agree that Dublin's literary scene was the poorer for his passing.

He was sadistic, undoubtedly, and with a tongue like a machete, but Brendan Francis Behan's slights were eminently forgivable, no matter how damaging the opprobrium. At the end of the day he was a loveable sinner, a man who preferred to be down in hell with his Guinness rather than up in heaven with his harp.

A world where the Brendans ruled would be a lot better than the stupid, chaotic one we live in now, but in the end there was nothing for him to do but die. And like everything else he did, he carried that to excess too.

He was like a great storm at sea that lashes up wild waves and rocks the ships at anchor, only to spend itself in some peaceful valley. There it will drop to a quiet murmur, twinning its tired arms in the tall pines.

He died a far too early death, but as Ma said, "Is it better to die young having led a full life and leaving behind *Borstal Boy* and *The Quare Fella* or live till four score leaving behind only a handful of dust?"

His star was brief and he flew too close to the sun, but God save us from a world that doesn't have room for the likes of Brendan Behan.

Brian Behan
October 1998

Chapter 1

Growing Up

We were born and reared in Russell Street, which was named after the Earl of Bedford. It was a short-arsed street running onto the Jones Road. We were on the fringes of Slumland, neither here nor there, neither heaven nor hell. A no man's land – and no woman's either.

Not very far away was the Phoenix Park with Johnson, Mooney and O'Brien down the road. We had a song,

> Johnson, Mooney and O'Brien
> Bought a horse for one and nine.

There were children by the dozen to play with, and we played with them until night came, driving us all back into our homes, for better or worse. Some of us were going back to lives of misery and abuse and some to deprivation. But I think we were happy.

Ma had thirteen children. Five died in childbirth and one lad at the age of seven. Such a number wasn't uncommon in those days: in fact a woman near us had 25. Anyway, seven of the Behans survived. For some people, that was seven too many!

Ma's first husband fought in the Jacob's Biscuit Factory in 1916, while she herself carried messages to Connolly and Pearse in the GPO. It was no surprise to anybody that her second husband would have republican sympathies. Da spent the two years of the Civil War in prison and saw Brendan for the first time from there. She used to sing us to sleep with lines like, "And labour shall rise from her knees, boys/And claim the broad earth as her own." The working man, she said, never got anything without having to struggle for it.

I can still see her bent over a scrubbing board with her big strong arms. And then, as we grew older, washing Brendan's and Dominic's whites. Such are the things that stay with us, these details that seem negligible at the time but haunt the life of the unconscious.

We came from strong stock. Da's mother had a mane of black hair and every tooth in her head at the age of 70 and Ma's ploughed the fields till she was well past 80, though she drove all her children away from her. When asked her for money to go dancing she'd say, "What need have you of money? The land is yours when I'm gone." So away they went to America, the land beyond the sea. They thought there

would be work for them all there, and that the sun would always shine,
but it didn't work out like that. Instead they wrote back telling their
friends not to follow them.

Ma had no interest in sex. All she did was lie back and count pawn
office tickets. She thought she would get pregnant if a man draped his
trousers over a chair at the side of the bed. She was slow to learn the
facts of life, but in other ways she was before her time. She was a feminist before the word was invented.

Some of the women that lived beside us thought she had airs and
graces because she wouldn't let me sit on the tenement steps with them
on the fine summer days. They called her Lady Behan. How could she
have notions about herself, they wondered, when her life had been so
rough?

She treated us all equally: she had no favourites. She said she would
never make a fish out of one of us and flesh out of the other. All her
geese were swans. Our world was the chip shop, the picture-house
and the four-penny rush of a Saturday afternoon. And swimming in
the canal in summer time, or being chased along the railway lines by
the cops.

Brendan and myself fought like buggers. We weren't happy unless
we were at each other's throats, but there was no lasting malice in it.
Sometimes we turned the mischief on Ma, ripping up her shopping
bags or whatever. Anything was fair game. We played all the games
everyone else did – Relievio, Every Inch a Pinch, you name it. Brendan
was as good as the rest of us, or better. He blinded a kid with a home-
made arrow one day and Da gave him a good hiding for it, even though
it was an accident.

We made use of every bit of the street, even making the lamp-posts
into swings. The gutters were our rivers and we floated matchsticks
into the drains. Ma watched us, pleased as punch that we were all thriv-
ing in our way.

Brendan was our leader, always wanting to be the centre of attention at any price. I remember him learning to play the mouth-organ
through his nose. He had to be different.

I went to school to the nuns in North William Street and then the
National School in Francis Street. I'm afraid I didn't find them very
Christian. Every other day I got the strap. I think they enjoyed it. They
tell us now it was some kind of substitute for sex. "There's another one
now," they'd say, "for telling a lie." You weren't hit just for misbehaving. Sometimes it seemed you were just hit for being there. But as the
man said, if you can survive that you can survive anything.

Although we weren't blue blood, we were never conscious of being poor. Da's mother, Granny English owned five houses (we lived in
one of them). She was a funny woman, every Christmas she'd march in
and fling a turkey and a goose on the table and then rush out again. Da

couldn't stand her because she took him out of school and put him to work.

Granny English owned three houses in Fitzgibbon Street and two in Russell Street. Most of them were unfit for human habitation, but she ignored closure orders by the dozen and merrily went on collecting rent. It was like pre-revolutionary Russia where the middle classes sank down into the pit of hell.

That was what happened to Ma. Her father had eight businesses on the go in Dublin but threw the lot away. He was a feckless man who suffered from mad delusions. He was a grocer, but somehow formed the conviction that he was really a High Court judge. Donning a long black top hat and white gloves up to his armpits he marched off to the law courts, sitting in the public gallery as he meted out sentences to fictional defendants.

He neglected his business so much that he became a pauper within a year and then the neighbours robbed his poor wife. "Oh Mrs Kearney," they would say, "can you let me have the bill on tick?" And she would give in. That went on until the whole eight businesses went bust. Ma ended up in Goldenbridge convent, the orphanage run by the nuns. That was why she hated forking out money throughout her life. In this she resembled everyone else on the street. She got four bikes from McHugh's shop on the Never Never – and that was exactly what it was for Mr McHugh! Granny had a son called Paddy. Uncle Paddy stood to inherit Granny's fortune so Ma told us all to be nice to him. This wasn't easy because he was thin and weedy. Paddy slept with Granny until the day she died. He was 40 by then. There was no harm in it, though, nothing as they say, went on. Her feeling for economy was behind it. Whenever anyone asked her the reason, she told them, "It saves a room."

Granny felt a normal job would be too challenging for her feeble Paddy so she kept him at home to look after the houses. This didn't involve much. His chief problem was blocked toilet bowls. When thirteen families are using the one bowl, you can imagine how this would be so. Paddy delegated myself and my brother Seamus to free them. We got nine pence a go for each one we cleared. That was my first job in life: a lavatory diver. I felt quite important in myself being such an asset to the community.

Our niceness to Uncle Padser didn't pay dividends, I'm afraid. Granny left all her money to him, about £3000 in total, but not a red cent did we see of it. Padser drank himself to death within nine months of getting that windfall. He collapsed in McGill's pub reaching for his last pint. As he hit the deck our aunt Jack Corr – so called because she drank pints like a man – is reputed to have cried out, "I hope he hasn't paid for that gargle!"

Brendan was Granny's favourite. She couldn't get enough of him. I think that was Brendan's first experience of hero-worship, and he lapped it up. It was her that gave him the craving for the drop. "Give him the taste of it now," she would say, "and he won't feel the want of it in later life." How wrong she was.

On rent day she would shout, "Come on now, Bengy, I have a sackful of money" and out they would go on a pubcrawl. It was to be the start of a pattern that would define his days. No wonder he would later claim he was born in a glass. The pair of them specialised in drinking during funerals, and ended up being barred from most of the pubs on the north side of Dublin. Even then the cussedness must have been there. "You're setting that boy a very bad example," Ma would say, waving an accusing finger at Granny, but she remained unperturbed.

Our house wasn't far from the sea. Ma would drag streels of kids out after her on the tram to Dollymount. From time to time do-gooders would invade the street and offer us free trips in what was called The Sunshine Coach. It was like something out of a cowboy film. A bar of chocolate was also offered, and some cocoa to take home. Alfie Byrne, the Lord Mayor of the time, was pictured with us as we set off from the Five Lamps in the North Strand. Alfie had the hand falling off him from pressing the flesh, God love him, but he had his heart in the right place.

From the top window of our house we could see into Croke Park. On All-Ireland days the street would be packed with thousands making their way to the match. Hawkers thronged around us selling their wares. We were in Croker when the Kerry team refused to come out and play as a protest against the internment of republican prisoners. Brendan was amongst them by then. It was in this same Croke Park that the Black and Tans opened fire on the spectators, killing the goalkeeper. Afterwards, the slogan "Remember the 77" was all around us.

De Valera spoke in our street when he won the election in 1932. He promised to create a country so prosperous he would have to tell our 24 million emigrants in the States to come back to fill the jobs. When Granny English heard him saying this she piped up, "Ah you bostoon: sure the country would sink under the weight of them!"

Da liked his drink. My aunt used to say he drank the value of a couple of houses. "You could have bought one from the dregs," she said. Ma complained to Granny about it and she gave her this tip, "When he comes in jarred the next time, hit him with the heaviest pot you've got." In fear and trembling Ma did precisely that, laying Da out. She thought she had killed him, but he was only asleep. He got up the next morning without a bother on him and sailed off out to work.

Brendan came and went. Half the time you wouldn't have a clue where he was, and you knew better than to ask. Whenever he entered a room he created an atmosphere – even then. You could sense he was going to be a force in life, but for what you couldn't tell. He was the type of lad you'd enjoy spoiling, as Granny discovered. Ma spoiled him too, at least on the odd occasions that she got to see him. But she knew he was a rascal, as any mother would. He was either an anti-Christ or a pussycat, depending on your attitude to him, but as difficult to ignore as Nelson's Pillar. He was a ball of energy unleashed onto the world, an explosion already getting ready to ignite.

I delivered milk one year for one and sixpence a week and saved up thirteen shillings, the price of a suit. But just before Christmas Ma told me the shop she was going to buy it in had burned down. I was in bits and cried my eyes out. Many years later my younger brother Seamus told me the truth. "You great lump," he said, "didn't you know she bought the suit after all, but gave it to Brendan for his confirmation?" So Brendan got the clobber. Not only did he get the suit, but he got a story out of it as well. I couldn't help being mad at him, but I knew it wasn't his fault. Years later he made it up to me, taking a Crombie coat off his back in the depths of winter and wrapping it around me. I was touched. He said to me, "There's a few stamps for ye," (that was his way of saying pounds) and stuffed 50 quid into my pocket. It was like socialism in action. He had it and I didn't and he wanted to spread it around. I was short at the time but hadn't mentioned it to him. I could never ask him for money but I didn't need to. At times like that he had a heart as big as all outdoors.

Da was a good painter, but our own door looked like the wreck of the Hesperus for want of a brush hand. The cobbler's wife often went ill-shod. "Would you not put a lick on it?" Ma would plead, but Da said he wouldn't do a Corporation workman out of a job. It was a handy excuse for laziness. Another time Ma got a load of manure for the garden and asked Da to turn it over. He refused. "It's far from shit I was raised," he said. But then he got a brainwave. He rang the Special Branch and told them he was sure Brendan had hidden guns in the garden. As he expected, they arrived out on the nail and proceeded to do his gardening for him.

I got a job working for a transport company in Summerhill. I had to drive a great big wagon with two heavy horses. In the middle of winter I set off for the docks, the frosty nails in their shoes spitting out sparks as we ploughed our way through icy streets.

Near the city centre we bought what was called 'fancy bread', which was just stale bread sold at half the ordinary price. We also got Mogerly sausages and pickled rawn. Ma always fed us well, "Out of your belly you'll grow," was her war cry. If you ever refused food from her she'd snatch it away from you saying, "See your folly out: you will follow the crows for that yet." She had a wonderful rich mix of language that would have proved a heavy soil for any writer.

I remember going shopping with her one day when she burst out crying. We were sitting on the top of a tram pulling out from Nelson's Pillar and she had a letter in her hands. It was addressed to Brendan but she had opened it.

She said she had a bad feeling about it and she was proved right: it was a letter asking Brendan to go to Spain to fight in the Civil War, with instructions about meeting a man who was to take him there. Ma tore the letter up and told me never to tell Brendan about it. I never did, but he found out about it a few years later and never forgave Ma. She didn't know if she had done the right thing or not. Some people said she had done the wrong thing, that he was of an age to make up his own mind and even though he was wild and all that, he might have come back a different Brendan. "That's all true," Ma replied, "but he might also have come back no Brendan at all." In later years I asked myself if a martyr's death in Spain mightn't have been a better end for him than the one in the Meath Hospital, but how are we to know the future?

Another thing we weren't to know was that our days in Russell Street wouldn't last forever – Granny died and we had to move house. We ended up in Crumlin, which was like Outer Siberia to us at that time. It wasn't yet a suburb. Da called it Barbarian Land. The Corpo were slapping up houses as if they were going out of fashion, with little thought of those who had to live in them, but the money situation meant we had to go.

The killing thing was that we could have avoided Crumlin. We had been offered what they called a 'purchase house' in Donnycarney, which was just down the road, but Da said no because it would have meant forking out sixpence a week extra. "I don't want to get into debt," he said, but what he really meant was that he wanted to keep the few extra bob for booze. So now you might have an inkling where wee Brendan came from.

We never paid rent in Russell Street, they wouldn't pay God Almighty there. It was like a little anarchic community. Everyone lived in everyone's ears and we all had the same game-plan. A man came to collect the rent one day and Ma said to tell him she wasn't in. I went to the door and said to the man, "Ma says to tell you she's not in." It was an unfortunate choice of phrase. He spotted her in the kitchen then and she went livid. She came out roaring at him like a mad thing. "How dare you not believe an innocent child!" she screamed at him. Ma won that particular round.

Crumlin posed two main problems. The first was that we didn't know a sinner out there. The second was that somehow we had to find ten bob for the rent every week.

It didn't have the the camaraderie of Russell Street either. Brendan said he missed the warmth, the friendly spirit – even the hallways. "The hallways," he said, "were where you learned as much about the facts of life as you ever could at the foot of the Dublin mountains." He used to go back to Russell Street now and again and try to pretend that we were still living there, but it was no good. Our friends were gone, the houses were pulled down, a way of life had disappeared forever. "Cities change," Ma said to him, "like people. They have to renew themselves." But he was inconsolable. He deplored the big, new estates that were sprouting up like Soviet encampments. 'Kremlin's Crumlin' he dubbed our new abode. It was not an inaccurate appraisal.

Brendan saw Crumlin as a place where they played Tip and Tig with hatchets, where even the bird's nests had padlocks on them. There weren't any schools there, so we had to pay bus fares to get to them every day. Was this all de Valera could offer, we thought – a little old dog box of a house and a shilling's worth of 'free beef'?

When Dominic asked Brendan why we were leaving Russell Street to go out there, he told him, "Me mother's country blood is unsettled and she wants to get back to the cows and cow-shite." He referred to Crumlin as the Wild West, which was ironic considering he was hardly the epitome of twee gentility himself.

I still remember my first day out there. It was like being at the end of the world. Every house the same, like some sort of surreal dream – or nightmare. There seemed to be thousands of them, all mean and dingy: the bountiful legacy of a soulless bureaucracy to the Behan family. De Valera how are ye. Devil Éire would be more like it.

To this day it makes me shiver to think of it. It was like being on a dump on the far side of nowhere. "Fuck this for a game of cowboys," Brendan said to me as he looked around him at the desolation. Maybe he should have put Indians in there as well. I felt we were in Commanche country. Granny English, to be sure, was gone to a better place. All you could do was keep your head down and soldier on. Or, if you were Brendan Behan, do something else...

"As sure as Jaysus," he muttered, "this is a livin' death. I don't know about you but I'm goin' to murder a few pints." It was so inevitable I laughed. You could always rely on the old bugger. No matter how hard or cruel the world got, there was always the Evostik of Arthur G to hold things together. Every cripple had his own way of walking, and by Christ, everyone looked like a cripple out there.

In a way you couldn't blame Crumlin. The whole country was in the middle of a slump that had begun in 1930. It's hard for people who never lived through it to understand how awful it was. It wasn't a famine, but maybe we'd all have been better off if it was. Your misery would soon be over then, but this was slow torture.

It was a long way from the hordes of shoppers you see nowadays teeming out of Tesco or Superquinn. If we had seen such a sight we would have pinched ourselves to make sure it was real. We couldn't envisage anyone buying a whole pound of sugar or a quarter of tea. We bought everything in ounces: miserable little two ounce twists of sugar and tea and the smallest possible amount of butter. Cigarettes we bought in ones and twos, with a match.

The pawn shop acted as our broker for everything, each stick of furniture we owned for that precious shilling or half-a-crown that was the difference between going to bed hungry or with a full belly. We had overcoats for blankets on the bed and flour-bags for sheets.

It wasn't as if we had been rich in Russell Street, but a kind of primitive communism kept us afloat there. It was a mutual-aid society, a society where everyone knew everyone else's business but here you knew nobody.

The dole had come in, but it was meagrely spread. Sean applied for it but was told, "You're looking for money for nothing. Well you won't get it here. You're living at home – let your parents keep you."

I remember Ma selling two flower vases to a neighbour just to get our evening meal. In the daytime I followed the banana and chocolate wagons to the tip, pulling half-rotten bananas away from shrieking seagulls who competed with me for them. At other times I burrowed into the ground for half-burnt coke or coal, a dangerous occupation because there wasn't any shoring.

At school we looked for the free dinners, Ma tutoring us well in the use of the Poor Mouth. "You're to say your father isn't working whether he is or not," she'd advise. In the house itself, bugs ran rampant. They were huge and red and looked better fed than us. Ma smeared the walls with Jeyes Fluid and we watched them falling dead as they reached it. I hated Crumlin and everything around it. I hated the deprivation and the loneliness and the crippling boredom. I started mitching from school in my misery. I was eventually sent to the approved school in Artane because Ma couldn't keep me. (Forty years before, the same thing had happened to two of my uncles.)

Some mothers terrified their children with threats, "Mend your ways or I'll send you to Artane." But to be honest with you I was glad to get into it. I was fed up with hunger, fed up with Ma telling me not to eat this or that because it had to be saved for Da's breakfast. Only those who have experienced hunger can tell you what it's like: a hunger that never leaves you, no matter how well off you become. Things were so bad that one night Ma had to unpick a cushion she'd filled with oats so that we'd be able to have porridge for breakfast.

Brendan wrote to me in Artane. He was in Hollesley Bay Borstal by now with his own problems. "Keep your heart up," the letter said simply. "The darkest hour is before the dawn." It heartened me. He asked me to write to him and I promised I would. The Brothers warned us to praise the school in everything we wrote. We were afraid not to, even though it was more like prison than Brendan's borstal. As Ma said, "After Artane, you could survive Belsen."

The Christian Brothers had no great love for me and my ways, nor me for them. They seemed to enjoy beating the crap out of you for looking sideways at them. I got a belt across the jaw one time for criticising Franco. Other times I ran away, but they always dragged me back. These were the three worst years of my life.

The discipline was the strictest I ever saw, even harder than Wandsworth, the maximum security prison. You woke to the clap of a Brother's hand, and if you weren't out of bed as soon as the clap ended, woe betide you. Then it was straight into the wash-room and after that to chapel for mass and prayer. Afterwards you went to the refectory, where everything was signalled by a whistle. There was a whistle to say Grace, a whistle to start eating, a whistle to stop eating and a whistle to walk out after your meal. This never varied.

The Brothers conducted two wars: one against the sin of impurity and the other against communism. Impurity was the main enemy. In the showers you had to face to your front for fear of getting a whacking. If you looked at the naked flesh of the boy beside you, you got a belt. They had false words for everything. You had to call your willy your finger and your bum your chest. If you did anything they regarded as impure they made you put a placard round your neck saying: 'I Am Impure. Do Not Speak To Me'.

I thought of Brendan a lot. I was wondering what it felt like to be captured by the dreaded Brits in a home far from home. I wondered if he was among strange people or boys just like himself whose mothers did the pawn on a Monday. When I finally left Artane, a qualified baker and proud as punch, he was just starting another jail stretch, this time for fourteen years for the shooting incident in Glasnevin. I found it hard to fathom and I blamed Ma for it, blamed her for rocking us in the cradle to those rebel songs. It was these that caused all the trouble, I told myself, these songs that had taken Brendan from us. "It's the mothers of Ireland that make the rebels," I thought, "and now I'll never see him again."

Chapter 2

Sweet Smell of Success

His uncontrollable desire to be always the centre of attention was obviously the direct result of his fear that he was unworthy of being noticed.

Ted E Boyle

Those whom the gods would destroy they first make famous. Brendan said that the thirst for beer was an awful curse, but still worse was a thirst that couldn't be satisfied due to lack of finances. "That," he declared, "would be a total crucifixion." I can see his point but, if he hadn't, become a victim of his own fame, nor had the wherewithal to drink himself into a stupor as often as he did, maybe he'd still be alive today.

No matter how famous he became, he still carried round with him the aura of the local-boy-made-good. Nor did he ever lose his wide-eyed innocence. It's probably safe to assume that most of the parasites who goaded him on to wilder escapades were cuter hoors by far, and that his failure (or inability) to come to terms with his celebrity status was what finally proved his undoing as he became the toast of everywhere from Ballymote to Broadway and beyond. Put a beggar on horseback, they say, and he'll ride to the devil. Brendan rode to the devil and back, confounding his critics each time they wrote him off as written out, but he finally succumbed to the rigours of fame in the early sixties when he realised he was becoming a self-parodying buffoon.

He fell victim to a syndrome Oliver St John Gogarty touched on in his book *As I Was Going Down Sackville Street*. "The moment our pubs become subjects of literature," Gogarty wrote, "that is the moment they are undone. Even we who patronise them would become self-conscious. The last thing drink should do is make one self-conscious." Combine that with the fact that Brendan had a low threshold of drunkenness, and a tendency to take any concoction for the same reason that the man climbed Mount Everest – because it was there – and you've got a man teetering between being Oscar Wilde and Johnny Forty Coats. His dalliances in pubs, like his life itself, tended to be composed of two distinct halves: the first articulate and user-friendly, the second volatile and (eventually) comatose. So when people came to interview him, it was almost *de rigueur* that he would disgust as well as discuss. It was all part of the evening's tapestry, the descent into inane pugilism like a mini-narrative of his future played in fast motion.

As Ted Boyle wrote in his biography of him:

> *The stage personality of the Irish drunk, which Behan had before used as a tool to call attention to his writing, became in the last five or six years of his life his reason for being.*

Anthony Cronin concurred with that viewpoint. "Brendan," he said, "had a voracious appetite for public notice. Wherever he was he sought it out and usually he got it. He would perform before any sort of audience willing to grant him its attention, even if that audience was, as it frequently turned out to be, uncomprehending, baffled, or – occasionally – hostile."

Joseph Cole put a different spin on events when he said, "The most pervasive myth fostered by the 'I Knew Brendan' school of journalists is of a Brendan Behan who was invariably the centre-piece of any company he chanced to be in, and that his wit, good humour and lovable drunken antics were enchanting to his (often captive) audience. This is a journalistic trick, and a good one as far as it goes, but it cheats in so far as Brendan was not always in the leading role in these incidents. As often as not, he filled in a bit part which only his subsequent fame caused to be built up in the minds of those writing about him into the star role."

In time he became a classic piece of Ireland's architecture, as much as The Rock of Cashel or The Giant's Causeway. Visiting Dublin and not having a pint with him was a bit like visiting Cork and not kissing the Blarney Stone. You could almost have put him in a cage and wheeled him down O'Connell Street, charging American tourists a dollar to take photographs.

Brendan might have hated ye olde Oirish cottage industry of begrudgery, but he also hated being ignored. I think if push came to shove he'd have preferred to be hated than that. As Oscar Wilde said, "There's only one thing worse than being talked about, and that's not being talked about."

As was the case with drink, he didn't so much *seek* publicity as *find* it. He was a natural performer and didn't need tape recorders or the pop of camera bulbs to get him going. In fact he spent a lot of his time throwing reporters off the scent. I'm surprised he didn't deck more of the paparazzi who dogged his footsteps. He much preferred signing autographs for what we might call 'ordinary people' for want of a better term. He got the better of a horde of journalists one time by speaking only in Irish all day. The venue was London and only one of them was a Paddy. He was happy to translate Brendan's witticisms for a fee, which delighted Brendan. He liked to look after his own. It was the ultimate two-fingered gesture to a country that was in the process of making him rich.

In a sense, he created around himself the cult of personality that writers like Norman Mailer were creating in America at about the same time, and for similarly scandalous reasons. They were kindred souls, and who's to say that if Mailer had been born in Dublin in the aftermath of the 1916 insurrection, he wouldn't have flirted with republican violence in the same way Brendan did.

I say 'flirted' because Brendan himself was the first to admit the IRA showed much *savoir faire* in never elevating him beyond the rank of courier. Maybe the surprise was that he did time for the cause at all. When he did, though, and when literature – not to mention pub legend – came out of the incarceration, his street cred was copper-fastened. Here was a man who lived his art as well as wrote it, who sang his grief rather than cried it, as Ma had always encouraged him to do. In Ireland, you see, the wars had always been merry and the songs were always sad.

In the Dublin of the fifties there was the kind of buzz about writers that we see today surrounding soccer players and rock stars. Brendan, Kavanagh and Beckett all ploughed separate furrows towards common goals. So did O'Casey, Flann O'Brien and Joyce. Whether they emigrated or not was beside the point. What mattered was their commitment, nay, obsession. And if it could be carried over into their private lives as well, so much the better.

With Brendan, the two were almost indistinguishable. His work poured into his life just like his Guinness. He would be seen around the so-called 'Left Bank of Dublin' with pieces of paper sticking out of his pockets as he regaled all who would listen with his treasured manuscript, in between singing ballads or abusing editors or pontificating, as only he could, on things sociological in his earthy argot. An exhibitionist to the core, he performed his writings almost in the same way as he did his songs. But most exhibitionists, particularly those who undergo dramatic personality shifts after drinking 'The Black Stuff', tend to be bashful souls at base. And so it was with Brendan, particularly the bellicose Brendan.

Discipline deserted him with the trappings (and traps) of fame. Writing is a lonely occupation at the best of times, and editing can be even more boring. When the bars were opened, or even when they weren't, they were to him like carrots dangling before a donkey's head. He also had money now, the lack of which – like prison – had often made thirst a necessary evil. A part of him also felt that the old brigade didn't so much want books from him as boisterousness. And as he often said himself, he was never one to let the people down.

He was like a child let loose in a sweet-shop. He was hungry, and he would gorge himself on fame, enjoying its blandishments, exploiting its possibilities and milking celebrity status for its free publicity. It wasn't long before he learned that his private scandals made better copy than his public successes.

When he became a media celebrity, first in Britain and then in the States, it was always only going to be a matter of time before he pressed the self-destruct button. He told Kenneth Allsop once, "Success is damn near killing me. I think a man should be allowed success for one month, and then given a pension and allowed to retire."

We may smile, but there's a rueful truth behind it. If Brendan attained modest success rather than becoming the Poet Laureate of the proletariat, he could have lasted into his seventies, a paternalistic scribe reflecting wryly over a Past Imperfect as he put the finishing touches to his memoirs. But because he became mega-famous at a time when writers weren't generally seen as public figures, but rather as grey men in cloistered rooms, he was always going to be the victim of his own poisoned fishbowl. He created himself in the mould the media wanted and was only too happy to milk it for whatever benefits accrued from such hellacious posturing, even if they were only short term. He claimed that journalists were only interested in him if he was in jail, in hospital or dying. Maybe there's truth in this, but if there is, he himself was primarily responsible for the aura of decadence that seemed to follow him wherever he went.

The drama critic Alan Brien said he began every play with his curtain speech, in a classic case of putting the cart before the horse. It was like an aspiring actor practising writing his autograph before he had his first screen test.

Brendan was a perpetual dreamer, forever reaching out through a clown's mask into the hearts of humanity, but he played the court jester once too often after fame came, painting himself into a corner from which there was no exit. The 'pleasure principle' became the 'pain principle' for him – and the so-called easy life a harder animal to negotiate than prison and poverty put together.

Fame always sat uneasily on his shoulders, despite the fact that he courted it with such exuberance. "God help the poor little famous," he said, quoting Keats, and we may assume that's how he saw himself underneath all the hype.

Once he created the image of the wildman, it became a monkey on his back. It meant he was expected to perform wherever he went. A part of him enjoyed this, the part of him for whom publicity became a drug, but it had to take its toll over time. Journalists loved him because an interview with him seemed to perforce mean a pubcrawl and pubs have a habit of loosening people's tongues. Not that that was ever a problem with this man anyway. Like his friend Groucho Marx, he could safely say he was inoculated with a phonograph needle.

He lived in an age before press agents had become important, but then he never really needed one as he was his own best self-publicist. Somehow it's hard to imagine him at a book signing, or being politically correct on a chat show about the motivation behind his works. He wrote like he ate, drank, slept and made love: on impulse. And how could you intellectualise that? The chat shows on which he guested, on both sides of the Atlantic, served to advertise himself more than his books, and if he was drunk in the process, so much the better. This, of course, is in marked contrast to today's generation of 'Ballygowan' writers, and our dearth of 'characters'. Can you imagine Brendan with a word processor?

It's somehow easier to see him frantically scribbling diffuse images with the butt end of a mangled pencil in McDaid's as last orders are being called. As far as the literary fraternity was concerned, he was the proverbial bull in a china shop – and boy how this bull loved to wreck china.

He witnessed the end of the bohemian culture and the birthpangs of yuppyism and designer angst. He admired Beckett more as a person than a writer. Indeed, if he didn't like somebody as a person, it's hard to imagine him admiring their works in any shape or form – particularly 'intellectual' writers. Like Boucicault crossed with O'Casey, or Dickens with Roddy Doyle, he acted like a bridge between those two cultures as he soaked up, like a sponge, every experience that came his way.

John Ryan said he was like that other BB the world had produced: Brigitte Bardot. He was hardly a sex symbol, but every-time he sneezed, the paparazzi of the time (though not then referred to as such) were on hand to capture the occasion for posterity. As Ryan put it, "He only had to drop his pants in Grafton Street for the teleprinters to cackle in Galveston, Texas or Osaka, Japan." And before long he started to believe his own publicity: the death knell of most writers.

In a certain sense his career trajectory paralleled that of Elvis Presley: from the early success of the *wunderkind*, the massive hype, the cult following, then the descent into addiction (booze for him, pills for Presley) and surrounding himself with all the wrong kinds of people before they both became 'fat and forty' and died a few years later. They were also both fascinated with guns, albeit for wildly different reasons, but as a sign of a fierce desire for control. And they were both so pampered with attention from a young age (one from his mother, the other from his granny) that they never quite grew up, or learned how to form a mature relationship with a partner. Both were incorrigible male chauvinists, but largely got away with it, as they did with many other vices, because of their charm. They were both basically gentle people, but given to sporadic violent fits.

Both of them were performance artists who needed to drug themselves up to perform, and the intake of such drugs got hiked up after they reached their mid-thirties. Both also needed to be alternatively nursed and mothered by their wives in the classic, chauvinist tradition. They were also both very generous with money, probably because they knew too well what it was like to have to do without it from their youths. Brendan wasn't exactly in the position to buy people Cadillacs, but he found it almost impossible to refuse anybody who asked him for a loan, or who was cash-strapped and too shy to do so. And of course there's that famous story of the day he frog-marched a dozen, frozen Dubliners into a tailor's shop and kitted them all out with overcoats free and gratis.

Elvis and Brendan became icons of what their critics would call 'limited talent', and for the last few years of their respective lives, both were on career auto-pilot. Each of them could have died well before they did because of their self-destructive lifestyles, but when death came it was still a shock to those who loved them – and even those who didn't. Brendan died more than a decade earlier than Elvis, but the reasons were similar. Both were suffering from premature burn-out, as they were from depression, and even a kind of self-loathing as it became increasingly more difficult to regain the fame that had once come so easy and so early.

Brendan described himself as a drinker with a writing problem, but what he really was a *painter* with a writing problem. No matter in what country of the globe he resided, or how many luminaries he met, he would always be a painter in his soul. If he had remained one for his livelihood, he could still be alive today.

The press knew nothing about him beyond the bluster, the bragadocchio, the unending piss and vinegar. They put him up to tear him down again (as the press will always do) but they could never divine his motivation, or what finally stopped that motivation in mid-canter. They saw him as the big fat Irishman that was always disgracing himself on the telly, an indigestible lump of rampant Paddyism. And how he loved to play that role for them. He performed on cue, right down to his final soliloquy.

Fame destroyed Brendan. The drink was a bad enough cross to bear, but literary notoriety was, to mix a metaphor, the twisting of another rope. Without it he could have lived out his life as a jolly house-painter, a man who fulminated about politics from a ladder rather than a pub stool or a television set, somebody who occasionally threw pennies to children when he passed them on the street. He may still have caused mild consternation when he broke into song on a bus or a building site, for he was always going to be a showman, but such showmanship wouldn't have become the burden it did if he didn't have the audience fame bestowed on him. It became his poisoned chalice.

The Irish-American Bill Slocum declared, after one of Brendan's escapades, "I am as Irish as Mr Behan, but I resent his contrived playing of an old stereotype character, the drunken Irishman. That role went out with the black-faced comic who got his laughs because he couldn't pronounce a three syallable word or the bearded Jew who built his act on a non-existent accent and a crooked shrewdness with money." Slocum went on to say that he'd seen Brendan all over New York dressed in carefully prepared disarray and as sober as a judge. The alcoholism was a ploy he felt, designed to goad his auditors towards headier seductions. Did Brendan have to die to prove the Slocums of the world wrong?

Parade chairman James Comerford banned Brendan from taking part in the St Patrick's Day Parade in New York in 1961 because of his unruly behaviour leading up to it, which Mr Comerford found boring. Brendan said he couldn't agree more. In fact he found it boring himself. But it was hard to avoid, because every time he bought a newspaper, there in front of him was a 'Behan Drunk and Disorderly' story. "The solution," he said, "was to stop writing stories about him and start tackling serious topics instead. Like unemployment, for instance. Or the finer points of carpet-weaving in the Himalayas..."

It almost became a cliché to say that Brendan courted his stage-Irish image and/or feigned drunkenness to pander to his audience. Author Jim King saw it differently. "He was like a man running away from a monster in his own backyard," he said. "He didn't deny the monster helped him get to the top of the literary mountain, but he didn't want it to bulldoze him down the other side."

Though he enjoyed the fame and adulation that came his way, he always remained bemused by it and knew a lot of it was associated with his boisterous persona. He said to me one time, "They'd praise my balls if I hung them up high enough."

Carraroe in Galway and the Aran Islands became a kind of spiritual retreats for him when fame became tiresome. Here he could indulge in his two favourite hobbies, swimming and drinking, without people bothering him about his next play or his last one. Here he was Brendan Behan the man, not Brendan Behan the writer. "Most of the people we met here hadn't even read his plays," Beatrice said, "and some of them didn't even speak English." Which made such sojourns all the sweeter.

Brendan believed that writers almost had to go to jail to prove their worth in the public's eye. Well not quite, but perhaps it helped in his case. He used it, as he used the drink, to bolster his ego, but by 1960 the image had taken over from the man and he was largely just playing out the role of a person called Brendan Behan as he might have played a character from one his plays. As somebody once said of Humphrey Bogart, "Bogie's okay until he has a few drinks. After that he thinks he's Humphrey Bogart."

❖

He enjoyed fame for a time, but eventually it became a bit wearying having every Tom, Dick and Harry coming up to him on the street shaking his hand. He made an exception for those who paid to see his plays, however. "Cash customers can shake my foot as well as my hand," he said graciously.

❖   ❖   ❖

Brendan was drinking with his good friend Ben Kiely one time and asked him if he worried much about what people generally thought or said about him. "Not much," Kiely responded, "the negative opinion of a friend would hurt, of course, but there wasn't much you could do about it in any case." He then turned the question on Brendan, who was looking into the malodorous Liffey at the time. "You're right," Brendan said, "if you and me worried about what people generally say about us, or think about us, we might as well give up and go down the stairs and cross the quay there and leap into the translucent stream."

❖   ❖   ❖

Frank O'Connor once claimed he was so famous that if somebody addressed a letter to him with just the words 'Frank O'Connor, Writer' on it and addressed it to the newspaper boy at the bottom of Grafton Street, he would get it. A correspondent took him to task on this, and one day a postman came up to Brendan's friend John Ryan and said, "The fella at end of Grafton Street says he never heard of O'Connor, but that you or that sign-writer Brendan Behan might." Brendan was as disgusted by this turn of events as was O'Connor. "Such," said Ryan, "is fame."

❖   ❖   ❖

When an interviewer asked him if success had spoiled him, he stroked his chin, sported a slight grin and said, "No, I've always been like this."

❖   ❖   ❖

When theatrical producer Joan Littlewood got her first play script from Brendan it was riddled with typos, beer stains and words careering off the page. However, she saw it was touched by genius despite (or maybe even because of) such unorthodoxy. She asked her colleague Gerry Raffles to send Brendan some money to pay for his fare to London so they could discuss it, which he did. Brendan, however, as was his wont, put the said money into his drinking hobby. He then wrote to Raffles saying: "Drinking with some Toronto Irish: send us an injection." Raffles duly posted off another fare, which also went west. Littlewood finally instructed him to change tack. The third missive Brendan received contained simply a ticket and an AA map . . . Ms Littlewood doesn't explain in her autobiography if the AA stands for Automobile Association or Alcoholics Anonymous!

❖   ❖   ❖

Comparisons between himself and Dylan Thomas were rife during Brendan's life, reaching their apogee in the oft-quoted statement that the only difference between them was that Thomas wrote *Under Milk Wood* and Behan wrote 'under Littlewood'. Brendan himself didn't like to be compared to anyone, feeling both himself and the other party would lose out from the analogy. He did say, however, that he had great respect for Thomas' poem *To a Child Killed in an Air-Raid Fire in London*. He couldn't have written it, he said, "if he was the proverbial monkey who was given a typewriter and 50 million years to write the complete works of Shakespeare".

❖   ❖   ❖

"Without Littlewood," a jealous author commented to him, "you wouldn't be who and what you are."

"Maybe not," Brendan replied, "but without me Littlewood wouldn't be who and what she is either."

❖   ❖   ❖

When Brendan learned that Dominic was having a play produced in Dublin in 1960 he exploded, saying to a friend, "What does he think, that genius is produced in litters?" When I produced my own memoirs he grunted, "The cat in Number 70 will be writing next."

❖   ❖   ❖

After leaving journalism for the headier realms of the theatre, he looked down on it as an inferior pursuit. Passing a columnist he knew on the street one day he roared at him, "That oul' column of yours is only retail business. Why don't you go into the wholesale trade like me?"

❖   ❖   ❖

When a fellow writer said to him that his own works would be remembered when Brendan was "dead and rotten", an unimpressed Brendan replied, "Number one, I'm not interested in having my writings remembered when I'm dead and rotten. And number two, I'm not particularly attracted by the idea of being dead and rotten anyway."

❖   ❖   ❖

This is the reason he gave for why he didn't write more letters: "Because when I'm gone, I figure there'll be one or two begrudgers about, trying to break into print by writing about me. And I'd like to make the whores search and shovel for their material – like I had to."

❖   ❖   ❖

Brendan said about the fairly ubiquitous press attention he received, "When I go for my tea, people break into print about me." He went on to elaborate, "The only reason they call me is because I happen to have a reputation. If I was the local milkman, or some poor cunt flogging turf from the back of a donkey's cart, the whores wouldn't even stop to give me a light."

❖   ❖   ❖

Ma was the one who started Brendan on this tack. "Was there ever a nation with such a spiteful face towards one another?" she'd say. "Our biggest industries are undertakers and glaziers."

❖   ❖   ❖

When a media hack said to him, "We made you and we can break you," he hit back with, "If it wasn't for people like me, people like you would be selling snowballs to little old senile ladies in the Antartic!"

❖   ❖   ❖

He generally felt there was only one thing to do with critics: bathe them in hot tar. "If I took any notice of them," he told a friend, "I'd have been in the madhouse years ago."

❖   ❖   ❖

Brendan said, "If you get six out of six good reviews you can ask the President of the United States to sell you the White House, but I don't think this has ever happened. If you get five out of six," he continued, "you're still doing fairly well, though you have to start worrying then about 480 Lexington Avenue (i.e. the income tax base). Four good reviews means you can throw a party – and even afford to attend it too. Three means it's time to go home to bed, but if you only get two," he advised, "you're best to stay there all day and don't show your face in public until after dark. If you get just one good review from six, make an air reservation. And if you get none? Take a sleeping pill."

❖   ♣   ♣

Brendan's passage from being an obscure writer to a household name can almost directly be traced to his appearance on the BBC in a Malcolm Muggeridge interview in 1956. This was always going to be controversial from the word go after somebody gave Brendan a bottle of the hard stuff in the studio.

Everybody was nervous about the show because of his condition, and Beatrice wanted it cancelled. "He was drunk," she claimed, "more from nervousness than anything else." Muggeridge prayed that he wouldn't use any four-lettered words and Joan Littlewood knelt behind his chair in case he keeled over.

The first thing Brendan did on the show was take off his shoes. The second was start to doze off. It was the first time anyone had ever appeared drunk on the BBC. He could hardly speak and Muggeridge was flummoxed, trying to coax words out of him without much success.

Muggeridge couldn't get him to talk but remembered reading somewhere that even if somebody was too drunk to talk, he might be able to sing. He asked Brendan to sing and of course Brendan obliged. The interview staggered on like that. Fifteen million people were watching it all, some of them disgusted and some just amused. At the end of it all Brendan said to Muggeridge, "What are we doing here? Why should fifteen million people be watching boring old farts like us when they could be making love, walking the dog or having a pint – or even all three at once." He became a media folk hero as a result of that night. Years later David Astor of *The Observer* told me he had never seen anything more honest in his life. (Anyway, as not many people know, Muggeridge was drunk himself during the interview!)

Muggeridge's other guests that night were two bomb disposal experts who rather fancied themselves according to Brendan's way of thinking. "Disposed of them, did you?" he said to them at one stage of the night. "Listen – I've planted more bombs than you've had hot dinners, you pox bottles."

Television made Brendan into a superstar. He was, as Ma said, "a child of the box". He told her he was determined going on to the show that after it was over, no-one would forget who Brendan Behan was. And they didn't.

On the morning after the interview, a man shouted out of a bus window at Brendan, "Saw you on television last night, Paddy, and I couldn't understand a fucking word of it . . . but then again I couldn't understand Muggeridge either!" Such an anecdote reminds us that he appealed to the working class of Britain just as he did to those of Ireland. Maybe this is why he said, "The famed British reserve is as much a myth as the idea of the broth-of-a-boy Irishman, he of the ready wit, the warm heart and the great love for a fight." Though there were those who claimed he epitomised those very characteristics himself.

Somebody else shouted out at him, "Why were you drunk at seven in the evening last night?"

"Because I'm drunk *every* evening at seven o'clock," he replied. Brendan knew he'd crossed a major hurdle despite having done little on the show. "Suddenly all London was at my feet," he said to me. "Everywhere I went I was hailed like a fucking taxi."

There was no West End interest in *The Quare Fella* until after that interview, but the next day two different managers rang him up seeking an option on it. The boy who used to spit at the King's head on pennies before he spent them was suddenly the toast of London. The people he wanted to blow up were now courting him. His gun had become transmogrified into a pen, his expletives into ejaculations.

Muggeridge said the interview was memorable to him because Brendan didn't utter "one single comprehensible word". What Brendan learned from the night, as Muggeridge said, was that, "One drunken and speechless television appearance brought more of the things he wanted, like money and notoriety and a neon glory about his head, than any number of hours with a pen in his hand."

I started to avoid Brendan after the Muggeridge show. I didn't want to be caught up in the whole circus. Even then I could see his personality taking over from the writing. It was like a distraction. This didn't bother me unduly. I was glad for him, but I wanted to go down a different road myself. I didn't want him to feel he had to be his brother's keeper.

Whenever I saw him afterwards his talk was rambling. Sometimes I felt he wasn't the brother I grew up with. He talked about smuggling marijuana in Paris, about talking the bollox off Samuel Beckett while Beckett just sat staring at a blank wall, about how Albert Camus had asked him if he could get him tickets for an Arsenal versus Tottenham match he hoped to go to in London. I didn't know if he was telling me true stories or trying to bamboozle me with bullshit. We always knew he was notorious for name-dropping, and now that he had people kissing the hem of his garment there was no stopping him.

Not long after Muggeridge, Brendan appeared on an American chat show with Ed Murrow but he was edited out before it was aired, except for a brief excerpt. But even this was publicity for him. Jackie

Gleason commented, "Behan came over 100 per cent proof. It was not an act of God, but an act of Guinness."

He liked to repeat the proverb, "A shut mouth will catch no flies" but this shut mouth was now catching quite a lot of them. His silence may not have been more profound than speech, but it was certainly more eye-catching.

He had arrived.

Chapter 3

The Write Stuff

In Behan we have the ancient culture of Ireland, the uproarious, boistering mixture of paganism and Catholicism, the latter subduing the barbarity, but not the ribaldry of the former. In him we have the Irishman who, while peripatetic, never abandoned Ireland, who spoke its original tongue, and wrote English with an exuberance denied to its native speakers.

Herbert Kenny

Most people's image of Brendan is of a man who liked to take potshots at the Brits in between guzzling pints and falling down drunk in the street. The reality is that he was a highly literate man who wore his learning (like his clothes) lightly. A man who, like the catcher in the rye, suspected anything ostensibly bookish as being, by definition, phoney. And this despite the fact that he himself was trilingual, and could quote liberally from Shakespeare or *The Bible* at the drop of a hat.

Da read Shakespeare and Dickens and Galsworthy and Eugene O'Neill to us, and then on Saturdays we went to the Queen's Theatre, so you can see where Brendan came from. If he didn't exist he would have had to be invented. Literary and political talk was flying round the house from when he was old enough to speak and he grabbed it with both hands. He was almost an inevitable product of his environment.

Brendan lit a bonfire under the arse of Irish literature. He took it by the scruff of the neck and dragged it kicking and screaming into the 20th century. His lifestyle made him an extension of his work, and it of him. That was both his blessing and his curse. It got him off the ground in 1956 and buried him under that same ground eight short years later. In those eight years he kicked up a storm everywhere he went, from Stockholm to Berlin. Fortune smiled on him and then turned the dagger. "Once I wasted time," he wrote, "now time wastes me." He went to hell and back but still wanted more. He drank the world and then vomited it up. And we're still trying to decipher the remains.

Theatre was in the Behan blood from the word go. From that point of view, it would have been more unusual if we didn't write plays than the fact that we did. Our uncle ran the Queen's so Brendan and the rest of us were given complimentary seats to it from a young age. Nothing could compare to the feeling of luxury, sitting in those plush red seats, or looking at the safety curtain with the adverts.

Brendan loved all the old come-all-ye's we used to see here. It's where *The Hostage* came from. I've always seen that play as music hall. In fact everything Brendan wrote for the stage has vaudevillian elements. That's not to take away from his plays but to praise them.

Ireland has traditionally been seen as a country that has two types of writers: those who beaver away at their desks day in and day out and those who talk their masterpieces away in pubs. Brendan was that rare specimen, a bit of both. A man who worked hard and played hard, there was always a very tenuous distinction between the two activities with him and, though he claimed he stayed on the wagon while writing, it's tempting to see him lashing out reams of republican Irish poetry on soggy beer-mats when the fit took. It's easy for us to say that his drinking and general lifestyle blunted the full fruition of his talent, but from another point of view it galvanised it into action, especially considering so much of his output was autobiographical.

Alan Simpson said of him, "He was an artist in spite of himself. His way of life was like that of an artisan, a house-painter like his father, who regarded work simply as a way of earning money. Whether he worked with a typewriter or a paintbrush was immaterial to him. He changed from the brush to the typewriter when he found that the typewriter could earn him more money. Then he discovered he could make money just by talking to people in pubs, so he didn't bother to type any more." This is, of course, a gross over-simplification of the complex parabola of his life, and also an evasion of Brendan's own description of himself as a man with a burning desire to write since as far back as he could remember. Indeed, he often said that if Ma sent him down to a shop to buy a loaf of bread, he would read pages of newspapers that were discarded on the pavement in front of him.

Simpson, strangely enough, had almost the very same view of Da as he had of Brendan on the subject of money. "Stephen Behan," he said, "operated on the simple basis of, 'If you have it, spend it. First on necessities such as drink, and then, if there was anything left over, on luxuries like food, clothing and shelter'." Of course that didn't apply to Da half as much as it did to Brendan.

Brendan said he discarded the paintbrush for the pen because the latter was easier to write with, and also somewhat lighter to hold. The money was obviously a factor too. Brendan would probably have agreed with Samuel Johnson's dictum that nobody but a blockhead ever wrote without getting paid for it, but I don't believe it was the prime reason he wrote. If it was, the passion that's in his work, and the undeniable love of words and the images they convey, wouldn't have been there. Instead we would have had a packaged, yellowpack writer. Whatever else Brendan's faults may have been from a literary point of view, being jaded and formulaic certainly wasn't one of them.

He said he wrote primarily out of 'muraphobia' (the fear of painting walls), but as his life progressed – or rather regressed – he drank out of scriptphobia (if I may coin an even uglier word). Most writers will dream up any excuse they can to avoid getting to their desks in the morning and Brendan had a better one than most.

When Sean O'Casey made a similar transition from pushing a shovel to pushing a pen, he said, "I just stepped from one kind of hard work to another." He knew what he was going into, but Brendan didn't. He expected it to come as naturally to him as the day job. He didn't realise a lot of the fun would go out of it when you had to prune and edit. Never a patient man, he only ever painted a given wall once, and if you asked him to do it over, you'd be told sharply what to do with yourself. The same went for editors who put red lines through his copy. The only time he didn't mind was when they took his plays and worked on them. That would be like someone else doing his re-painting.

Neither did he mind the fact that his mentor Rae Jeffs was content to be a sounding-device for him towards the end of his life. He did books like *Brendan Behan's Island* and *Brendan Behan's New York* merely by speaking them into a tape recorder, which she subsequently edited.

The taped books weren't a surprising development, considering he was essentially a bardic talent. In a sense, all of his books were spoken or at least they read that way. However, the spontaneity was missing from these later books. In many ways they read like a series of journalistic interviews cobbled together which is, of course, what in essence they were. When he talked in bars he never felt the compulsion to be quotable, and often that's the very time you are, because of the absence of pressure.

The watched kettle of Rae Jeffs did boil sometimes, having said that, but somehow the idea of a performer speaking into a machine didn't seem to jibe, especially when there was a witness present watching him for developments. It would have been like Beatrice looking over his shoulder in Anglesea Road as he typed out the earlier books. It was like writing-by-numbers, a muted attempt to capture life in fast motion using technology. But maybe Jeffs reasoned that sub-standard Behan was still better than no Behan, and she was right in that, even if the finished products fell beneath both of their expectations.

Brendan never read these books, and really only did them as stop-gaps, like a prize-fighter getting into training for his next bout. Alas, the rehearsal became the main event as he drowned himself in a sea of booze and self-parody and his inspiration became mangled somewhere inside his demented pub performances.

Brendan wasn't a great writer in the strict sense of the term and his output was as fitful as his life. Indeed were it not for the cult of notoriety that dogged him everywhere he went – at his own instigation as often as not – it's doubtful if his work would have garnered the close attention it has since his passing. On the other hand, the same cult of notoriety warred against any semblance of discipline he might otherwise have had when it came to knuckling down to work.

So it cut both ways. In creating himself as a legend, Brendan did a career hara-kiri. His high profile stultified his inspiration even as it secured his plays and fiction a sure place on any shelf marked 'Contemporary Irish Literature'. Even the casual reader couldn't help feeling that here was a writer who wanted to bring everyone to his party, that his work was almost an extension of his drinking, an activity where yet again he gave vent to that Falstaffian joviality. He wanted his audience to be not just McDaid's and The White Horse Bar but the world.

J P Donleavy said that Brendan "believed deeply in publicity and the fact that it had some sort of reality of its own – but he forgot the fact that newspapers and TV appearances don't last as long in the public memory as one's books". True enough, but the books are there too. What he was doing was merely giving them a bigger window than most writers got the chance of creating as most of them didn't have his colour or versatility.

Author Ted Boyle claimed that if the critics had demanded more of Brendan, he would have dug deeper into his creative reservoirs. The exuberance of his genius, he added, was a function of his magnificent lack of self-control. Had he been able to stop drinking, his creative capacity would probably have dried up as well. Clearly, there are more questions than answers, and every theory about what direction his career could have taken invites another one that's almost its anthesis.

Rather than attempting a third, it might be easier to simply describe what his gift was. Kenneth Tynan came close, "If the English hoard words like misers, the Irish spend them like sailors. And Brendan Behan, Dublin's obstreperous poet/playwright, is one of the biggest spenders in this line since the young Sean O'Casey."

Long before Roddy Doyle, he took writing away from academia and gave it back to the people. For good or ill, he was 'The People's Champion', both hero and heartbreaker, poet and pillock, genius and jackass . . . but always himself, from page to stage and cradle to premature grave.

Francis McManus put it this way:

> I remember Brendan Behan in the morning, as it were, of his writing life when the dew was still on him. He used to ramble in to see me in old Radio Éireann in the very late-forties and early-fifties. Alone or in company, he let the whole place know with a hullaballoo that he had arrived. With his gap-toothed grin and his fat, round-

*cheeked, country woman's face he looked utterly harmless, like an
overgrown cherub.*

David Nathan was more complimentary when he said, "The laughing
storyteller with the gap-toothed smile was a far greater writer than he
ever was a drinker. And a far greater man than either."

Hold Your Hour and Have Another, to use Francis MacManus' phrase,
captures him in the spring of his life. It has a light touch that's difficult
to square with the man he became. This is mainstream family fare with
a slightly off-beat edge, a far cry indeed from the kind of man one could
imagine wrecking bars – or his own head.

The un-blessed Trinity of *Brendan Behan's Island, Bredan Behan's New
York* and the posthumously published *Confessions of an Irish Rebel* are
really the marginalia of his career, the indecorous footnotes to a once
vibrant talent. They were books he could have written in his sleep –
and, if we're to believe some of the stories told about Brendan around
this time, he very nearly *did*. He was, by then, trying to clutch at literary straws the same way he tried to clutch at old friends for support,
but the harder he tried, the more the magic eluded him. Rae Jeffs was
like his new Joan Littlewood, the midwife who would string together
the diffuse strains of a fast-diminishing talent, unleashing it upon the
public as she vainly sought to re-inspire that beleaguered psyche. But
Brendan's soul wasn't in these books. They were like *Hamlet* without
the Prince, like a man playing mind-games with himself, and his readers. Without her input, they wouldn't have been done at all. With it,
they were like half-cooked soufflés.

There's an argument to be made for the fact that writers are people
who never grew up. The same is also said about alcoholics and uncon-
scionable showmen. Brendan was all three. He brought joy to life and
literature, even in the midst of misery. Like Ma, he had learned to smile
through his tears, to sing of grief. Gone was the *ochón ochón* tradition.
This is a pagan affirmation of life in all its vicissitudes. It could even be
encapsulated in the comment he often made when people asked him
how he was. "Jaysus," he'd say, throwing his head back, "if I was any
better I don't think I could stand it" – a far cry from the "Not too bad"
that was almost a catch-phrase of his contemporaries when asked the
same question.

"Behan's belief," Colbert Kearney said, "was in the power of generous laughter to raise the hearts of the faithful, and lower those dull,
scruffy creeping jesuses, the begrudgers of life."

"Behan is the one Dubliner who has expressed himself in his writing," claimed Terence de Vere White in his book *Ireland*. "Even O'Casey,"
de Vere White continued, "was an observer, always slightly removed
from his neighbours. Brian O'Nolan was a great patron of bars, and he
had a wonderful ear, but Behan was the thing itself and he combined it

with a self-granted licence to enact the stage-Irishman of legend. With
him died two traditions."

Too often posterity has described him as a drinker who wrote rather
than a writer who drank but, for as long as I can remember him, I knew
of his passion for word-making. I never saw him but he was writing
something. Propped up in bed with the typewriter on his knees, he
never thought of food or drink till he was finished what he was doing.
Then he would come down to a great bowl of soup. Worn and unshaven
he looked like a proper Bill Sykes. That's the way I still remember him
today.

Brendan, of course, wasn't the only one of the Behans who wrote.
Our uncle Peadar Kearney, composed Ireland's National Anthem. That's
a nice thing to have on your CV. Sadly however, the same tune seems to
have fallen into disfavour in recent times. A few years ago John Bruton,
who was Taoiseach at the time, launched a campaign to have it replaced
by a "less militaristic" ditty. This, he thought, would better suit the
peace process. Bertie Ahern thought *A Nation Once Again* could be a
good alternative. I myself suggested *Danny Boy* crossed with *London-
derry Air* . . . provided Orangemen stopped singing the British national
anthem. Ulster Unionist MP Clifford Forsythe was unimpressed with
my idea. "I like *Danny Boy*," he admitted, "but then I also like Mozart.
Neither, however, would be a proper substitute for *God Save The Queen*."

And of course Dominic was a writer, as am I. In fact one of the
reasons I was never threatened by Brendan's literary success is that I
was famous before he was. (In 1951, my photograph was on the front
page of *The Observer* standing with Mao Tse Tung. I had also shaken
hands with Stalin in Russia by that time.) Sometimes people even call
me Brendan by mistake. This doesn't bother me either. We should turn
life's millstones into stepping stones.

Seamus, God love him, is given to saying, "I'm the luckiest of all
the Behans because I'm the only one of them who never wrote an effin'
book." And do you know something – the lad is probably right.

Seamus compares writing to hard labour. Being a Behan, he has
also seen enough of writers to know that he prefers to walk the other
side of the street from them. "A curse on all their houses," he proclaims.
In fact one time when Brendan was swinging the lead about how he
was such a great writer and all that, Seamus looked him squarely in the
eye and said, "I don't give a shite if you are or not. I'm a great sparky
and that's much more important to me than your books." Brendan was
a bit taken aback but didn't pursue the matter.

"I loved Brendan's bones," Seamus says, "but he was of a different
ilk to me. I wasn't a republican, and my reading tastes were different
too. I read everything from *Boy's Own* to R M Ballantine's *Coral Island*.
Not exactly the sort of stuff you'd find Brendan with." Seamus insists
there are too many writers in Ireland, and I tend to agree with him. "I

have no public to please," he says, "so I have no public to enthrall or disappoint." Wise man.

Then there was Dominic. Brendan and Dominic never saw eye-to-eye. Brendan broke up a production of Dominic's play one night by shouting obscenities up at him from the audience. He deeply resented competition from his own family. He fell asleep at the play and when he woke up he started roaring at the actors, saying the play was like folk-singing, like a bull farting through a comb.

When Brendan heard my memoirs were being translated into Japanese he said, "Good fuckin' job – nobody else would understand them."

After my first play, *Boots For The Footless*, became a hit, Dominic went ballistic. His jealousy was a sight to behold. He wrote a piece in *The Sunday Times* where he said he had never seen me *reading* a book so he didn't know how I could *write* one. Personally I didn't see the connection. Each man has a library inside his head. If you read too much it dulls your inspiration and you find yourself aping other writers. I prefer to write from my experiences and my imagination.

I've always been proud of *Boots*. It got its title from a story I heard about a man who was asked what he had ever done for the working man. "I put boots on the footless," he replied, "and specs on the blind." That anecdote amused me. It was a Dublin Labour Party Councillor who said it, a big docker called Barney Conway.

Boots was compared to Brendan's *The Hostage* for its ballads and blarney, its hilarity and humbug. The critic Claire Armistrad said I hadn't pushed back the frontiers of drama, but there was something immensely refreshing, in those days of dour bearings of the Irish soul, about seeing the whole shebang sent up so toweringly as it was by me.

Unlike Brendan, my passage to the pinnacle of the literary tree wasn't smooth. After *Boots* was accepted for staging, the theatre burnt down. I told them it would have been simpler to reject the play. They didn't need to go that far as I'm not easily offended. It was the worst rejection slip I ever received. But it did get on eventually and played for seven weeks to rave reviews and sell-out houses. I ended up selling the rights for a grand.

Most of my plays invite caveats from sensitive souls, such as "Lock up your daughters" or "Stock up on the mouthwash". No higher praise can one heap on me. I have made it my life's business to rattle cages – and begrudgers. *Boots* was condemned as endorsing paddywhackery by people like Frank Delaney who epitomise 'High Seriousness' – a disease whose sufferers, I think, should be avoided. There are already too many of them in the world, and life is too short for that kind of thing. Like Brendan, I like to enjoy life, and I like the characters in my plays to have spirit. They don't 'stand' for anything. They're just themselves. It's like when Brendan was asked what were the messages of his plays. "Messages?" he barked. "What messages? I'm not a fucking postman."

I have also been accused of plagiarism in my work, but as I always say, every writer robs. Shakespeare lifted all of his Roman plays from Plutarch.

The critic Alan Titley even coined a new term to describe *Boots For The Footless*: 'fromp'. I quite like that. He meant it was a cross between a farce and a romp. I don't really care what people call my plays as long as they go to see them and I get paid.

Tom Widger commented, "I found it a cross between the storm scene from *Lear*, the mad scene from *Lucia* and the closing chapters from *Alice in Wonderland*." Don't some people take literature very seriously all the same? These are people, as Brendan commented, who go to the theatre every other night, and know how it should all be done, which makes you wonder why they don't compose a few themselves and get rich, instead of wringing out other people's dirty laundry. But there you are.

Fintan O'Toole wrote in *The Irish Times* that people who regarded the play as offensive were over-reacting because it was in reality "about as offensive as an old drunk sitting in a corner of a pub shouting incoherent curses at nobody in particular".

Initially I had one of the characters, Padser, having sex with the Queen Mum at the end, but I decided that would have been a bit vulgar. Still, it would have been nice to get the reaction of Fintan to the scene, if nothing else.

No matter how bad the abuse got, however, I knew I was going to tough it out. Dammit, I had been a hod-carrier for 27 years and I wasn't going back to that even if I got a court injunction banning me from ever putting pen to paper again for the rest of my natural. No siree. The learned critics of the day would have to find a new whipping boy. A bit like Maggie Thatcher (or Attila the Hen as I like to call her) this lad was not for turning.

Another woman described my play as, "Two hours of psychological torture." I hope I haven't misunderstood, but I take that to mean she didn't enjoy it. Others called it racist. All I can say to this charge is that the plays of Synge and O'Casey were labelled the same way, so it appears I'm following in an honourable tradition. A gaffer in London's *Evening Standard* even suggested that, if I weren't Irish, I would have been hauled up before the Race Relations Committee. Some members of this Committee actually picketed the theatre in which *Boots* was being staged. I believe they had good fun out on the street. As the play itself was street theatre, a discussion ensued as to which provided more entertaining action: my play or the picketers. I am open to opinions on this, though I'm reminded of the party that was thrown in Hollywood in 1966 for the wrap-up of the Marlon Brando film *A Countess from Hong Kong*. The party was such a success and the film such a flop, one wag suggested they should dump the film and release the party.

Criticism of the play told me more about the critics themselves than anything else. Frank Delaney acted as if I had committed some unpardonable sin by daring to write a play that people could actually enjoy (a definite no-no for all self-respecting modern playwrights, apparently) whereas most of the others damned it as a pastiche of everybody from O'Casey to John B Keane to Boucicault to, yes, Brendan Behan. To which I say: so bloody what? I was never a great fan of the pretentious 'Theatre of Misery'. If Brendan took the *ólagóning* out of Irish literature, I hardly felt it incumbent on me to put it back in.

Ferdia MacAnna, the son of Tomás and a sometime rock star with the Rhythm Kings in a previous incarnation, slammed it as "lobotomised paddywhackery" on Mike Murphy's *Arts Show*. That was a new one on me. He said Billy Boyle's Padser reminded him of "a punk Val Doonican" a definite sight to contend with. Ferdia expressed surprise that the Kentish Town Ladies Sodality hadn't skipped across the pond to picket it, and I have to admit I was a little disappointed by this too. However, maybe the Stalinist clique that orchestrated the pickets in the first place didn't have a budget that covered the mailboat for the rent-a-picketers. (Our Sean went up to one of them at Kilburn, outside the Tricycle Theatre, and asked him what he was picketing. The answer he got was "I don't know", which put the whole matter in a certain new perspective for me.)

In time I myself joined one of the pickets protesting against the staging of *Boots*, yelling along like the best of them. And of course it produced the desired effect, as more and more people streamed in the more I shouted. I knew it was what Brendan would have wanted.

Another play I wrote, *Halleluah, I'm A Bum* was about a Tory Minister who's having a homosexual affair with another member of the Cabinet. When this came out in England, a state of national emergency was declared. People were getting heart attacks in their beds at the sheer thought of it. Can you imagine it – gay men in the House of Commons! Unthinkable. Anyway, everybody was anxious to make sure I didn't get a farthing from the Arts Council to help me stage this unadulterated filth. I think a lot of politicians did novenas to Our Lady that year hoping I would retire. Once again the curse of the Behans was in danger of hitting the West End with this new Scud missile. The very least these people would accept was that my play be banned and/or censored.

At this juncture let me state that I disapprove of censorship in any shape or form. Last year I wrote a play that was called *The Fatwa*. It was about the plight of Salman Rushdie but it never reached the stage because the actors kept pulling out for fear the death sentence on Rushdie would transfer itself to them. I find it extraordinary that a condemned man with a life sentence hanging over him, with no possibility of appeal or reprieve, can't be discussed on a platform or stage.

To those who criticise my works for being too light, I say, I'm not into the theatre of misery like that miserable old hoor Samuel Beckett. He made a fortune out of it. I prefer laughter. It's more effective than any sword, yet all narrow-minded cults fear it.

Anyway, *Boots* played to packed houses in the West End, and many of the critics who saw it said it was as good as anything Brendan ever wrote. It was subsequently staged in the Tivoli Theatre in Dublin's Francis Street. (I used to go to school in that street as a nipper, getting the halfpenny bus in from Crumlin.)

If people see my works as anti-Irish, then that's their problem, not mine. Let them carry me away screaming if they must. If they want to see me as a thick Paddy, that's okay too. I will then join the ranks of other 'thick Paddys' like Yeats, Joyce, Sam Beckett, Oscar Wilde and George Bernard Shaw. For we are all, in our way, unpatriotic sods and so was Brendan.

The point is that I'm not afraid of criticism. Some years ago Susan Raven of *The Sunday Times* rang me up to say that they were considering running an article in which Dominic called me a Provo. The article suggested that I was involved in the assassination of some Dublin officials, and that I used socialism as some kind of a cover for international terrorism. "Will you sue if we publish?" she asked me. "I'll sue if you *don't*," I told her, "I have a book coming out and I could do with the publicity."

I don't want to write smug plays about things that don't matter. I don't want to write drawing room comedies like Noël Coward or linguistic gobbledegook like James Joyce, despite Mr Joyce's undeniable gift in that area. Joyce wrote middle class literature after those same classes fed him with their money. He justified it on the grounds that he was a genius – which, fortunately for him, he was.

One critic described me as Dublin's verbal equivalent of Semtex. He said he took an atheist, a left-wing schoolteacher and a very religious relative to see *The Begrudgers* and they all laughed throughout like leprechauns on LSD. Can you ask for anything more than that in life?

When I first sent that play to Les Smith at the Bristol Old Vic, he wrote back to tell me he thought it was "hilarious, sprawling, life-enhancing and a total mess". As well as summing up my play, I think that's a pretty good description of my life so far.

Neither has such a life been without its ironic touches. I wrote a play called *Barking Sheep* in 1994 which concerns three prison inmates, but I ended up acting it myself because one of the actors playing an inmate was, you've guessed it, arrested just before the play was due to start. Like all good playwrights who believe the show must go on, I doubled for the unfortunate gentleman.

The title of that play came from a comment a lorry driver made to me. I was saying to him we should have a referendum on the withdrawal of British troops from Northern Ireland and he said, "You're wasting your time talking about referendums. The people of this country are born for slavery. Sheep can't bark." I thought it was a great title for a play.

It's also, in case you care, a pretty good description of my personality. Like a lot of writers who get their mugs into the newspaper for groaning on about this and that, I'm basically a shy person (I can tell you Brendan was too). It's a quality I've noticed in many alcoholics. It's the confident people and the cute hoors who can handle their drink. But that's to go off the point. I'm just saying I never thought I would become as well known as I am. I haven't courted headlines for the sake of them. Neither did Brendan. Neither of us went looking for trouble. It just seemed to find us. And as regards tipping a Behan to become a world-famous author in the fifties, well you'd probably have had a better percentage of success putting a fiver on a 100/1 shot in the Grand National.

After seeing *The Hostage* for the first time, I was gobsmacked. I sat in the audience thrilled skinny. I wanted to shout for everyone to hear, "My brother wrote that!" Just like Brendan himself used to say at rehearsals. You see we're a childish lot, us Behans. We always get a bit of a surprise when an editor accepts something from us. It must be something to do with the national inferiority complex.

I get disturbed, on the other hand, when people go for me. I don't mind criticism of my work, but I don't like when it gets personal. I realise that asking for it not to get personal in Ireland is asking a lot, we Irish being famous for our internecine squabbling, but sometimes critics seem to want to hit below the belt for the sake of it.

Hugh Leonard took particular exception to my (ab?)use of expletives in *Boots* when it played the Andrews Lane Theatre. "Mr Behan's late brother," he wrote, "effed, blinded and bejaysused profusely wherever he went, and as a result, it was presumed he must be 'one of our own'. People mistook that for talent." Hugh accused me of sullying Irish theatre with the same lavatorial curses as Brendan. It seems he wanted me to adopt a gentler form of abuse, which was never going to be easy.

Even when Hugh knows he's up against a hit play, he refuses to quell his stream of invective. He acknowledged that Joe Dowling's 1994 staging of *Borstal Boy* was a triumph of acting, but after taking the mandatory number of digs at Brendan's stagecraft (or rather lack of it) he finished his 'review' with: "It is a show that will run on and on like a gurrier's nose-bleed."

Hugh conceded that Brendan was a good writer of narrative, but accused him of being an imposter as a playwright, leaning all too heavily on the likes of Joan Littlewood and Alan Simpson to get his plays to the producable stage. He also called Brendan "a sad man, a mess and a messer, a bully, a nuisance, a poseur and a great pudding of *schadenfraude*". I think we can assume Hugh did not like my brother.

On another occasion, Hugh said Brendan was phonier than Richard's cork leg. That hurt. And he said Celia Salkeld wrote the famous last line of *The Hostage* in a dressing room. I disparage remarks like that. It's easy to slander the dead. Corpses don't sue, as you may have noticed. Some time ago Hugh, carrying on his favourite hobby of badmouthing my dead brother, wrote a piece in the *Sunday Independent* about Brendan where he wrote: "His place in the pantheon seems to be founded on the axiom that loutishness and chronic drunkenness are evidence of genius. Put Behan in a colander, shake him over a sink, and what is left is one arguably good play, *The Quare Fellow* and a far better book *Borstal Boy*."

Hugh went on to write about being on a ferry bound for Liverpool with Brendan where he "loudly lacerated" a waiter because he wanted Veuve Cliquot wine and it wasn't forthcoming. "What kind of a fuckin' culchie bastard are you?" Brendan asked the waiter. Things got worse afterwards, and Hugh crept away to his cabin, away from the corrupting influence of Brendan's tongue-lashing.

Fair enough, Hugh. Nobody ever pretended Brendan was an angel, least of all himself. He had a hair-trigger temper, and if you were on the business end of it when he flipped, you would be advised to wear a big pair of ear-plugs.

Hugh seems to have devoted his life to the demolition of 'Behandolatry', as he calls it. But why? What harm can our Brendan do him in death? Maybe Hugh feels he himself should be given the distinction of taking Brendan's place in the literary pantheon, I don't know. I regard *Da* as a very fine play and have no interest in criticising Hugh as he criticises me.

Revenge writing in the grand manner (*à la* Joyce and Gogarty) is only effective against the living. Journalists attacking the dead are simply living for spite. They're inverted necrophiliacs, exhuming corpses for some sort of grandeur by default.

A man in The Beachcomber pub on the Howth Road said to me once, "You're nothing but a has-Behan." I replied, "That's better than a never-was." You have to learn to laugh at yourself Hugh, whether you're past your sell-by-date or not.

My most vicious critics come from Ireland, Hugh included, and I'm just wondering if it's something in the air. Even John Behan, a good and generous man – he's no relation – said to me at dinner in Dublin one night, "You're a traitor for leaving Ireland." "If that's the case," I replied, "then I'm among two million traitors over in England, and a further 24 million in the States." Despite this, John, like many another Irish artist, is only too willing to put his work on show for the Brits to fondle and drool over. Paddy Kavanagh put it well when he said, "The defeated rule in Dublin." A lot of beggars over there were never given the chance to go on horseback and ride to the devil. If they were, they'd be singing different tunes in different vernaculars. As Oscar Wilde said, "the most vociferous critics of society are those who can't get into it".

Sam Beckett declared on the end of Dún Laoghaire pier, "Better France at war than Dublin at peace." I think I know what he meant. I asked Paddy Kavanagh why so many great writers fled Irish shores. "Because they were exiles in their own country," he said. "In Ireland we're ruled by race-course touts." Paddy said of Dublin's literary critics, "I'd love to blow up the whole shaggin' lot of them, providing no one would know."

The same thing happened with Joyce. Ireland paralysed him but he got out in time. The only trouble was he wrote a lot of rubbish abroad. Money destroyed Joyce just as it would Brendan. He wrote three fine books as a pauper but once Sylvia Beach took him up he lost the run of himself and produced that woebegone dirge, *Finnegans Wake*. Ezra Pound sent it back to him saying, "This book is neither a divine revelation nor a cure for the pox." Even his own brother Stanislaus said it was the last witless wanderings of a literary lunatic. And yet the scholars can't get enough of it today. But then that's Ireland for you: drive a man out of his country and then laud him after he's gone.

Hugh and Brendan, in many ways, were really at the same crack. With one difference: Brendan was always out of control when he abused people, whereas Hugh does it in a cold and sober manner. I'm not saying that excuses Brendan, but to my mind it makes his conduct (or should I say *mis*conduct) more forgivable. When Brendan bit you, it was from the front and he wasn't afraid of retaliation.

We used to call Hugh 'the little leprechaun' at school. He is now something of a green Orangeman. Begrudgery comes from people who are so lacking in self-confidence that they hate everyone. It was this that drove Joyce and Beckett, to name but two, from Ireland. It's particularly virulent when applied to people like myself, who left the Old Sod and made a success of my life in hated England.

Anyway, we will let that particular hare sit for the minute. I bear no ill-will to my detractors, short of the occasional wish that they have lighted matchsticks placed under their fingernails. The point is that even when they're denigrating me, it's all grist to the mill. As Brendan said, "there's no bad publicity except your own obituary". I think if I'm going to be bad, I'd prefer to be bad in an outrageous way. It must be something in the Behan genes.

I would also prefer to write a bad play than no play – nothing ventured nothing gained. This may be hard luck on the poor bastards who have paid to see it, but they know where the exit door is, I presume. And there's always the chance that they'll get a laugh out of my nonsense.

Some people seem to be enjoying my work, in any case, because so far nobody has arrived at my door with a pair of handcuffs to stop me doing any more writing. I also understand that the odds against getting a play read are a thousand to one, and the odds against getting it accepted for production something beyond that again. That's why I feel so privileged to have been allowed to do what I like doing in this vein, whether it's due to luck, talent or the fact that I'm my brother's brother. Or all three.

I published my aforementioned memoirs in 1964. They were called *With Breast Expanded* in case anybody wants to rush out and procure a copy. I take some pride in telling you this book was indeed translated into Japanese – the thing that annoyed Brendan so much. The two people responsible were called Suzuki and Giiuchi respectively. Might I add this volume is also utilised as a textbook for Japanese students endeavouring to master the figaries of the English language. Some people who don't like me will probably baulk at this notion, suggesting a better use for it would probably be propping up the dodgy leg of the kitchen table or something like that but, as I've been saying, I've never been unduly bothered by critics. When they give out about me, I cry my way to the bank. The full title of *The Begrudgers* is *Fuck The Begrudgers*, which is a phrase minted by my better-known brother. I called it that in his honour. It's meant to apply to curmudgeons everywhere, but particularly hurlers on the literary ditch. Or as Brendan phrased it, "eunuchs in the harem".

I write what I see and what I feel. I improvise. I use music hall, vaudeville, snatches of conversations I've heard, song and dance, whatever you're having yourself. I'm not a precious writer, and I don't expect scholars (I use that term advisedly) to spend the rest of their natural pouring over my work, looking for hidden symbols. If they do – sorry, boys and girls – they won't find any.

Joyce is up there in that big library in the sky as I write, but I'm sure he takes the occasional time out to chortle at the pathetic efforts of the literary *cognoscenti* to 'interpret' him. He claimed he wrote parts of his books to keep these lads and lassies busy. It was his ultimate revenge on donnish fossils. Likewise, when somebody said to Beckett about the tramps in *Godot*, "They sound as if they've been to university." He replied, "How do you know they haven't?" Another adorable reply.

When Flannery O'Connor was asked if she felt universities stifled writers, she said, "They don't stifle half enough of them." My sentiments exactly. And, I would wager, Brendan's too. The Behan family is a scavenger at the literary feast. We've come in by the tradesman's entrance, if you like. Not, like the Cypriots, bearing gifts, but as our own men. There's more enterprise in walking naked, as Yeats observed in one of his more lucid moments.

I will continue to push the boat out in any case, and to rock it when-ever I can. Most English plays are about middle class love affairs. I think there are more important things in the world to be writing about, don't you? Funnily (or tragically) enough, I've had more success with my work in England than Ireland, just like Brendan. I think that's be-cause the Irish take themselves too seriously, nose-picking their griev-ances.

One of the reasons Brendan was so popular in England is because the English are such miserable buggers they get a big adrenalin rush when somebody says something outrageous – especially if he's drunk at the time. They're reacting the same way to those Oasis lads at the moment.

Before I get side-tracked into that topic, let me stop here to make way for some more Brendan stories. . . .

❖

When Brendan gave a reading in America once, he was informed by the master of ceremonies at the event that he would have to put down the glass of Guinness that was in his hand before he took the stage. His response? "Listen, if you think I'm goin' out there alone, you've got another think comin'!"

❖   ❖   ❖

When Paddy Chayefsky's play *The Tenth Man*, which is set in a syna-gogue, was praised at a performance attended primarily by Jews, Brendan poured cold water on their adulation by grunting, "That's a bit like showing *National Velvet* to an audience of jockeys."

❖   ❖   ❖

Benedict Kiely tells a story about a time he was in Gerry Ryan's pub with Brendan, who was fulminating against the evils of censorship af-ter yet another of his books had been banned. Suddenly, a man with a Northern accent approached them and asked Brendan what size this banned book was. When Brendan gave him a rough idea of the cubic content, the man said, "I could run you over 2,000 copies." He was a butter-smuggler from across the border and wanted to estimate how many copies would fit into his truck coming down!

❖   ❖   ❖

In an *Irish Press* article called "Dialogue on Literature" a character says of Brendan, "Sad case. Only went to school half the time, when they were teaching writing. Can't read."

❖   ❖   ❖

He went into a shop one day looking for Plato's *Symposium* and received this rather daunting response from the bookseller, "We saw a
slight run on it, and the same sort of people looking for it, so we just
took it out of circulation." This was not *Lady Chatterly's Lover*, mind,
nor Dante's *Inferno*. The man went on to say, *vis-à-vis* a recent change in
Ireland's censorship laws, "We don't have to be made decent-minded
by an Act of the Dáil. We have our own way of detecting smut, however ancient."

❖   ❖   ❖

Brendan had such respect for Kerry journalist Michael O'Halloran, according to Ben Kiely, that one day when the pair of them were drinking
together in Skerries and O'Halloran walked in, Brendan commented,
"Get that man a double brandy – he's coming from an ambush."
O'Halloran had been writing a series of articles on the violent Irish
events of the early-twenties for *The Sunday Press* at the time, which was
what led to Brendan's jocular remark. The articles were so vivid,
Brendan claimed, "tin hats were supplied free to all regular readers of
the paper".

❖   ❖   ❖

When asked for the difference between prose and poetry, according to
Peter Costello, he recited this limerick:

> *There was a young fellow named Rollocks,*
> *Who worked for Ferrier Pollocks,*
> *As he walked on the strand,*
> *With his girl by his hand,*
> *The water came up to his knees. . .*

That was prose, Brendan argued, but if the water had got any higher, it
would have been poetry.

❖   ❖   ❖

Colbert Kearney called to see him one day before *Brendan Behan's Island* was published and said he had heard about a forthcoming book.
"There's no new book," he said, "the newspaper reports are all fucking
rubbish." At this point Beatrice said that there was indeed a new book

coming out. "There's a sheaf of shit called *Brendan Behan's Island* due out soon," Brendan admitted, "but it is neither a fucking book nor is it fucking new."

❖ ❖ ❖

Before Alan Simpson and Carolyn Swift produced *The Quare Fella*, Brendan submitted it to Ernest Blythe, the Managing Director of the Abbey Theatre. Blythe said he was interested in the play in theory, but that Brendan should see producer Rita Mooney with regard to making some editorial changes. Brendan, who proved more than amenable to any changes Simpson suggested in later times, told Blythe angrily, "I am a playwright. Miss Mooney is a producer, and we don't speak the same language. If there are any revisions I will do them myself."

❖ ❖ ❖

When Brendan was asked where he got his inspiration, he said, "In the ordinariness of people – because it's often extraordinary."

❖ ❖ ❖

Asked what an author's first duty was, he said famously, "To let down his country." This was his responsibility, he maintained, because every writer knew his own country best, so no foreigner should be allowed to criticise it in the same way without that first-hand knowledge. He went on to ask rhetorically, "How can any writer attack another man's fatherland if he doesn't attack his own first?" So you see Brendan wasn't prejudiced against any nation: he insulted them all equally.

❖ ❖ ❖

When somebody asked him if he was a working class writer he replied, "Go and ask Evelyn Waugh if he's a middle class writer. If he says he is, then I will be a working class one."

❖ ❖ ❖

Brendan asked Bryan MacMahon what was the difference between a true artist and a phoney one. "The true artist," McMahon replied, "is mad and has a helluva' problem trying to appear sane, while the phoney artist is sane and has a helluva time pretending to be mad." Whenever MacMahon met Brendan afterwards, Brendan would say to him, "I'm still pretending to be sane."

❖   ❖   ❖

He was so innocent about his talent that, at productions of his plays he would often nudge the person in the seat next to him and coo, "I wrote that you know".

❖   ❖   ❖

Ma was a maid in a house in which W B Yeats sometimes ate. According to her, he would put sugar in his soup and salt in his coffee. One day she served him parsnips and he sniffed them and said, "This is a very peculiar pudding."

Brendan was telling this story to a rather studious American academic, and after, the latter individual had assiduously jotted down the anecdote in his notebook (under 'Parsnips; attitude of Yeats to'), he enquired further of his interlocutor, "And you say he didn't like Stephen's Green either. What kind of vegetable is that?"

❖   ❖   ❖

Brendan defended the profanity in his work because it came from the world he was writing about. He exclaimed frustratedly, "How the hell can I write the way Irishmen talk if I don't use the 'F' word. After all that effer Lawrence got away with it."

❖   ❖   ❖

Brendan liked Sam Beckett, he said, because he kept him going when his readies were low. (Greater love than this no man hath). He wasn't too sure about the man's literary abilities. He confessed he couldn't understand his plays any more than he could understand a swim in the Forty Foot, but he enjoyed them just the same – probably for that reason.

❖   ❖   ❖

"If my plays show anything," Brendan claimed surprisingly, "it's that no ideal is worth the shedding of one drop of human blood."

❖   ❖   ❖

Asked what kind of people he liked best, he replied, "Those who don't buy books very much and who don't live by literature – except newspapers with the racing results."

❖   ❖   ❖

When he was asked who, if anyone, influenced his writings, he placed himself in august company, "Shakespeare said pretty well everything, and what he left out, James Joyce with a little nudge from myself put in."

❖   ❖   ❖

He said *Richard's Cork Leg* wasn't a comedy or drama but a 'dramedy'. It's interesting that the title *Richard's Cork Leg* came from an aside by Joyce himself. "I didn't lick me words from the bricks of Dublin," Brendan said. And, when asked where he got the inspiration for *The Hostage* he snapped, "Ah sure of course I stole the fuckin' thing." After *Exiles* had been rejected, Joyce commented, "If I'd given Richard (one of its characters) a cork leg, it might have been accepted." Brendan took him up on the point – and improved it, after a fashion.

❖   ❖   ❖

In 1947, someone suggested he write a play about the Rising of 1798. "Fuck '98," he said. "Why not a play about our own time?" So *Borstal Boy* was born.

❖   ❖   ❖

Despite his own large body of prison work, he was given to say, "Anything written in jail is rubbish. And that includes *The Pilgrims Progress*."

❖   ❖   ❖

Ma spent a short time with some of our relatives in MacCafferty's Estate when she was pregnant with Brendan. Nobody is quite sure if her decision to leave there was her own or forced upon her, but Brendan liked to say that he was the only writer who was ever evicted before he was born.

❖   ❖   ❖

He once wrote this letter to his Hutchinson publisher Iain Hamilton regarding a book he was working on: "I sat at the typewriter till 8 pm without eating or drinking till I finished the job. I can't drink if I'm working because it will be rubbish, and I can't eat because I haven't been drinking."

❖   ♣   ❖

On his way to France one time, an immigration officer asked him what he did for a living. He said he was a journalist "on my way to write an article for the *Irish Times* on the attitude of the French to football at Dalymount Park". He mustn't have sounded very convincing because the immigration officer then enquired if he knew Brendan Behan. "Oh yes," he beamed, "I've seen him over in Dublin but I don't know much about him. He's a loud-mouthed bastard." When another immigration officer asked him if he was Irish, he said, "No, I'm a Yemenite Arab!"

❖   ❖   ♣

Even though Brendan wrote a song about Michael Collins, he never sang it "because I can never remember anything that I write myself".

♣   ❖   ♣

Brendan confessed to his friend Bill Kelly one time that he wrote some pornography when he was in France, adding that he was relieved it appeared in French. If anyone in Ireland saw it, he said, they'd probably "drown me in holy water, swimmer an' all that I am".

❖   ❖   ❖

Brendan met a man who said one of his plays was rubbish. "Did you pay to get into it?" Brendan asked him. When the man said he did, Brendan said, "That makes me feel a bit better."

❖   ❖   ♣

An American poet informed him that he earned $100 a month from the Government for being mad. "In Ireland," Behan retorted, "our poets go mad *all* the time and get sweet fuck all for their efforts."

❖   ❖   ♣

He had mixed views about the riots surrounding JM Synge's *Playboy of the Western World*. He didn't have a problem with the play being objectionable to certain sections of the audience. He would probably have joined in the shouting if he was there . . . because he enjoyed shouting.

❖   ❖   ♣

He often laughed at the fact that, while *Borstal Boy* was banned in Ireland as a book, you could see it on the stage without any problem whatsoever. A very Irish type of censorial logic.

❖ ❖ ❖

Just as Brendan used to go a bit mad in pubs in the early days for the publicity, so he liked to write contentious material in his books. "If you're not on the banned list," he said to me once, "you're nothing." It was like getting membership of an exclusive club. Joyce and Beckett had known the feeling. "My name is Brendan Behan," he crooned, "I'm the leader of the banned." Well maybe he wasn't quite the leader, but he was right in there with the big boys.

❖ ❖ ❖

In other moods, though, he became incensed at being censored. After being informed that *The Hostage* had been banned, he fumed, "Fuck the censor. I've set up my own Censorship Board, and I hereby censor all censors."

❖ ❖ ❖

When John Ryan spoke of Brendan as being a writer to Pa O'Toole, an old friend of my father's, O'Toole said querulously, "A writer? No, there's only one writer in that family and that's his father Stephen. Did you ever see the sign for Guinness he done up there on the gable over Slattery's in Phibsboro? Them letters is seven foot high. And the pint he drew beside it, with the shine down the side and the big foamy head? Now that's writing. No, Stephen was the only one that ever wrote in that family."

❖ ❖ ❖

Actually Da had no problem about the fact that he didn't do that kind of writing. He was never the jealous type. When he appeared on *This is Your Life*, Eamonn Andrews said to him, "I believe Brendan is doing well for himself."

"Indeed he is," Da replied, "last year he wore my cast-offs, and now I'm wearing his."

❖ ❖ ❖

When an interviewer asked him why he had never produced a play, Da replied, "I am too busy producing playwrights."

❖   ❖   ❖

Evelyn Waugh said to Da in Neary's pub in Chatham Street, "How
come a man like you, a tradesman and house-painter, can have such
brilliant sons?" Da replied calmly as he removed the pipe from his
mouth, "A case of pure biology, sir."

❖   ❖   ❖

There was one other kind of writing Da was talented at, however. "I
write better fiction than any of my sons," he claimed, "and it's good
stuff too. Otherwise how could my timetable have fooled the boss every
week for years?"

❖   ❖   ❖

When *The Hostage* first appeared at the Theatre Royal in 1958, Brendan
told the rapturous audience, "My play is a comment on Anglo-Irish
relations. As to what it is about, you will find out from the critics in the
morning."
     Examine both cheeks for tongues.

Chapter 4

Brendan the Voyager

There is more difference between a Manchester man and a London man then there is between a Belfast man and a Dublin man.

Brendan Behan

Brendan had many homes, and hung his hat in all of them with equanimity. Whether he was in Kildare Street or Crumlin or borstal or the continent or the back room of a bar, he never asked for much in the way of comfort. When he became famous he said, "I go to better rooms, but I sleep less well." He preferred to be in a familiar environment rather than a sterile one, but success meant he had to relinquish some of these 'privileges'. Michael Douglas once said, "My children didn't have the advantages I had in life: they were born rich." Brendan would have known the feeling.

But he had known hunger and thirst. So when he swanned around the world as "Brendan Behan, Celebrity", he milked that too, both for the novelty value and because he had suffered so much from the resentment of his would-be peers.

Begrudgery is so rampant in Ireland, there's an oft-told story about this geezer who says in a pub, "Behan a great writer? Impossible. Jaysus, sure *I* knew him!" Hugh Leonard has defined an Irish literary movement as "two writers on speaking terms with one another". For George Moore it was "half a dozen writers who cordially detest one another".

Brendan described Dublin as the biggest parish in Europe, and he also said that if you got three Irish writers together, two of them would most likely be backbiting the third. In such an environment, it was surprising he didn't get even more of his teeth knocked out in bar-room brawls. He dived into literature the same way he liked to dive into the Forty Foot: from a height and without looking. A swim in the Forty Foot usually left him feeling invigorated, but the murky waters of Irish letters soured him. And yet he never became an exile like Joyce or Beckett or O'Casey, always returning to the city that spawned him like a salmon swimming upstream. He had a love-hate relationship to Ireland as he had to its inhabitants – and indeed with himself.

Brendan described Ireland like this: "It's a village in Trieste with James Joyce, Devon with Sean O'Casey, Paris with Sam Beckett and all tied together, from O'Neill in America to Wilde in Reading Gaol to an

elderly degenerate proselytising umbilical lasoo known as the Archbishop of Dublin."

He agreed with O'Casey that Ireland was a great country to get a
letter from. Such a healthy cynicism helped him keep his sanity among
the people he both loved and hated, and who loved and hated him.
Suprisingly enough he disputed the notion that his fellow countrymen
were cynical. "It's rather that they have a lack of respect for everything
and everybody," he explained. So now you know.

He needed Ireland to fire his inspiration. He needed it for its pubs
and its characters and its easygoing ways. And of course its tolerance
of him when his behaviour became riotous, which was most of the time.
If every tinker had his own way of walking, to quote himself, every
writer should have his own way of embellishing his legend. And
Brendan, when all was said and done, preferred to do it among his
own people. Absence from Ireland didn't necessarily make the heart
grow fonder, but it made him return to it like a comfortable old boot he
wore. It was a place in which he didn't have to strike poses. Everybody
knew him for what he was – and wasn't.

Having said that, he loved travelling abroad, especially to America.
It was a country where he found relief from Ireland's parish-pumpery.
It was also a place where he drank less, because there were less daily
temptations in the times between play openings. He once stayed sober
for nine months solid in New York. If he had stayed there during the
sixties, it's possible he wouldn't have descended into the human wreck
he became for the last few years of his life.

A plaque on the Chelsea Hotel in New York quotes a dedication
from *Brendan Behan's New York* that he wrote in the spring of 1963: "To
America, my new-found land," it says, "the man that hates you hates
the human race." Which pretty much summed up his feelings.

He was as at home in Third Avenue, New York as he ever had been
in 14 Russell Street, having that talent for transforming every community he graced with his presence into an extension of his personality.

It was a long way from Sundrive Road to Greenwich Village, but
Brendan performed the hardly negligible feat of acting the maggot in
similar fashion in both locales. A pub was a pub no matter where you
went, and if they let you sing an old ballad, what did it matter if it was
the tricolour that was hanging outside the window or the Stars and
Stripes? Clifford Irving said about him, "He was a vicious tank of a
man rolling relentlessly through the minefield of America, crushing
everything in sight until he blew up." (This is not – and I repeat *not* –
an overly romantic appraisal of my brother's life.)

In Norman Mailer he met his alter ego. There may not have been
many similarities between Brooklyn and North William Street as regards getting a rudimentary education, but here were two little men
with two big mouths, a pair of Raging Bulls if you like, with the ability

to make steam rise off the pages they filled with their spleen. They also knew how to tell a story. And if somebody put them together in a boxing ring, there wouldn't have been many empty seats. Not that they needed to, for they did enough horse-playing in bars without having recourse to the boring detail of having a referee intercede when the going got rough.

One of the funniest encounters between the pair of them was when Mailer asked Brendan if he usually had a police escort on public occasions back in Ireland. "Indeed I do," Brendan told him, "but I'm usually handcuffed to the bastards!"

❖

Brendan was never what you might call a snappy dresser, which made it occasionally difficult for him to get a cab when he was in New York. He didn't realise this until a cab-driver said to him one day, "You look like a bum, but I'm going to take you because you look like a bum with enough to pay the fare." And there you have the contradiction that was Brendan.

❖   ❖   ❖

Brendan found the French very civilised. He said, "You can break up a cafe and as long as you pay for the damage you're perfectly welcome to come back the next night and do it all over again." No wonder he enjoyed his Parisian escapades. Would that Irish society was so understanding of those with a penchant for the transference of furniture from one end of a room to the other when a pint went down the wrong way.

❖   ❖   ❖

Of the Spanish Civil War Brendan said, "The Irish who fought for that fascist cunt Franco at least had the good sense to come home with more men than they went out with."

❖   ❖   ❖

Brendan believed it wasn't Christopher Columbus that discovered America but his namesake Brendan the Navigator. Not being overly impressed with the place, though, he hushed it up.

❖   ❖   ❖

In *Brendan Behan's Island* Brendan tells of a murder in Kerry where everyone kept tight-lipped to the Gardai. Finally a Garda said to a woman

"Tell me, mam, do you know the names of these three islands out there?" as he gazed out over the Atlantic Ocean. She thought for a moment and said, "I couldn't tell you, sir, but they weren't there when I went to bed last night." Now that's loyalty.

❖   ❖   ❖

Brendan had a plausible theory that was more justification for partitioning England than Ireland because there was more difference between a Liverpudlian and a Cockney than there was between, say, a Belfast man and a Dublin man.

❖   ❖   ❖

Our Granny once said to him, "Do you know the difference, between having an Irish Republic and being a section of the British Empire?" When he asked her to tell him she said, "From one you'll get an eviction order written in English with the lion and unicorn and from the other you'll get an eviction order written in Irish, with a harp."

❖   ❖   ❖

Toronto, he once said, would be a fine town when it was finished. He had no love for Montreal either. Arriving there in 1960 for a lecture, he was unimpressed with its dullness and freezing temperature. As he stood on the top of a mountain one day looking down at the city in all its frostiness, he made two typical Behanesque gestures to sum up his feelings about it. The first was to make the sign of the cross, the second to pee in the snow. He hated Toronto so much he said the New York Tourist Board should spend a weekend there to get some advice on how *not* to attract tourists.

❖   ❖   ❖

He wrote this in a letter written to Rory from Hollywood in 1961: "Broadway is a great place for a quiet piss-up, the secret being to get the newspapermen pissed too."

❖   ❖   ❖

One of the things that most amazed him about Americans was the fact that they boasted about bribery and corruption as if it was their own invention. "They boast of the heartlessness of the multitude, and how a man could lie in Time Square for a month without anyone going near him, except to rob or rape him." Brendan concluded that Americans had come to such conclusions as a result of seeing too many movies.

❖   ❖   ❖

An acquaintance of his told him he knew of a woman who said once, "My husband was all right until he discovered he was a bleedin' Irishman!"

❖   ❖   ❖

He knew an Irish-American girl who sent a bundle of teabags home to her mother during the first World War. Her mother hadn't a clue what they were for so she hung them up on the wall as Christmas decorations.

❖   ❖   ❖

When a magistrate asked him how he had got into England in the first place, Brendan's answer was original even for him. "By umbrella," he exclaimed, "me grandfather had a noble umbrella with powerful ribs on it. We were flying over London and I says to the pilot, 'Let me out here, mate'. So he slides back the door an' I opened the brolly an' out I stepped."

❖   ❖   ❖

Brendan met a New Yorker who informed him that the Irish National Anthem was a song called *Who Put the Overalls In Mrs Murphy's Chowder*. Considering that our uncle Peadar Kearney wrote the anthem (as I mentioned earlier) he was trying to schmooze the wrong guy.

❖   ❖   ❖

Brendan said this about Piccadilly at midnight, "Unless you're a policeman, a criminal or a prostitute, you have no business there."

❖   ❖   ❖

I was with him at Dublin airport one time and I asked Brendan why he was going to America. He answered me in what I deemed to be a succinct fashion, "To earn money to support some ignoramus in the government who couldn't tell a pig from a rabbit."

❖   ❖   ❖

The author Ben Kiely likes to tell the story of the day he was walking with Brendan from Rathgar to an establishment called The Old Grinding

Young. It was the day of a big game in Croke Park in which Wexford were playing and Brendan listened to the "rural hurrahs" of passing cars with increasing disapproval. He finally said to Kiely, "I want to tell you something. I have a pathological horror of country people. And no harm to Pearse McGuinness or yourself, but the North of Ireland people are the worst. They are of two varieties: Catholic and Protestants. The Protestants are all right. Up where they are they've grabbed everything, so they stay at home. But the North of Ireland Catholic would come here into Dublin and lift the sausage off your plate."

❖   ❖   ❖

When Brendan was in America one time he made this rather politically incorrect comment on disapora, "People who are compelled to abandon their homelands in search of a better way of life are troglodytes and low class scum. I'm here at the invitation of Hollywood moguls and Broadway producers."

❖   ❖   ❖

He liked to tell the story of the commander of a Japanese submarine who came to Cork and was asked what he thought of it. "The only difficulty," he said, "was that my crew failed to distinguish one Corkman from another."

❖   ❖   ❖

Overall he described America as a "the land of permanent waves and impermanent wives".

❖   ❖   ❖

He liked The Big Apple, though with some reservations: "There are three things I don't like about New York: the water, the buses and the professional Irishman. A professional Irishman is one who's terribly anxious to pass as a middle class Englishman."

❖   ❖   ❖

Brendan made an unusual analogy between two unlikely groupings when he said, "Other people have a nationality. The Irish and the Jews have a psychosis."

❖   ❖   ❖

After meeting Louis Armstrong at a party, he asked the legendary musician what he thought of Dublin. "What's Dublin?" said Armstrong. "Is it something I can play?"

❖　　❖　　❖

This was Brendan's take on Dublin snobbery: "It started off with hats and white ties and getting into the 'gentry', and then to chatting about the servant problem with the Anglo-Irish horse Protestants. It went from that to late dinner and now it's ang'st, no less."

❖　　❖　　❖

After reading rebel leader John Mitchell's description of Dublin as "a city of genteel dastards" Brendan remarked to Da, "I suppose he really said *bastards*, but they changed it to *dastards*, for reasons of respectability." Da replied, "No it's nobody's fault to be a bastard, but to be a dastard you have to really work at it."

❖　　❖　　❖

Adhering by his own dictum that an artist's first duty was to let down his country, he said that if it was raining soup, the Irish would be out with forks.

❖　　❖　　❖

Englishmen weren't much better. They were a pacifistic race, he believed, because they always had their wars in other people's countries.

❖　　❖　　❖

An Englishman said to him that every time the British find an answer to the Irish Question, the Irish change the question. "Not so, *a mhic*," Brendan replied, "because there isn't any such thing as the Irish Question for us Irish; there's only the English Question."

❖　　❖　　❖

"I knew a man from Nicholas Street," Brendan wrote in one of his *Irish Press* columns, "that sat on the Throne of England." Come again? Well actually he was a painting contractor doing up Buckingham Palace…

❖　　❖　　❖

He's alleged to have believed that Cork people would steal the cross behind Jesus' back and leave him hanging in the air.

❖ ❖ ❖

Corkmen were also, he thought, the hardest people in Ireland to hang: because they have such bloody hard necks.

❖ ❖ ❖

Cork comedian Niall Toibin says a lot of Brendan's alleged anti-Corkness, like a lot of other things about the man, was really just a pose. When Toibin mentioned to him one day that he had been at Dalymount Park at a soccer game, an exasperated Brendan exclaimed, "What the fuck were you doin' in Dalymount? You should have been in Croke Park. You're from the country, and soccer means nuthin' to you fuckers." Toibin, not to be outdone, replied, "I beg your pardon, I'm from Cork city and for your fuckin' information we won the Free State Cup more times than anybody else." Brendan conceded grumpily to this.

❖ ❖ ❖

Cartoonist Bob Pyke met Brendan in the fifties in a Dublin pub and the pair of them found themselves discussing – among other things – the joys of France. Not long afterwards Pyke remembers Brendan hailing a taxi and before he knew where he was (the amount of drink he consumed had made his mind hazy about the details) he found himself at a Paris airport. Boulevardier Brendan took him on a pubcrawl for the next two days and then a pole-axed Pyke returned to Dublin, and started to wonder if he had imagined the whole escapade...

❖ ❖ ❖

Brendan said he would have loved to have lived in America in the last century, adding, "I would have been a carpetbagger or a scallywag, whichever was the most obnoxious."

❖ ❖ ❖

At the New York premiere of *The Hostage* in 1960 he told an interviewer that if the play bombed, he planned to join the Fire Brigade as an alternative lifestyle. Asked how he planned to amuse himself in his spare time, he said he intended to pay a visit to the Empire State Building "in honour of King Kong". He also said he wanted to have a swim at the local Jewish boy's club. Asked why, he replied, "Because I'll be the only one there with a foreskin."

❖   ❖   ❖

Moving from Russell Street to Crumlin was for Brendan like being transformed into a reconstructed culchie overnight. He professed a pronounced disdain for anybody beyond the pale – which, by his estimation, meant within an asses roar of The Pillar. He met a man in a pub who was of uncertain geographical origin and said to him, "Are you from Dublin? You don't effin' well sound like it. Come back when you're born in Dublin."

Chapter 5

Shooting from the Lip

Behan sends language out on a swaggering spree – ribald, flushed and spoiling for a fight.

Kenneth Tynan

Even though Brendan finally became a victim of premature burn-out, in the short years he spent sullying and embellishing the tapestry of literary Dublin in about equal measures, he created a treasure trove of stories for those with whom he fraternised. Many in Dublin have a Behan yarn to tell. Most likely it will be apocryphal, but it's a long time now since that has been a cause for concern. As Irish-American film director John Ford once put it, "When the facts conflict with the legend, print the legend." Or, in the vernacular of one of those with whom he had a troubled relationship, Paddy Kavanagh, "Gods make their own importance." Brendan obviously was not a God – he told most of those he knew he would prefer to end up in "the other place" because that was where all his friends would probably be – but he was certainly larger than life. Most of those who knew him (or pretended to) had a love-hate relationship to him, and one senses this was as he wished it.

He was able to toss off one-liners as if they were going out of fashion, which made newsmen lick their lips (and pencils) when he was about. To quote Flann O'Brien, "He was always more a player than a playwright."

❖

He said to a priest one morning after a swim in his beloved Forty Foot, "You know, Father, after this early dip I really feel I've earned my break-fast." When the priest agreed, Brendan said, "Aye – a large brandy and a plate of Benzedrine!"

❖   ❖   ❖

He had this to say about being only allowed fish one Friday when he was in hospital, "There appears to be in this hospital a sort of weekly solstice, an occasion where you are not allowed to partake of flesh. Now, where I come from, which is the slums, there are only two times when you don't eat flesh. One is when you're too damned broke to buy it. The other is when you're too damn sick to eat it."

❖   ❖   ❖

After being discharged from hospital with diabetes and given an insulin dose, his doctor advised him to always carry a couple of lumps of sugar with him wherever he went. "Is that in case I should meet a horse?" he enquired.

❖   ❖   ❖

When asked about his relations, he replied, "The only relations I care to encounter or know are sexual ones."

❖   ❖   ❖

He described Paris thus, "It's a city everyone should live in when they're very young or very old. It's no place for the middle-aged, but then, where the hell is?"

❖   ❖   ❖

Asked why he rarely made plans, he replied, "People who make it a practice of keeping one foot in the past and the other in the future wind up pissing in the now."

❖   ❖   ❖

He was in an elevator with Groucho Marx when the latter prefaced some story with, "I was making *A Night at the Opera* when . . ." Brendan cut in with, "That's like Michelangelo saying, 'I was doing the murals in the Sistine Chapel when. . .'"

❖   ❖   ❖

When Ma told him she'd like to see Paris before she died, he shot back, "You'd better hurry up. Your chances of seeing it afterwards aren't too good!"

❖   ❖   ❖

When he was in borstal, a fellow prisoner who was about to be hanged for murdering his wife asked him if hanging hurt. "I don't think so,"

Brendan replied, "not that I've ever talked to anyone who went through it, but if I do I'll let you know."

❖   ❖   ❖

Brendan once found himself in a pub with a friend who had been a boxer, but the barman refused to serve his friend. He was outraged at the barman adopting the high moral ground because he knew that up until recently, the pub had been a notorious hang-out for prostitutes. One of the latter had been murdered and, frightened by the subsequent publicity, the owner had adopted a new ultra-clean door policy. To bring him back to earth, Brendan, spying a man going to the toilet, expounded, "Watch you don't pull the chain too hard, or you'll be drowned in a sea of contraceptives."

❖   ❖   ❖

After he was spotted with a very uncharacteristic bottle of milk in his hand one time, he remarked, "I'm on the wagon. It's not easy to smile when you're drinking this stuff. I may need a stomach pump."

❖   ❖   ❖

When he was asked if he believed the Irish language was of use anywhere in the world, he replied, "In Nova Scotia it is. It's the only language they use there. They publish a daily paper in Cape Breton in Gaelic."

❖   ❖   ❖

This was his considered view of Clontarf, "It retains a curious, unpleasant odour, because it was here that Brian Boru beat the shite out of the Danes."

❖   ❖   ❖

He was no great fan of learning Irish at school, probably because of the teaching methods. "The Education Minister is making us illiterate in two languages," he bristled once, "Irish and English." But of course he developed a fascination for the language later, when mastery of it became his own choice.

❖   ❖   ❖

This was his greeting to the ornithology correspondent of *The Irish Times*, "How's the blue tits today, missus?" Her reply hasn't been documented.

❖   ❖   ❖

After *The Quare Fellow* premiered in London, a journalist due to interview Brendan appeared in front of him with two pet poodles. "I see you laugh at your own jokes," he said, having heard Brendan guffawing broadly during rehearsals some time before. "Maybe I do," Brendan shot back, "but I don't fuck me own dogs!"

❖   ❖   ❖

When he heard of a gunner who had been shot in the Dardanelles, he muttered, "A very sore place to be shot down there, very sore indeed."

❖   ❖   ❖

After being asked by a foreigner if there was any bullfighting in Ireland, he replied in the affirmative. When the foreigner acted surprised, he explained what he meant. "This isn't a fight between a bull and a matador I'm talking about. It's a fight between two bulls over the affections of a cow." (When asked which of them won, he replied, "Both of them.")

❖   ❖   ❖

After being sentenced to fourteen years in prison for one charge and three months for another on the same day, he said to the presiding judge, "I prefer the three months sentence, Your Honour. Can I have a choice?"

❖   ❖   ❖

He was in the company of American comedian Jackie Gleason one night when Gleason asked him to say something in Irish. "Where the hell did you learn Irish?" Brendan enquired "Oh, I can count up to ten," said Gleason. "A *haon*, a *dó*, a *trí*, a *ceathar*," came the reply.

❖   ❖   ❖

Brendan told a ribald story in front of Dominic and then said, shaking his fist at him, "I shouldn't have said that in front of the skinny bastard because he'll write it down."

❖   ❖   ❖

When an interviewer said to him, "I believe writing runs in your family," Brendan replied, "Well it certainly ran by Dominic!"

✤   ✤   ✤

Groucho Marx said that he would never deign to belong to any club that would actually have him as a member. No doubt Brendan would have concurred. One of his favourite Parthian shots after being chucked out of yet another pub for obstreperous behaviour was, "You're doin' me a favour, *a mhic*. I've been thrown out of better places than this kip."

✤   ✤   ✤

When Brendan was informed that Sweden had the highest suicide rate in the world he said that was a lot of bollox. Sweden was the only honest country for giving out the figures, he said. "It's just as bad in Ireland, except if someone tops himself here we say, he didn't know the gun was loaded, or that seven million pills could tip you over the edge."

✤   ✤   ✤

After alcohol started to take its toll on his health, many of his friends began to worry that he might be tempting fate with his reckless lifestyle. "Do you ever think about dying?" Alan Brien asked him, and he replied in typical Behanesque vein, "Begod, I'd sooner be dead than think about dying."

✤   ✤   ✤

The journalist Proinsias Mac Aonghusa interviewed him in Baggot Street hospital one time, and a very easy interview it was. Brendan told him, "Just sit there and read the papers and I'll write the funny remarks I'm supposed to have made. I know what the crowd want."

✤   ✤   ✤

This was Brendan's definition of an Irish queer: "A man who would trample over twelve bottles of Guinness to get to a woman."

✤   ✤   ✤

In his 1960 interview with Eamonn Andrews he was asked what he would like said about him in 50 years time. He thought for a moment, and then, breaking into hysterics at his own wit, replied, "That I've celebrated my 86th birthday!" No death wish there. Another time he said he wanted to live to be a hundred, "and then be killed by love bites".

❧   ❧   ❧

Asked why he took up writing in the first place, he said, "Because it's easier than house-painting."

❧   ❧   ❧

When one of the Guinness family said they'd been very good to the people of Dublin, he replied, "The people of Dublin have been even better to them."

❧   ❧   ❧

When he was only five years old, Brendan was in a neighbour's house watching a woman cooking eggs for her family. She couldn't afford to give him one as well, so she just gave him a cup of tea and some bread instead. Brendan looked disgruntled, and when she said to him, "Have you lost your appetite, child?" he looked from his bread to the egg and said longingly, "Hello egg."

"Even at that age," Ma said to me, "he had more humour than most men develop in a lifetime."

❧   ❧   ❧

During Brendan's house-painting days, a snob asked him if he was using the inside or the outside of the paint. "I'm putting it on the fucking edge," he replied, "so that you can see the two sides at once."

❧   ❧   ❧

When a fellow house-painter asked Brendan if he ever considered doing an unofficial job, he replied, "The only thing I like better than an unofficial job is an unofficial strike. And the only thing I like better than an unofficial strike is an unofficial lightning strike."

❧   ❧   ❧

On a pavement one day he tried to pass a woman as stout as himself without success. "The spirit is willing," he told her, "but the flesh is in the way."

❧   ❧   ❧

Somebody mentioned to him that Siobhan O'Casey, Sean's daughter, was a nice girl. "Why shouldn't she be a nice girl?" he roared back. "Isn't she an effin' communist like her father?"

❖   ❖   ❖

He met an emigrant in America who was waxing lyrical about the harp. "If you lived in Ireland and saw a letter with a harp on it coming through the letter-box," Brendan told him, "your heart would stop, because a harp usually means the Government and that generally means income tax."

❖   ❖   ❖

He said this of New York cab drivers, "They try to live up to the reputation all taxi drivers have, of being a wit. As I am in the wit business myself, I object to competition."

❖   ❖   ❖

When Art Buckwald queried him about his dress for his weekly column in the *New York Herald Tribune* Brendan said, "I wear a red tie for my school, a green tie for my country and a blue tie when I have a hangover," adding, "I have been partial lately to blue."

❖   ❖   ❖

Regarding his scraps with French police, he told Buchwald, "The newspapers quoted me as saying I did not want to die for France. What I actually said was that I did not want to die for *Air* France."

In the same interview, he blamed his troubles on whiskey and Guinness. "I don't necessarily drink them together," he said, "but there's a very short interval in between!"

❖   ❖   ❖

When Buchwald asked him if he was married, he said, "Yes, to a very dear girl who's an artist. We have no children except me."

❖   ❖   ❖

Brendan believed that capital punishment did him a big favour because its theme made *The Quare Fellow* a success, and he, its creator, into a household name. When our cousin Séamus de Búrca wrote in one of his plays, "He has the face of a hangman." Brendan quipped, "I object to a gratuitous insult to my good friend the hangman."

❖   ❖   ❖

Addressing a committee one time, he asked if it was a republican one. When he was assured it was, he said, "Let's prove it; let's have a split."

❖　　❖　　❖

Da and Brendan argued a lot of the time. They were alike in many ways but different in more. As Ma put it, "Da was content to drink beer, but Brendan was for the champagne of life." One night Da said to Brendan, "You should have more respect for them that kept you." Brendan replied as quick as a whip, "You *had* to keep us. It's against the law to starve children."

❖　　❖　　❖

He fancied himself as something of a Stephen Roche of his day, and said once, "I could cycle from the city to Dún Laoghaire while you'd be saying Lennox Robinson."

❖　　❖　　❖

He was on a painting job for a snobby woman one time. "There's a lot of dirt in the room," she declared at one point. Brendan replied, "I didn't bring any of it in with me, ma'am."

❖　　❖　　❖

"I always know my capacity for drink," he confessed, "it's just that I get sozzled before I reach it."

❖　　❖　　❖

Brendan said he wanted to "paint the town red" neatly encapsulating his political, economic and career ambitions for Dublin.

❖　　❖　　❖

When a priest asked him why, as an ex-IRA member, he chose to represent Britain rather than Ireland favourably in *Borstal Boy*, he replied, "For the same reason, Father, that you're not married: nobody asked me."

❖　　❖　　❖

He was impressed with the cheapness of Spanish beer, saying, "It's for nothin'. You could wash your feet in it."

❖   ❖   ❖

He said of the Black and Tans, "The only man I ever heard admitting he was one of them was a Liverpool lad who said he joined up because he hadn't the fare for the Foreign Legion."

❖   ❖   ❖

After being asked how he planned to spend a certain New Year's Eve, he replied, "Ebbing and flowing. Ebbing in the morning and flowing at night."

❖   ❖   ❖

When a black man said to him that he seemed to understand the problems of negroes very well, he replied, "Why shouldn't I? Sure amn't I a negro myself?"

❖   ❖   ❖

After he became famous, a former acquaintance who knew him in the hungry years asked him for a loan, which he (uncharacteristically) refused. "I remember you when you hadn't a shaggin' farthin' to your name," the outraged acquaintance roared as he passed by. To which Brendan replied, "You don't remember it half as well as I do, me oul' flower."

❖   ❖   ❖

Brendan wasn't the only witty member of the Behan clan. He inherited his sense of humour from our parents. When Ma was annoyed with Da sometimes, she used to try and spite him by extolling the virtues of her first husband. Da would drone dryly, "Yes, Kathleen, it was a sad day for me when he died . . ."

❖   ❖   ❖

Sometimes things got really bad between them. When the sparks flew Ma would say, "What a pity you're not like my first husband Jack, a model of a man, a jewel. He never drank or smoked, not like you, who smokes like a chimney and would drink Loch Erin dry." And Da would reply, "It's a pity the old fucker died. Otherwise he'd be down here now, suffering the torments of the damned like me. You know sometimes I think the Almighty God put you on the earth with the sole intention of persecuting me. If Jesus Christ came down off the cross and married you, he'd be back up there in five minutes hammering the nails into himself."

❖   ❖   ❖

In fact the wit even goes back a generation further. Our grandfather met Nora Barnacle on a train bound for Galway during the Civil War when she was, as Ma put it, "up to her eyes in muck and bullets". "A funny looking woman," was his estimation of her, "Barnacle by name and nature. Joyce can be sure of one thing though, she'll stick to him through hell or high water."

❖   ❖   ❖

During the Spanish Civil War, priests came to our house looking for money for the Fascists. Ma's father told the priests what to do with themselves and they shouted back. "You'll all burn in the flames of Hell for eternity!" Our unperturbed grandfather regarded this as some-thing to be looked forward to rather than feared, considering the threat was made on a freezing winter's night. "Well at least we'll be effing warm," he said, "which is more than we are here."

❖   ❖   ❖

Ma carried on that toughness into her own life. When a priest came round to our house one day with a collection box for the black babies of Africa, she refused to contribute. "What's wrong Mrs Behan," the priest said to her, "Do you not want to help a heathen see the face of God?" Ma looked him straight in the eye and said, "Don't they have enough gods of their own without us giving them another one? And besides, aren't there enough white children running round the streets of Dublin in their bare feet. Shouldn't you collect for them first?"

❖   ❖   ❖

Da's coarse tongue exhibited itself at its most vivid the night a drink-ing chum spilt a pint over his trousers. He exploded, "Jaysus! May the Lamb of God stick his hind leg out through the golden canopy of heaven and kick the bollox off ye." Them's fightin' words where I come from and they were probably the origins of Brendan's cyanide-laced verbal bullets in later years.

❖   ❖   ❖

I've been quick on the verbal draw myself betimes. When a college principal called me to a meeting one time and said he was in need of fresh blood, I piped up, "Are you Dracula, perchance?"

The poor man then went on to shout, "Any man or woman over 42 is redundant to my staff requirements."

"When are you leaving, then?" I asked him. "Seeing as you are in excess of that magic age. Or are you like the gods, immortal?"

Chapter 6

Paddyland

It's better to be fightin' than lonely.

Brendan Behan

The acrimony between Brendan and the poet Paddy Kavanagh gave rise to one of the most legendary (and long-lasting) feuds in the Irish literary scene of the forties and fifties. It was merciless, unrelenting . . . and very, very funny. Paddy was permanently in the wars, either with himself or the world. He met J P Donleavy one day and said to him, "You see before you the soul of a man fighting through the raging waves of misfortune." It was, in a way, the story of his life.

He said another time, "I have lived in poverty for twenty years in the illiterate and malignant wilderness that is Dublin." Which fairly puts it on the line. But he could never cut it abroad, at least not until after he died. It was yet another irony of his tragic life that posterity would claim him as our best poet since Yeats, Mr Heaney notwithstanding. Paddy may have had short arms and long pockets when it came to buying a round of drinks, but it wasn't due to meanness as much as penury. "Joyce has Sylvia Beach," he droned, "and Behan has the Guinness family, but I have sweet Fanny Adams." And the sad thing is, he was right.

He was poxed with bad luck. If Paddy had had ducks, they'd have drowned on him. Ironically, Brendan and Paddy became friends shortly after they first met. When Paddy was trying to impress a girl he knew, who was visiting him from America, he asked Brendan to paint his flat. Brendan did so, but painted it in a wicked dark colour that fairly turned the Monaghan man's stomach. "That's as black as the Earl of Hell's waistcoat!" Paddy said, but Brendan was as happy as if he had just painted the Sistine Chapel. Amazingly, considering the circumstances, Paddy made Brendan a present of his book *Tarry Flynn* with the dedication: "To my friend Brendan Behan on the day he painted my flat."

Brendan didn't only paint the walls black, but the windows and doors as well – and even the ceiling. The night it was done, Paddy was a bit jarred and the bulb was gone so it was the next morning before he saw what Brendan had done. It was so dark he thought it was still night-time!

I first met Paddy in a pub in 1962. He was a large man, his crumpled black hat giving him a priestly air. He would sit in the corner of the pub telling people either to buy him a pint or fuck off. Sometimes they did neither, sometimes both. Paddy and myself had been published by the same man, Tim O'Keeffe (who also published Brendan's *Borstal Boy* and Flann O'Brien's *The Dalkey Archives*). I was a little apprehensive when O'Keeffe introduced me to him, and with good reason, because shortly afterwards Kavanagh started spitting like a stranded whale. "I know who you are!" he exploded. "You're the brother of that man Brendan Behan, a man who is evil incarnate, who goes about the streets abusing me like the town bull."

He then told me Brendan carried hate around with him like a pet dog. This news I received with some amusement. Now that he had got it out of his system and I hadn't retaliated, he seemed to quieten down. He calmed himself and we started talking normally. It turned out he was familiar with my own work. After a while he said I was the only Behan who could write, adding, "The only journey your brother has made in life has been the one from being a national phoney to an international one." I suppose I should have been annoyed, but I couldn't help enjoying Paddy. I knew he was winding me up, but I have a long fuse.

Paddy paid Brendan a fairly characteristic back-handed compliment when he said, "I have been friendly with Brendan Behan only in the hope that I would thereby be free of the horror of his acquaintanceship." Maybe we could call this a peculiarly Irish form of camaraderie. Brendan's response to the jibe wasn't recorded. It would probably have been unprintable. He felt the same way about Paddy as Paddy did about him. Brendan referred to him alternately as either 'That Monaghan Wanker' or (equally charmingly) 'The Fucker From Mucker.' When Brendan heard Kavanagh had visited the zoo he said, "I'm surprised they didn't keep him there. Maybe they were afraid he'd frighten the animals."

Life was always more lousy than savage for poor old Paddy. Brendan hated what he believed to be his rather tortuous soul-searching and navel-gazing. When Paddy went to London in 1952, Brendan wrote to Sinbad Vail: "The disciples he left behind still line the bars, and give me an odd pint of porter or glass of malt if I can listen respectfully enough to the old chat about Angst." Such a breed, to Brendan's way of thinking, wouldn't have had two words to put together before 1922. They would have been arsing round the nearest bog with a bowl of stirabout and a plateful of spuds. But now, God love them, they were gettin' notions. Truly, Michael Collins had a lot to answer for.

Kavanagh, of course, added fuel to the flame as well. He was in the Phoenix Park one day when the National Anthem was being played. Everyone stood to attention except the bold Paddy. "I'll not stand up

for an old come-all-ye written by Behan's granny," he announced. He
knew full well it was our uncle that wrote it. He was trying to be thick
to annoy Brendan. Anyway, the crowd got angry and threatened to
hang Paddy from the nearest tree. The unfortunate man had to run for
his life to escape the lynch mob. He was finally rescued by a police
superintendent from Inishkeen.

Paddy said in 1964, "The big tragedy for poets is poverty. I had no
money and no profession except that of small farmer, and I had the
misfortune to live the worst years of my life in a period when there
were no Arts Council Foundations or Fellowships for the benefits of
young poets." These were the years, he said, when he often pretended
to borrow a shilling "for the gas" when what he really wanted it for
was some food to put into his mouth.

Paddy kept his flat like a tenement, his one item of cutlery being a
can-opener. He practically lived on cans of soup, depositing the emp-
ties in the bath afterwards. It was one of the few flats in Dublin, Brendan
said, where you had to wipe your feet on the way *out*. It hurt Paddy to
breathe the air Brendan breathed – and vice versa. Brendan, though,
was always more on top of the situation than Paddy he didn't let it eat
into him. It was more like fodder for fun. "Take the shit off your shoes
before you come in here, culchie," Brendan would snarl at him or,
"Spongin' again for pints, are we?" Brendan was often in the position
of cadging pints off people, but he was never sensitive about the fact
because he knew when he was flush he could pay them back. But Paddy
never became flush and never looked like becoming so. He was the
classic struggling poet in search of the big windfall.

He wrote in *The Green Fool*: "I used to hear people, saying that 'God
never sends a mouth but He sends something to fill it'. A true saying
only it seemed to me God sometimes sends the food to the wrong address." The food never came to Paddy's address right through his life.
The drink did, but it was hardly God that provided it. Or even Brendan.
Part of Brendan's problem with Paddy rested on the fact that he was
from the country. "The first time I met Brendan," Mick McCarthy (a
house-painting colleague) says, "I was reading Thomas Paine's *The
Rights of Man*. Brendan came over to me and looked at the cover. 'Where
are you from?' he asked me. 'Listowel,' I said. At that he started to
laugh. He threw himself on the ground and started banging his fist on
the grass. 'A fuckin' Kerry man readin' *The Rights of Man*!' he roared,
'that's the most incongruous thing I ever heard in my fuckin' life! Are
you sure that's not a comic book you have there?'" That's how deep his
feelings went on country people.

Da had advised him as a nipper, "Son, there's three places to keep
out of when you grow up – the country, the continent and the benighted
blankin' city of Belfast." Of the three, I think he feared the country most.
Granny English told him country people were so sly they'd steal the

eyes out of your head and come back for the eyebrows. The first time
she said it he burst out crying saying, "We'll all be blind!" Granny said,
"God love you, child that's only a saying, so it is." She never expected
Brendan to take her pronouncements as seriously as he did. She over-
cooked it with him though, leaving him with a lifelong prejudice against
country folk. That was one of the main reasons Brendan saw red every
time Paddy approached. He couldn't square it in his head that a bog-
trotter could write such hauntingly beautiful lines as Paddy did. It just
didn't work for him.

It worked the other way too. Brendan felt Paddy, like many other
authors he knew, was jealous of his success. "When he hears good news
about me," Brendan said, "something in that fella dies." And then he
added, "If there's ever a Begrudgery Olympics held in Dublin, he'll
clear the board at every event."

"When God made us he matched us," he said to Paddy once. "Your
face and my arse." Paddy couldn't take it, couldn't match him. Sometimes I thought he was going to get a heart attack in the pub. I could
see him falling down like a sack of potatoes in my mind's eye. Paddy
took out his problems with Brendan on Da. Da met him on the street
one day and said, "Good morning Paddy." His response was, "Kiss my
arse." He'd use anyone to have a go at Brendan.

Paddy had a tongue that was almost as rasping as Brendan's. He
said to me one time, "I regret the day the British ever left Ireland, there's
no such thing under the skin as Protestant or Catholic, we're 98 per
cent chimp and who ever heard of anyone asking a chimp his or her
religion?" Another time he told Yeats he could kiss his arse and also
said that his purpose in life is to have no purpose. His ambition in life
he told me, was to move Irish literature from the tenth rate to the merely
mediocre. The flights of fancy in his poetry were in sharp contrast to
his biting tongue. This was shown to some advantage the day an American academic – a breed he despised but occasionally indulged, at least
if they were buying drinks for him – asked him if he had ever tried
using "the Alexandrine hexameter with the internal rhyming scheme".
He thought about this for a moment and then replied, "No. But I once
nailed a pig's liver to the back door of a haggard and fucked it!"

Another time he was in McDaids scrutinising some poetry when
the barman spilt a glass of beer across the table. The page was ruined
but Paddy saw the funny side of it. "You may not ever make much of a
barman, young man," he said, "but you're a fucking great judge of
poetry." He had a healthy ability to criticise himself, but he didn't like
Brendan doing it. Paddy was the only man I ever knew who could use
the words 'God', 'arse' and 'poetry' in the one sentence without seeing
anything strange in it. He could range from the sacred to the profane
while you'd be batting your eye. He'd even merge them.

Remember, this is the man who referred to World War Two in a poem as "that bit of Munich bother". "There's a great future for the Beat writers," he said, "you have only to roar and use bad language. I'm thinking of having a go myself." Such a breed, he claimed, knew "as much about literature as my arse knows about snipe-shooting". Brendan once told Paddy he was a coward, whereupon Paddy retaliated by saying he had volunteered to fight in the First World War. "That's right," Brendan shot back, "on the day it ended."

He went on to say that Paddy could have been a great help to the war effort if he signed up on time. Hitler would have been devastated with the news, he said. He would have said, "Listen to me, Eva. Paddy Kavanagh's coming. Fuck this for a game of marbles – pass the cyanide." Brendan and Paddy would verbally abuse one another on a nightly basis until each was exhausted. It was like going fifteen rounds with Jack Doyle listening to them. The onlookers would judge the winner. That was usually Brendan. He sent shock waves through poor Paddy whenever he barrelled in through the door of McDaids.

Brendan also delighted in ribbing Kavanagh about sex. Niall Toibin claims that the sex urge in Ireland is either "sublimated by religion, dissipated in sport or drowned in drink, or in the case of Paddy Kavanagh, all three!" (Paddy was once a goal-keeper for Monaghan.) After he put a masturbation sequence into his poem *The Great Hunger*, Brendan had a field day. "There's yer man who makes love to his fist," he'd say. "He's married to the five-fingered widow." Kavanagh would answer, "The world and his wife knows I only wrote about masturbation when I thought I couldn't get a woman: now I know it's a damn sight worse to have too many." But Brendan thought he was protesting too much.

Things got worse when the Special Branch called to Paddy's flat about the selfsame poem's alleged obscenity. That put the wind up Paddy and fortified his notion of Dublin being a city of myopic philistines. But then the poem was banned and that became a new kind of honour. He now had the martyr's crown – an object beloved of all Irish writers. "Why do you let Brendan get away with torturing you?" people would say to him sometimes. "Because I have to," Paddy would reply. "You don't know the man. When he's in a temper he can blow himself up like a frog. Then he threatens me with a Ringsend upper-cut." (That was Dublinese for a kick in the privates).

Kavanagh also had problems with Brendan's politics. He felt he was one of those 'wrap the green flag around me' boyos. He quoted Shaw's dictum about patriotism being the last refuge of a scoundrel. "The only freedom worth having," he claimed, "is the freedom from want." God knows, the poor bastard knew all about that. If anyone said to him that Brendan suffered imprisonment for his beliefs, he'd say, "Sure prison is easier than having to earn your living, easier than having to suffer the winds of the world. Prisoners live like nuns. They have a bath and laundry and three square meals a day and all the time in the world to do what they want. It's like a holiday camp. In fact I know a man who tried to strangle his wife so he could get locked up for life." If you told him Brendan was nearly sentenced to death, he'd throw his eyes up to heaven and say, "It's a pity he wasn't. It would have saved us all a great deal of trouble."

"You'd put your mother on a spit for a shilling," Paddy would say to Brendan, "and turn her over for another." And Brendan would reply, "Fuck off back to Monaghan you thick culchie and impregnate some sheep." It was hardly refined chit-chat but Brendan had to be fighting – with his mitts or his mouth.

"Go back to the stony grey fuckin' soil of Monaghan you thick cunt," he'd say. "You love those fuckin' hills so much it's a pity you ever fuckin' left them to plague me." I captured all of this in a play I wrote, *The Begrudgers*. I almost felt guilty getting the royalties because the two of them all but did the work for me. If Brendan wrote a play set in a pub featuring himself as the main character it could have been his most memorable work.

A lot of their problems came about because both of them had deep-seated unrest within themselves. Most hatred, psychologists inform us, is *self*-hatred. Brendan had a schizoid relationship to the fame game, as we know, and Paddy was also bedevilled with contradictions that unnerved him. As a country person, he believed that nature's replenishing cycle was the basic theme of mankind – that everything came from the soil. But as a peasant he also harboured a hatred of the land. He had, after all, known 'The Great Hunger'. Brendan might have called one of his own books 'The Great Thirst'. Put the two of them together and you had a highly combustible union.

I actually played Paddy in *The Begrudgers* and you can't get closer to a man than that. I would have been a good referee between them in McDaids if anyone let me. I would have separated the 'Borstal Boy' from the 'Fucker from Mucker' telling the former to come down from his high stool and the latter from his high horse. It probably wouldn't have made a damn bit of difference, though. Hell wasn't hot enough for Brendan as far as Paddy was concerned.

An acquaintance of Paddy's said to him one night in McDaids, "I believe you haven't worked much since you came to Dublin." "I took early retirement," Paddy replied. This caused Brendan to guffaw with mirth. "Very early," he roared in his ear, "so early in fact that he never fucking started." Abuse is a two-way street, like I said about Dom, so you have to expect the backlash. That's where Paddy fell down. Unlike Brendan, he was super-sensitive as well as being a crank. Brendan played at slagging as if it was a game with hard-and-fast rules, and if someone else upped the ante it adrenalised him. "Fuck you, Brendan" led to a "Double fuck you" back. That wasn't Paddy's way at all. He took criticism far too seriously – as he demonstrated by running to his lawyers every time he felt somebody slagged him off. The funny thing was Brendan and Paddy were alike in more ways than either was prepared to admit.

Despite the urban/rural divide, both of them had grown up in impecunious circumstances and both flirted with writing for many years before being recognised. When they were, they both experienced a lot of resentment from Irish readers and none at all from foreign shores where they pedalled their wares with some zeal. Both also liked drink, needless to say, and hated the bullshit that went with fame. Both were also highly irascible and had problems with everything from sex to the Church to a nine-to-five lifestyle. Both of them also had a bit of sibling rivalry – Paddy from his brother Peter and Brendan from Dom and myself – and neither liked it one little bit.

Both of them also suffered large insecurities, Brendan because he was having a lot of trouble getting published when he first met Paddy, and Paddy because he had something of a persecution complex with many of the literary figures he knew. Rightly or wrongly, he felt they were out to get him – or gut him. When Brendan and Paddy met, these insecurities manifested themselves as defensiveness and then naked aggression.

One day Paddy had the misfortune to drop a letter out of his pocket in McDaids. It was a reply from no less than the then-Archbishop of Dublin, John Charles McQuaid to Paddy's request to do a film column in the Catholic newspaper *The Standard*. The letter said: "I'll try to get you that job in *The Standard*." It was signed, "Yours in Christ, John McQuaid." Brendan exploded with laughter when he read it. It was like the last craven compromise of the Monaghan wanker. He wasn't going to let it pass in a hurry. Afterwards you'd see Brendan down on his knees in McDaid's with a fellow called Sean Daly acting out a scene of Paddy trying to kiss 'Plug' McQuaid's ring. "Let me kiss it!" he'd roar out at Daly for Paddy to hear. "Which ring do you want me to kiss? Yours in Christ!" Paddy was livid. That was the end of any chance they had of making up.

John Charles McQuaid – the J Edgar Hoover of the Catholic Church – epitomised the parochial insularity of the Ireland of his time, attempting to run both the Church and the State from his mansion and brooking little interference in either ambition. But he displayed sympathy for Paddy. He was also immensely generous to him and prevented Paddy from being evicted from his lodgings on more than one occasion by coming up with long overdue rent arrears. Paddy used the kind of language in pubs which was guaranteed to give any priest, never mind an Archbishop, double hernias, but he took care to be on his best behaviour when he was in McQuaid's presence. Like most starving artists, he knew which side his bread was buttered on, and was content to take the clerical shilling even as he vilified McQuaid behind his back.

You could safely count the number of films Paddy had seen, before the job at *The Standard*, on the fingers of one hand, but 'any port in a storm'. Even poets – *especially* poets – had to take the soup. He was also a bit of a chancer when it came to writing about films. In fact he walked out of *Gone With The Wind* and reviewed it by culling press releases. John Charles, I daresay, wouldn't have been too pleased.

McQuaid actually called to Paddy's flat in Pembroke Road one day but His Grace's timing wasn't the best as Paddy was in the company of a lady of the night. He saw the Archbishop's secretary knocking at the door through a car mirror he had placed strategically beside a window (a somewhat rudimentary version of our modern peepholes) and started to panic. If word of this got out, he knew he might as well kiss *The Standard* goodbye forever. He thought fast and said he wouldn't insult the Archbishop by having him come in to his lowly abode, which was in a despicable condition. (This part of the excuse was probably true.) Instead, he suggested going out to McQuaid's car to chat to him there. This course of action was agreed upon, much to the relief of Paddy. When he emerged from the car, his female friend saw him carrying a bottle of whiskey, a carton of cigarettes and an Aran sweater. She opened the top window of the flat and let out a roar to wake the dead. At this stage, McQuaid's secretary stepped on the accelerator and sped away to the relative sanctuary of the Palace.

When McQuaid died, Paddy gave this less-than-salubrious eulogy, "The long miserable streak of piss – now the old bollox knows there's no God." It was hardly the type of thing that would put the Curia in mind of canonisation – for either of them. "That's lovely talk indeed," Brendan said when he heard it, "good old-fashioned Irish gratitude for a man who took you off the streets." The theology was also a bit suspect. If God didn't exist, then presumably there was no afterlife of the soul either, *ergo* no John Charles either. Paddy wasn't unduly perturbed about such eschatological nuances.

Anyway, things reached a head between the pair of them in 1954. That was the year Paddy took a libel action against the *Leader* magazine for defamation of character in an article. The article portrayed Paddy as a kind of literary guru sitting in the centre of a bunch of bird-brained acolytes who hung on his every word without half knowing what he was on about. The famous Paddy Kavanagh voice was described as being reminiscent of "a load of gravel sliding down the side of a quarry", and his bouts of coughing were said to be so violent as to stop the traffic outside the pub. The article, he said, "nearly laid me low in tragedy's muck". Brendan offered to testify on Paddy's behalf but Paddy told him to fuck off, which proved to be an unwise choice in retrospect. He gave out stink about Brendan in his testimony but then Rory Furlong produced the copy of *Tarry Flynn* that he had signed for

Brendan with the words: "To my dear friend Brendan Behan". This seemed to make a liar out of him.

Paddy lost the case and never forgave Brendan, even though Brendan denied writing the *Leader* piece. He also had no idea Rory was going to produce the book in court, and indeed roundly descended on him for doing it after the case was over, saying it was none of his effin' business. Paddy called Brendan a Judas for doing the article. He wouldn't even entertain the idea that he didn't write it. He even claimed to know how much money he got for it. Brendan eventually told him that it was a poet called Valentin Iremonger that wrote it. But that still wasn't enough for Paddy. "Then you were behind it!" he thundered. Brendan couldn't win. Paddy felt Brendan approved of the article even if he didn't pen it: he saw him as a kind of *agent provocateur* to Iremonger – who was aptly named considering the circumstances.

Paddy's big mistake was over-reacting when he was asked his opinion of Brendan. He should have played down his problems with him. But the very words 'Brendan' and 'Behan' used in any form and in close proximity was enough to send him into a fit. He fairly exploded with venom about him, which may be all right in a pub but doesn't go down too well in court. If Paddy had been cuter he could have claimed that being a former good friend of Brendan's strengthened his case rather than weakened it, on the basis that he had entered the relationship in good faith and had afterwards been betrayed by the "drunken bowsie", as he called him. But he was too angry (and, of course, surprised) to think straight. The fact that he had been undone by his own hand – literally – merely served to compound his dementia.

The jury watched him explode, and formed the view that he had a vested interest in the matter. In that one moment the whole issue turned on its head. From being a case in which Brendan was judged to have had a grudge against Paddy, it now looked decidedly the other way around. Once again, Paddy had shot himself in the foot. Anthony Cronin, another literary acquaintance of Brendan's, thought Brendan was behind Rory turning up with the book and refused to talk to him. Brendan offered to buy him a pint on a few occasions, but Cronin didn't want to know. Brendan got fed up of this and ambushed Cronin one night when he was coming out of McDaid's, grabbing him by the scruff of his neck and ramming him into a lampost. Cronin rallied, and then Brendan headbutted him a few times. It was hardly the Queensbury Rules: more like a bullfight, Irish style.

Brendan was on the receiving end of a few punches himself, and when Cronin related the incident back to Paddy, the Monaghan man quipped, "I always knew the bacon would be no match for the slicer." Afterwards Brendan accused Paddy of suing for the easy money rather than sensitivity over having his name besmirched. This was hardly true, though, considering his track record.

Paddy had been in court a few years before when Oliver St John
Gogarty took exception to a harmless comment Paddy had made in his
book *The Green Fool*. Paddy had written that, after calling on Gogarty's
door as a callow country boy, "I mistook Gogarty's white-robed maid
for his wife – or his mistress. I expected every poet to have a spare
wife." Gogarty didn't see the funny side of the remark and sued – and
the court found for him. And now history had repeated itself. Paddy
had been given an advance of £20 from the publishers for *The Green
Fool* but now that was eaten up by his legal costs, which topped the
£200 mark – a phenomenal amount for an indigent poet in those days.
He referred to the case as 'Trial and Error'.

After he lost the case, Paddy fell into bad health and had to go into
hospital for the removal of a cancerous lung. He said to his sister-in-
law, "Most likely it will kill me but to tell you the truth, I don't give a
shite." Well it didn't kill him, but he came out a different man. His
vocal cords were damaged by the operation and he could only speak in
a hoarse whisper now. His breathing was laboured too and he had to
keep clearing his throat every few minutes. He also had problems with
his heart and liver and even his bladder and kidneys. It was a long way
from the days of jumping round the Monaghan six-yard area during
soccer games.

Aggressions with Brendan were temporarily suspended for the
duration of his stay in hospital, but when he came out it was back to
square one. Brendan would nearly have bribed the doctors to keep him
in longer, he claimed. But in another way I think he needed the buzz of
it all. Four years later in an article in *Vogue*, Brendan fanned the flames
again by mocking Paddy speaking about Edith Sitwell. He had the
Monaghan accent down pat when he wrote: "Hah sure Aydit is a naice
semple wamman at the back avitt shewerly." And so on. Paddy was
livid, which only goaded Brendan further. But there was yet another
twist to the saga . . .

In November 1958 an enemy of Paddy's spiked his drink and then
when he was leaving McDaids, pushed him over a fourteen-foot wall
into the canal he loved so well. He was expected to drown or, if not
that, to die of pneumonia as he had only one lung by this time. Paddy
was reciting a poem to himself as he ambled along. "Lord commemorate me where there's water," he intoned. At that point his abductor
stole up behind him saying, "I'll give you water, you fuckin' mad poet
you." And dumped him in the drink. As he went under, he heard a
voice say, "That's the end of him, the old bollox," and somehow, his
anger gave him the will to survive. Drawing on all his resources, he
pulled himself to safety and went to the flat of a female friend to re-
cover. Before long, he was back on the piss again. One night when Paddy
sat down to have a drink, who walked in but the man who pushed
him! Paddy relished the moment, likening it to Macbeth seeing Banquo's

ghost at the feast.

Some years later, though, in another twist to the tale, these two became good friends. It turned out the man had objected to an article Paddy wrote denouncing Dublin's Underworld, but he was now consumed with remorse over what he had done. Paddy told him not to worry, that there were no hard feelings, but the man was inconsolable. Shortly afterwards the man's wife gave birth to a slightly handicapped child and the man believed this to be a sign of God punishing him. You wouldn't see the like of it in The Abbey! He asked Paddy to come to his house and try to heal the baby by a laying on of hands and what's more, Paddy obliged. Who needed John Charles McQuaid when you could have Paddy Kavanagh, working miracles on your progeny? When Brendan heard of these developments, his reaction was, I suppose you could say, to the point. "There's no way that clumsy bastard dragged himself to safety," he roared, adding equally endearingly, "I just can't wait to get me hands on the fuckin' bollox who pulled him out."

Chapter 7

Filthy Lucre

He would give you shirt off his back – and then tell you what horse to put it on.

Sheila Greene

Brendan was capable of haggling over a few pennies for many hours, then blowing a fortune at the races (or, more likely, in the pub) at the drop of a hat. Beatrice used to say that he liked to walk round looking like a vagrant, but would spend 30 guineas on a dress for her. She also said he was capable of inviting a gang of tramps he had just met down in the local home for lunch and that he would give his last penny to a hobo. He earned a lot of money in his life but it was like water in his hands, drifting away even as it came in. Most of his book advances he spent before he wrote the books, either on drink or senseless whims.

Money was made round to go round, he felt, or as Fr Cormac Daly put it, "His personal touch was his willingness to always fall for the latest offering of the Knights of the Hard Luck Story." His acts of generosity were legendary and, one imagines, the lion's share of them were uncatalogued. He could be an anti-Christ with drink, as we all know, but he was also, as he put it himself, "an oul' softie" when it came to down-and-outs. He was known to scatter billfolds to all and sundry when he was flush, or half-crowns and pennies when he wasn't. He even gave money to spongers, confessing that he had been one himself, so understood the breed and their needs. One story tells of him cashing a Radio Éireann cheque to buy a bottle of port for a sick woman, then giving a further shilling to a small boy to deliver it to her. There are countless other examples of him paying the rent and electricity bills of those less well-off than himself, and throwing coins to children on the street like some Dickensian philanthropist.

When he met Allen Ginsberg in New York they went to dinner together and when Ginsberg excused himself to go to the toilet Brendan followed him down. "Do you need any ammunition?" he asked Ginsberg, meaning money. Ginsberg was hard-pressed for cash at the time and was flummoxed at his spontaneous generosity. Brendan gave him 80 dollars on the spot. He made it nice and handy from *The Hostage*, he said, "Easy come easy go." When Ginsberg heard the word "ammunition", considering Brendan's IRA background, he got a fright, but Brendan then translated and all was well.

Brendan's generosity sometimes manifested itself in strange circumstances, like for instance the time he sold the English rights of *The Quare Fellow* to Joan Littlewood – an unethical act considering they were owned by Alan Simpson and Carolyn Swift of The Pike. He felt justified in doing this considering he only received a pittance from The Pike, but he went behind Carolyn Swift's back to do it. In fact she only heard the news as she herself was preparing to launch the play in Piccadilly Circus. She forgave Brendan for biting the hand that fed him and, even though they took him to court and lost, there was never really bad blood between them. Two years after the court case, Brendan got a chance to pay them back. It was at a time when Simpson was going to court on another theatrical matter and was short of cash for his defence.

Brendan heard about this one night. "I know I did you over the rights of my play," he said to Carolyn, "but you should have known I'd do anything for money. Why didn't you make sure you had me sewn up legally?" He said he had always regretted the event "because you and Alan really invented me". Before he went away, he pressed a wad of dirty notes into Carolyn's hand with the words, "Here's something for your auld defence fund." Carolyn was deeply touched by his act, though not altogether surprised. As she said herself, "Unseen I had often watched him distributing half-crowns to every child in sight, and he must have kept half the soaks in Dublin in drink when he was in funds." Too true.

Barman Paddy O'Brien remembers Brendan in McDaid's creating havoc as he rambled in with his shirt hanging out and his hair flying, getting it up for Paddy Kavanagh or whoever, but with a big heart beating in his even bigger frame. He asked O'Brien for a loan of five bob and as he was on the way out the door with it, he happened to meet two impoverished children who were looking for their father. He gave them a half-crown each. That was his nature. Other times, as Bill Kelly commented, he was "slow on the draw" when it came to paying his round. It all depended on who he was with and how he was feeling. As with most things in Brendan's life, there were no rules, no predictable behaviour patterns. With money as with everything else he was a loose cannon – going where the wind took him. And this didn't change when he became famous. He hassled publishers for advances just as he hassled editors for fees for his articles. Rich or poor, he seemed to thrive on recalcitrance, trying to drag blood out of a stone. But if he won the Lottery he'd still have been broke soon afterwards. The more he earned, the less he had. Like Groucho Marx, he worked his way up from nothing to a state of extreme poverty.

He wrote better when he was skint than when he was flush. Money may not be the root of all evil, but it certainly seems to stem the tide of inspiration. That's not to say I go with the old nonsense about poverty being ennobling for a writer, or great creativity as springing more spontaneously from the gutter than the mansion. But just as the thought of death concentrates the mind wonderfully, so also does the thought of where the next meal is going to come from. Journalism was different from book-writing in this respect. There were no advances and sometimes you didn't get paid on the nail for your articles. Brendan couldn't abide this. When he needed the few shillings for some serious drinking, newspaper editors quaked in their boots for fear of a visit from him, demanding they cough up for articles they had printed. He expected the pay for these to take place almost by osmosis. Not for him the drudgery of accountancy procedures. Brendan was even known to throw pebbles at editor's windows at the dead of night, demanding payment for services rendered, even if his piece had only been published that very day. Maybe it's just as well he didn't live to see the credit card age.

Money was more predictable in the world of painting than publishing. In painting you did a job, were paid and went home. You knew where you stood. Publishing was different. Many of Brendan's writings were rejected in his early years – works he had sweated over and loved dearly – whereas others were tossed off frivolously and remunerated generously. He was short of cash one time in London and waltzed into the office of Donal Foley, the London editor of the *Irish Press*, looking for an advance on four articles he had been commissioned to write. Foley told him he couldn't part with any money until he got the articles upfront, so Brendan promptly went off and wrote up the four of them in one fell swoop. This was like literary prostitution. It was as if he was on steroids. Putting black marks on paper, like putting different coloured marks on walls, meant instant cash. Journalism taught him that being succinct was the key – that and the ability to meet deadlines.

Writing plays was deeper, but the pay-off was less certain. You were also dependent on actors and directors to transmit your words successfully to the public. The other variable was the fickleness of taste. There were few guarantees here, at least before his name became a byword for controversiality. Later the advances were large, and, by definition, came more quickly. He drank many of them, which meant that it became more difficult to motivate himself to the work in hand afterwards. It would be like a householder saying to the young Brendan, "I'm going to pay you to paint that wall before you paint it." Dangerous words indeed to an alcoholic, but part and parcel of the writing game. After Brendan's hitherto unpublished story *Christmas Eve in the Graveyard* was sold for a phenomenal £5,400 last year, Ulick O'Connor quipped that if he were alive he'd probably have said, "Wasn't I right to give up the poetry?" Indeed. But it's a pity he wasn't around to spend it.

J P Donleavy has said that the greatest sin imaginable to Brendan was to shirk your round in a pub, or to hide from your acquaintances the fact that you had money. This very bone of contention led to Brendan and Donleavy having a set-to on Fleet Street one day. Another time Brendan seemed to have X-ray vision and divine that Ben Kiely was concealing £1 from him when he touched him for a loan. Drunk or sober, he had a strict code of what people should do with their money, and woe betide anyone who broke it. It was unforgiveable to him to leave a pub with money in your pocket. All good Irishmen drank until they fell, were turfed out for misbehaviour, or ran out of 'stamps'. Anything else smacked of cute hoorism.

♣

Asked if he was a bourgeois decadent, he replied, "No – but I'm savin' up for it."

♣   ♣   ♣

He was with a couple of boozing pals in a taxi one night in Dolphin's Barn, "I don't need friends," he said tapping his wallet, "I can buy them with this." Ironically, at the time, it was empty.

♣   ♣   ♣

When Carolyn Swift accepted *The Twisting of Another Rope* for a four-week stint at The Pike Theatre she told Brendan she would offer him £30 on the condition that he allowed her to change the name of the play to *The Quare Fellow*. "For £30," he told her, "you can change it to 'The Brothers Fuckin' Karamazov'."

♣   ♣   ♣

He claimed the most enjoyable writing any author ever did was signing his name on the back of a cheque.

♣   ♣   ♣

A reporter asked him, when exactly he stopped writing for the *Irish Press*. "The day before I became famous," he said, "and that was the day when I could afford, at long last, to pay for me effin' gargle."

❖   ❖   ❖

When he was asked if he could ever curb his roguish ways he remarked, "If people want me to behave like Cardinal Spellman or Billy Graham, why don't they pay me the salary these fellows are getting?"

❖   ❖   ❖

He was frequently in the habit of singing to crowds lined up outside theatres queuing up to see one of his own plays. He would sing republican songs and then pass the hat around, either pocketing the proceeds afterwards or presenting the money to the nearest available busker.

❖   ❖   ❖

No matter how horrendous Brendan felt the morning after the night before, money could dramatically change his mood. His friend John Murdoch recalls calling to his flat in Waterloo Road one morning when he was so hungover he was hardly able to speak. He was lying on his bed with his bloodshot eyes half shut, but when Murdoch produced a cheque for a piece he had submitted to *The Sunday Dispatch*, Brendan leaped out of bed and grabbed it "like a hungry child grabbing a crust". A few moments later he was in his trousers, and had stuffed his sockless feet into laceless shoes. Unshaved, unwashed and with a vice-like grip, he took hold of Murdoch and frog-marched him down to the nearest hostelry for yet another hair of that famous dog.

❖   ❖   ❖

On Brendan's first visit to New York, he phoned our aunt to ask her where he could find our Uncle Jimmy, who lived on Staten Island and had often sent him a few dollars.
    "In a bank off Wall Street," our aunt said.
    "Which floor?" Brendan enquired.
    "*Every* floor," she announced.
    "God bless us and save us," said an astounded Brendan, "he must be the bank's vice-president."
    "No," our aunt informed him, "he's the elevator man!"

❖   ❖   ❖

A Canadian club offered him a thousand dollars to sing, which amused him greatly. "For doing the same in Dublin," he announced, "I get thrown out of pubs!"

❖   ❖   ❖

A British editor offered Brendan 75 guineas for an interview but he said he wanted 100 or nothing, and he wanted it in hard cash so the taxman wouldn't get a cut.

"I can't promise you 100," the journalist doing the interview said, "and accountants never pay in cash."

"Then tell the bloody accountants to write the article themselves," Brendan snapped back.

❖   ❖   ❖

Brendan often called on Samuel Beckett in Paris, much to the latter's chagrin because he knew his reputation all too well. One night after a brawl in a Parisian bar, Brendan was arrested by the gendarmes and forced to spend the night in jail. Beckett called on him the next morning and paid the fine, thereafter giving Brendan a few pounds for himself – but not before he delivered a stern ear-bashing to the contrite scribe. "That's what I like about Sam," Brendan said afterwards, "he knows exactly in what order to take care of a man's needs!" (Brendan has less time for Beckett's writing than he had for his largesse, I might add. He called *Krapp's Last Tape*, 'Tape's Last Crap'.)

❖   ❖   ❖

No great lover of Queen Victoria, Brendan claimed she donated a fiver to the Famine Relief Fund during the 1840s . . . but on the same day also gave the same amount to the Dog's Home in Battersea.

❖   ❖   ❖

Brendan was walking along Baggot Street one night when a nun rattled a box at him.

"What are you collecting for?" he asked.

"The night shelter," she replied.

"Oh fair enough," he said, dropping some money into her box, "as long as it's not to convert the poor Africans. Jaysus, haven't they enough to put up with, being black, without having to be fucking Catholics as well?"

❖   ❖   ❖

When Ma was pregnant with Brendan she met Michael Collins on O'Connell Bridge. He was a wanted man at the time, but he still stopped to talk to her. "How are ye, Kathleen?" he said, "How are the children?"

After they were finished talking, he pressed a £10 note into her hand, saying: "Take care of yourself." It was the last time she ever saw him. Brendan loved hearing that story. It was as if Collins had given the tenner to him personally. He wrote a song for Collins in gratitude, the only one of its kind ever written. It's sung in *The Hostage*.

Chapter 8

Hell's Bells

My interest in the next life is purely academic.

Brendan Behan

We'll never be sure if there's any truth to the rumour that, when asked for his religion, Brendan replied, "I'm an alcoholic." However, in 1959, he confessed, as he laced five pints of Guinness with large whiskies, "I write in order to keep myself in liquor." He went on to say, "I have nothing against the Church as long as they leave the drink alone."

Brendan wasn't fully certain such a state of affairs could continue in an ecumenical universe. After Pope John XXIII called for the unity of all churches, he fumed. "The day the Catholic and Protestant churches combine, it's the end of all drinking. I'll have to go to Rome to sabotage the affair." Notwithstanding all these quips, Brendan was a dye-in-the-wool Catholic. In fact one of the things that most bothered him about his republican involvement and subsequent spells in prison was that they meant that he was ex-communicated and so unable to receive the sacraments. No matter how explosive Brendan became, he carried a penny catechism theology with him to his grave. He told Beatrice on his deathbed that he had received confession and communion, which lightened his heart considerably.

A familiar catch-phrase throughout his life was, "I'm a daylight communist, but a Catholic after it gets dark." This was a frank – and decidedly un-macho – admission from one who to so very many epitomised the 'Hard Man' ethos. But then Brendan was always ambivalent in this regard. He loved the pomp and ceremony of religion, but there was nobody quicker to have a go at particular members of the cloth. "All my plays are blasphemous," he proclaimed, "but I still want Cardinal Spellman to see them." He didn't think there was any inconsistency in this. Every self-respecting clergyman, he felt, should be able to see the mote in his eye, or his institution's eye. And Jesus wouldn't love him any the less for pointing it out.

Only the truly passionate become rebels and Brendan was as ardent in his early religious devoutness as he was in his later anti-clerical pronouncements. He liked to recite this dubious paean to Protestantism:

Don't speak of your Protestant minister,
Nor his Church without meaning or faith,
The foundation stone of his temple, you see,
Was the bollox of Henry the Eighth.

Brendan had more problems with the philosophy of the Church than its priests. There was a drunk slagging priests in Tom English's pub on the North Wall one night and Brendan stopped him in his tracks. "Listen man," he said to him, "I have met more priests than you are likely ever to know. I have had reason to disagree with them over politics, socialism, economics and other matters too numerous to mention at this particular period of time, but I want to say here and now: I never met a bad priest in my life."

"I enjoy the society of Catholic priests," he said in a different mood, "so many of them know everything about everything and are so jolly about it." He liked to keep in with them, he joked, because he had had the Last Rites a few times and thought they might have a bit of pull if he ever made it as far as the Pearly Gates. He needed all the help he could get because he wasn't one to wear a hole in the knees of his trousers on Sundays or Holy Days of Obligation. "I believe everything the Catholic Church teaches is true," he allowed, "but I let Beatrice go to mass for me."

He had it covered all ways, didn't he? He didn't believe in putting the clergy down like some of his left-wing friends, but he had no awe of them either. Meeting a bishop at a literary luncheon in the sixties he chirped, "How's your racket?" The bishop's reply was almost as good, "Not as profitable as yours, I'm afraid."

One of the surprising things that depressed Brendan in the early sixties was being banned from attending the St Patrick's Day Parade in New York. I don't know why he took it so hard. St Patrick is always a good excuse to get drunk, but I can't say much for him beyond that.

Brendan lived like a pagan, but he wore his First Communion suit under his painter's overalls. He was a prodigal son who liked to read the lives of the saints, an excommunicated gunman who used to be a weekly communicant. Like many writers, Brendan tended to boast about being a "bad Catholic". This despite the fact that after he received his First Communion he prayed that God would take him so that he could go straight to heaven. What happened after that, you might ask? The three Gs, I suppose: Guinness, guns and girls. Though not necessarily in that order. Maybe I should have put guns first. Let's not forget his pronouncement, "You must understand that the freedom of Ireland to me is a second religion." Maybe it was even his first one. Brendan needed mass as much as *meas*, the old Irish respect, his wild years saw this bad Catholic deprived of both. He saw no disjunction between the Bible and the balaclava, but ex-communication made him re-think his position slightly.

When he dubbed himself a "night-time Catholic", this was his way of saying there are few atheists in the trenches. But when the bell finally tolled for Brendan, he didn't die screaming for a priest. "I'd love to see my funeral," he said once, "it's a pity I won't be there." He saw it as his final performance. He would have loved it even more if he could have leaped out of the coffin to sing a republican ballad. "I want to die when I'm 90," he also said, "with a mountain of pillows beside me and 60 priests and 40 nuns praying fervently that I'll go to heaven." A modest enough ambition, by his standards.

Nobody could break the Behan spirit. I witnessed Ma at the age of 94 deserting a Church she had worshipped in since childhood. Another time, leaning up out of her bed she asked me: "Who made the world?" Surprised, I stuttered, "God". "Well then," she cried, "who made God?" I told her at her age she should be down on her knees taking out religious insurance, not cashing it in. She virtually gave up her religion in the last years of her life, keeping her inquiring mind to the last. "Laugh and the world laughs with you," she used to say, "weep and you weep alone. The sorry old earth must borrow her mirth, for grief she has enough of her own."

Ma was the first feminist I ever met. She believed in the good of women everywhere, but starting with herself. She demanded one day a week off work and overtime for weekends. "I'm living in a house full of trade unionists," she said, "so I demand some trade union rights myself." And more power to her. But sometimes she sprung a few surprises on us. I asked her where my dinner was one day and she said, "Can you afford servants?" I said no, whereupon she blurted out, "Then get it yourself." So I did. Other times she would disappear we knew not where – and I knew better than to ask. How could you criticise a woman like that?

My fondest memory of her is an image of her sipping whiskey in a home for retired bishops when she was in her eighties. "I believe in heaven," she said, "but will it ever be as good as this?" For once, theology let me down and I was dumbstruck. Ma had no shyness about speaking her mind on matters of religion, no matter where she was. I took her to mass one time in Norwood, in England, and at the end of it, the priest called for blessings for the Queen. Ma jumped up and shouted out, "She's blessed enough, with lands that she's stolen from the Irish! I'm not staying here while she's being blessed." And out she waltzed. I didn't know where to put my face. The whole chapel was in an uproar.

I had seen this attitude exhibiting itself at certain stages during my youth. A particular instance springs to mind after a nun smacked me hard one day as a child at school. After I told Ma, her face went all the colours of the rainbow. "I'll sort her out," she told me. "But you can't hit a holy nun!" I pleaded. She hared off down the road and that was all I ever heard of it so I don't know what was or wasn't said, but I'll tell you one thing: my life in William Street was somewhat more pleasant as a result of their altercation. She said to a priest one time, "Tell me Father, isn't it true that pagans in Africa can't commit sin because they don't know the meaning of it?" When he said that was true, she said, "Why bother converting them then when what they don't know can't hurt them?" He had no answer for that.

Like Brendan, she lived for the moment. One of the reasons she went into the nursing home was because she'd been knocked down by a motorcyclist. She got £3,000 in compensation but it was gone within a year. "What did you do with it?" I asked her. "Sure that lasted no time," she said, "we'll be dead long enough." Ulick O'Connor used to say it was like an electric charge to be in the same room as her, "A cemetery could be lit up in her presence."

At the age of 93, she appeared on the Russell Harty show on television and a year later, launched a record of some of her favourite songs. She sang her heart out for an hour. She didn't think much of the next world. "I'll be singing a song when I'm dying," she said, "an old come-all-ye." She didn't want any tears when she was gone, just a decent wake, and the rest of us to have a few jars. As regards the hereafter, she remarked, "Even if we come back as seeds isn't that better than nothing? Or even a head of cabbage."

Da was actually in to be a priest at one point. Could you credit that? Imagine: no little Behans if he was. (Or maybe not, considering what we hear about some priests these days.) His mother yanked him out of the seminary saying, "It's no priesthood for you, but the painter's overall and rising at the crack of dawn winter and summer to serve your master." Brendan heard that story when he was young and it had an effect on him. In a way, I think writing became for him what the priesthood never became for Da: a ticket to Easy Street. Or so he thought. Little was he to know that the cure would become worse than the disease.

Da hated Granny for taking him out of the seminary. And, by extension, he hated the Church as well. He actually claimed he'd only go back to it if he was made Pope. "I won't be one of the flock," he'd say. "I'm not a sheep. A sheep has four legs but I have only two. And I have no wool – I'm bald." Ma tried to get him to go back to the Church but he refused point blank. "My knees are worn out," he told her. Still, when we were growing up he pretended he went to mass. When he'd get us up he'd say he had been already – to the one at half-six. Da was very sceptical about the hereafter, which caused Ma to bellow at him one day. "You must believe in something – even a pig has religion!" she shouted. Da replied tartly, "Pigs end up as bacon, Kathleen."

Granny Furlong had a funny attitude to religion as well. She went on a bombing mission to England in her seventies, but never lost her devoutness. When she found herself standing in the dock after a cache of explosives were found in her house, the Angelus rang out. Down she went on her knees, which caused the astonished judge some concern. "What are you doing down there?" he asked. "I'm saying the Angelus!" she barked back, "if you know what that is, you bloody oul' heathen." Brendan inherited this devotion to The Angelus, interrupting himself no matter what he was doing to go down on all fours when the bell pealed for the 60 seconds. Such piousness wasn't shared by the rest of the family.

Dominic was the most anti-clerical of the lot of us, which is surely saying something. At Rory's funeral he interrupted the priest just as he was about to give an oration, saying it was all a load of balls and hypocrisy. He said Rory had been an atheist for 30 years and the only reason he was in a church at all was because he was dead and couldn't get up out of his coffin and walk out. He abused the priest something awful – a bit like Nora Joyce did at James' funeral.

After Ma died. Dominic refused to go into the chapel. "There are more Marxists on the front seats of the church," he said, "than there are in the Soviet Union." (He was talking about Sean and myself.) After the funeral mass for Ma was over, an old friend of ours called Jim Fitzgerald (a one-time theatrical producer who ended up a drunkard) rapped on the coffin and shouted, "Come on, Kathleen, get up out of that and stop making a cod of us all." She would have liked that.

You have to look at the double standards. I don't want to go on about Eamonn Casey but I can't help feeling it's not good enough for the Church. They never stopped giving out about the sin of impurity when I was a lad and now they're hoist on their own petard with all the scandals. It'd make a cat laugh.

When I was at Artane school, two boys were discovered performing a sexual act together and all hell broke loose. The Director said to us afterwards, "I want you to shun these boys as you would the devil. For the next three months, no boy will contaminate himself even by talking to them." When I was with the Brothers, I was taught to see sex as the biggest enemy of the Church since Luther. Then I came out into the world and I realised that Catholics had indeed whittled down the Ten Commandments to two, as Jesus advised. But the two they chose were the sixth and the ninth.

Eamonn Casey was a man who re-defined the rules of chess to read, 'Bishop can jump anything'. But I have to say I felt sorry for his predicament. There he was, sandwiched between an American feminist and a Scotch Calvinist, and bound to the secrecy of the confessional. What chance in hell had he got? Maybe he was lucky to escape with his life.

Brendan, strange as it may sound, was the most religious member of the family. Da like all IRA men, was ex-communicated in his twen-

ties and never had much time for religion after that. Sean lost his through
Marxism and Seamus for no reason at all. Carmel says it doesn't really
matter one way or the other: that all roads lead to the same end. I told
Brendan I had no religion after leaving Artane and he was scathing
with me, "I've heard of clever arses like you before," he rasped, "but
the Church has survived the passing of empires and is still flourishing." He saw it as a flickering candle in a sea of darkness and none of
us wanted that light to go out. "You'll die fucking roaring for a priest,"
he told me.

He saw religion as one of his few certainties in life and something
he couldn't bear to part with for that reason. Brendan told me he loved
its magic and warmth. Joan Littlewood accused him of writing Catholic propaganda under the guise of anti-clericalism: she had a point. For
just as Brendan never really outgrew the ideals of 1916, which we may
deem naïve and simplistic in many regards today, neither did he out-
grow the saccharine pieties of the penny cathecism – despite the general air of blasphemy that laces his work.

There's a difference, you see, between being a "bad" Catholics and
a non-Catholic. In fact I would go so far as to say that bad Catholics
ensure the perpetuation of institutions like the Catholic Church even
more than "good" ones. The latter group certainly spend more time in
church – unleashing in the confession boxes if not imploring in the pews.
Bad Catholics need the Church as a crutch just as much as reckless
spenders need banks. And Brendan needed both.

The rest of us saw religion as an oppressive force. It was anti-com-
munist and anti-progressive. In fact I regard religious nationalism as
the main enemy of mankind – be it fundamentalism or what the terror-
ists in Ireland pedal. The slogan by which I live my life is this one:

> *No Saviour from on high deliver,*
> *No trust have we in priests or peer,*
> *Our own right arms the chains shall shiver.*

The Church is in a bad state today; we all know that. The first thing
that has to go is celibacy. It's a vow that's outdated and stupid and you
can see what damage it causes. The obvious example again is Eamonn
Casey. He took the Commandment 'Love Thy Neighbour' a bit too literally.

In *The Begrudgers* I actually have him becoming a woman in a bid
to advance the cause of feminism – to paraphrase Brendan at the end of
The Confirmation Suit, I felt this was the least he could do to re-establish
his credibility with the female of the species.

❧

This was one of Brendan's favourite stories:

A Catholic farmer married a Protestant woman one time, to the blindingly clear displeasure of the local parish priest. However, within the year he had converted her to Catholicism and she was down at the church every other day, but, a few years later she died tragically. Not too long afterwards, the farmer re-married, again to a Protestant, and the parish priest was equally aggrieved. But lo and behold, within a few months, she became a Catholic and was a regular attender at church services. When she died, the farmer said he was going to marry a third Protestant. The parish priest by now was quite chuffed at the turn of events, imagining his trusty farmer would effect a trinity of conversions. It was not to be, though, and some months afterwards the priest called to the farmer's house to find out why. "What's happening?" he said dejectedly, "your new wife hasn't been in church even one time since you married her." The farmer was now in his sixties, and said to the priest as he looked down at his nether regions, "Musha, father, sure the oul' converter isn't what it used to be."

❖   ❖   ❖

Brendan hated name-droppers, even though he was partial to that weakness himself. He visited Kruger Kavanagh's pub in Kerry in the late-fifties and Kruger showed him photographs of himself with various celebrities. Most of them were signed with messages like "To Kruger, from Jack Dempsey" or "To Kruger from Mae West". Brendan was under-whelmed, and went over to a picture of the Sacred Heart, upon which he scribbled, "To Kruger, with love from Jaysus".

❖   ❖   ❖

Brendan often described Kilbarrack as the healthiest graveyard in Ireland because it was so near the sea. That crack wasn't original though: he got it, like a few of his other ones, from Da. "People are dyin' to get into it," Da would say, continuing with the old corny line. "It's been a long time here now and there was never a complaint from a corpse yet."

❖   ❖   ❖

He didn't only read the Bible . . . but *smoked* it. This feat he achieved by putting a piece of mattress between two of its "lovely thin" pages while in prison. He wasn't the only inmate with this habit. A man he knew in Brixton claimed to have smoked his way through the whole Book of Genesis.

❖   ❖   ❖

Brendan was short of cash one time when he was in Paris and thought he could touch some Irish pilgrims he spotted on their way to Lourdes. He wasn't very successful however, as they seemed to be more intent on getting rid of their money on Paris wickedness than seeing to the needs of an indigent ex-patriot like himself. "All their effin' charity," he concluded, "must have been reserved for buyin' candles at the shrines."

❖   ❖   ❖

In Brendan's *Irish Press* piece "Overheard in a Bookshop", a man asks for a copy of the New Testament and the woman behind the desk says to him, "Desperate sorry I am sir, but I'm afraid it's not out yet. We have the old one, of course, but I suppose you've read that." When another customer asks her if she likes Kipling, she replies, "How could I know when I've never kippled?"

❖   ❖   ❖

After a mad drinking binge in New York in 1962, Brendan was hospitalised, but walked out without being discharged. Shortly afterwards, looking for "the cure" in a friend's house, he accidentally went to the house next door instead . . . which turned out to be a nursing home for alcoholics! Perhaps seeing this as a sign from above, he admitted himself and allowed himself to be treated there.

❖   ❖   ❖

At the funeral of a former girlfriend of Dominic's, Brendan was surprised his brother wasn't crying. "I didn't care for her that much," Dominic confessed finally, "it would be hypocrisy." Brendan thought for a second and then piped up, "Will you not shed even a few crocodile tears to encourage the relatives to buy a drink?"

❖   ❖   ❖

He never regarded himself as a prize pupil at school, which was probably just as well. This is how he described leaving it, "That was the day the Christian Brothers realised that if you pray long enough, your every wish will be God's desire."

❖   ❖   ❖

One time Ma was very sick and a priest was called to the house to give her the Last Rites. The priest asked Brendan to kneel down and pray beside her bed. Instead of that, he started spouting obscenities from Brian Merriman's *The Midnight Court*.

❖   ❖   ❖

When Brendan was a young man, a neighbour of ours wouldn't stop annoying him boasting about her "darling boy" walking in the procession in Lourdes. Brendan's version of the situation was somewhat different. "She sent him equipped with a pair of wooden hands," he claimed, "which he wore clasped in front of him, while he picked pockets with the real ones."

❖   ❖   ❖

How is it, he used to wonder, that members of the cloth, who were all supposed to be experts on the next world, never seemed to him to be in any special hurry to get to it – unless they head heard something very unpleasant about it? He could understand the fear for sinners, or "daylight atheists" like himself, but even saintly priests seemed to him to be afflicted with this reluctance.

❖   ❖   ❖

He was at the funeral of the journalist Terry Ward with Ben Kiely in Skerries and the mood of all concerned was despondent so he tried to lift the general spirits. The Pope was also sick at the time, and having constant medical attention. "I'm a little doubtful about the future life," Brendan enunciated "because I don't see The Pope in any hurry to get there, and surely to God he should be well expected." When it came to his own time, Brendan declared, he'd lay on his bed, strongly resisting the Church for three or four months, but then, gradually growing good-humoured, he would submit and depart upwards to the cheers and congratulations of friends and relatives.

❖   ❖   ❖

John B Keane says that Brendan burst into his kitchen one day where his wife was painting a chair. "Why don't you hire a painter?" he asked her, the hint being palpable. When she didn't reply, however, he acknowledged that she was "better than most daubers". He sat down and had a cup of tea then. Seeing a statue of the Infant of Prague, he looked up at it and said, "She often came to my aid; there was always money under her."

❖   ❖   ❖   ❖

John B says Brendan was also responsible for the following verse, which
is something of which I wasn't aware:

> *Oh the winds that flow across the roofs from Kimmage,*
> *Bring perfume from the knackers as they blow,*
> *And the women in the boozer drinking porter,*
> *Speak a language that the clergy do not know.*

Chapter 9

Confessions of an Irish Rebel

The IRA didn't take sides. We were neutral in favour of one side only – our own.

Brendan Behan

Considering Brendan was the son of a man who was a cellmate of Sean T O'Kelly and the grandson of a woman who was imprisoned in Manchester at the ripe old age of 82 for republican activities it's hardly surprising he would have had a certain patriotic zeal. Ma used to boast that not one of her family were in their homes during Easter Week 1916. I believe her. I've heard it said that if everyone who was supposed to be in the GPO during that week was really there, instead of cowering under their beds, we would have had no problem taking out the Brits. My family takes proud exception to such duplicitous claptrap, and we have the track record to prove it.

Sometimes that record takes a colourful turn, as in Brendan's case. When he was a boy, he convinced himself he'd actually taken part in the 1916 Uprising even though it happened seven years before he was born. He knew what garrison he belonged to, who he fought with and what his main duties were . . . and felt quite superior to anyone who hadn't been a part of it, whether they were born at the time or not.

Brendan got most of his socialist tendencies from Ma, a campaigner for equality to her last days. After she moved to Crumlin, which never held a candle to Russell Street for her, she used to turn up the radio and open the windows every time the Russian National Anthem came on the radio. As a baby, she rocked him to the tune of *The Red Flag*.

"We became members of the Fianna," he once wrote, "the way other kids became altar boys." In other words, in our circle it was a part of growing up. He couldn't wait to get involved in the 'Armed Struggle'. As Dominic said, he didn't play long under the street-lamp with us, and at the age of six he had joined the young IRA. By sixteen, an age at which most of us haven't even started to live, he was already in prison. It was an ominous foretaste of what was to come. Just one day before his 17th birthday, he was served with his first borstal sentence for being part of a bombing campaign.

"National freedom, as far as Brendan was concerned," said Cathal Goulding, "was looked on as unfinished business." And as Rory added,

"England's difficulty was Ireland's opportunity." Brendan listened to Ma and Da feeding similar sentiments to him from the cradle.

None of us will ever know all of the republican exploits Brendan got up to, but it's probably safe to say most of them are in the public domain. He once dubbed himself "the most captured soldier in Irish history". He had a talent for getting caught with his finger in the cookie jar.

When it came to ideas, he was always a stirring stick. He never accepted communism; it was too cut-and-dried for his liking, and the idea of party discipline was anathema to him. But like many writers who came out of toil and travail he supported the Russian Revolution, believing it would eventually bring world freedom. Like the rest of us he longed for the day we would establish a brave new world free from hunger and poverty. In his case it was more a longing for the big rock candy mountain, a kind of tired man's heaven.

He dearly wished to go to Russia, but never made it. During the Cold War the communist party couldn't get enough tame clods to visit that country and report back. Brendan came to me and asked if I would use my influence to see that he got on to one of these cultural delegations. I couldn't because they wouldn't risk sending him. They couldn't be sure what he would say when he came back, and a Brendan let loose in Red Square could have hastened Stalin's heart attack by a few years. Brendan ranted and raved about the idiots they were sending while "real" men like himself were being left behind. He was right too: all they wanted were a few castrated scribblers who would see only what they wanted them to see.

Brendan had no politics. He made them up as he went along. He used to say the first communists were some monks in Prague who agreed to hold everything in common long before Marx appeared on the scene.

Politics took me down a different road than it did Brendan. He was a more direct descendent of Da, a man he first espied through the railings of Kilmainham Prison. Like both of them. I have spent time behind bars, but for somewhat different reasons and also for different lengths of time. The time I spent in Wandsworth was, as a fellow inmate put it, about the length of the average pee, but that is neither here nor there. Suffice to say that I have garnered more headlines for my trade union activities than for trying to blow up English people.

Ma could never understand my politics. When I told her one time that she had no need to worry about me, that I wasn't going to count the hairs on Trotsky's beard, she looked at me and said, "Who's Trotsky? He sounds like a horse."

I have joined, and left, political parties for many reasons, some of which may surprise you. I used to belong to the Worker's Revolutionary Party when it was known as the Socialist Labour League, but we closed down one branch of it in Nottingham because everybody was drinking too much and sleeping with anyone else. Not that that surprised me. To be a revolutionary, I think you have to relate to human beings.

Dominic described me as a "Voltaire Republican", which has some truth in it. I was a Marxist from an early age, and looked down my nose at republican adventurers like Brendan. Brendan viewed anarchism as "singing Red songs to the amused toleration of the police, and getting in with millionaire's daughters". There was a time I would have reared up on him for a comment like that, but now I can just smile. Who knows, maybe the old bugger was even right.

I was never a great proponent of the 1916 business. I thought we should have stayed with the British. At least they would have had to keep us, I thought – and we would have fared better on their dole than ours. All governments, I used to argue, amount to the same thing in the end. When all the screaming and shouting is over, what have you left but a load of fat-arsed politicians arranging the next big scam from the comfort of their local watering holes.

Dominic had it down cold when he wrote, in *Teems of Times*, "A wise-after-the-event British politician said that Pearse and his comrades should have been brought before a civil court, charged with disturbing the peace and sentenced to seven days." Nothing more, he predicted, would have been heard of an Irish Republic.

The looters of 1916 had more sense than the fighters, I've always said. If there's ever another war, I shall become a looter and get myself a country mansion.

Da was a looter too, but not a very successful one. Once during the Troubles when the family were practically starving due to financially straitened circumstances, he raided a building that had been hit, making off with two boxes he hoped would contain food. He risked his life running home and dodging bullets but when he opened the box he found it contained twelve wigs and six pairs of ballet shoes. Unbeknown to him, the building had been a theatrical supply house.

Ma was a mother first and a republican second, I'm glad to say, but we were all still suckled on patriotic ballads like this one of James Connolly:

> *Come workers sing a rebel song,*
> *A song of love and hate,*
> *Of love unto the lowly,*
> *And of hatred to the great,*
> *The great who trod our fathers down,*
> *Who steal our children's bread,*
> *Whose greedy hands were e'er outstretched,*
> *To rob the living and the dead.*

Ma was a vibrant woman, a socialist without using that word, a woman who had a passionate concern for fair play. A mountain of energy, she was forever scooting somewhere. She always told me to ignore what people thought or said about me, and to never look up or down at anyone. When I was infected by anti-Jewry one time, I pointed to a little Jewish boy and said, "Look Mammy, there's a dirty Jew." She whacked me across the mouth and said, "Never call anyone a dirty anything again. Everyone is some poor mother's son." From this woman we all inherited our love for the little man. I like to think of her as the wellspring for my Marxism, even if she couched it in different terms.

Ma wasn't blinded by Anglophobia, either. She was well aware that you could starve just as easily under a green flag as you could under a Union Jack. She was able to see through the nonsense that once you had your own State, somehow or other you became free. On our wall we had a picture of the Sacred Heart sandwiched in between Lenin and Jim Larkin: an unlikely trio. "Christ between two thieves!" Ma declared.

In my youth, politics wasn't so much an ideology as a question of survival against the economic odds. When I was 16, Ma pointed out an advert for miners in Nottingham. Da told me I could do whatever I liked with my life so long as I never asked him for money. Between Ma's gentle hint and Da's liberal parenting I felt this was about as much career guidance I was going to receive, so off I went. And the rest is history. Brendan also advised me to go to England, quoting an old saw. "Sell the pig," he said, "and wander far away, for in Paddy's land but poverty you'll find."

Ma said there was no work in Dublin, so it would be better for me to take a skip across the water. I reminded her of her old slogan, "Burn everything English except their coal." She snapped back, "I never said you weren't to dig the stuff." She had all the angles covered. I looked at Da to see if he was of a similar attitude but he just waved his pipe at me and said, "Watch out for the women." So I knew the die was cast.

The very next day I found myself aboard the *Princess Maud*, a cattle-boat full of great beasts from the grasslands of Meath, bound – like myself – for the stomach of John Bull.

I landed in England with three shillings and four pence in my pocket. The first thing I did was to go to the Salvation Army. I asked the man behind the desk if he had any rooms and he burst out laughing. "We don't have rooms, old Pat," he said, "but we have dormitories or cubicles." I asked which was the cheapest? "The dormitory," he replied, "but I must warn you – it's dog-rough." I told him I'd take a chance. When I got inside, this old dosser said to me, "What are you doing with your shoes?"

"Taking them off," I said.

"Well put one under each leg-iron of the bed," he said, "and lay on it. Because if you don't, you'll get up in the morning and by Christ, you'll be barefoot."

The next thing I did was take off my trousers, which made my few remaining coins rattle. Suddenly, ten heads looked up out of the surrounding beds. I looked round at the poor buggers coughing and sneezing and I felt sick inside. Some of them were drinking a concoction called 'Jake', which was milk with gas blown through it via a tube. Some of the others preferred boot polish. They lit a flame under the tin and drank the melted polish down, sometimes burning their insides. Many of them were old navvies broken on the wheel of labour. They had poured out all their great strength on rivers and reservoirs, had tramped the earth "from Boston to Buffalo making other people rich as they scrimped to stay alive". And now in the autumn of their years, drink was their only companion. It was like a foretaste of what was going to happen to Brendan, though I wasn't to know that then.

I went on from there and made some kind of a life for myself. I had gone to England for three months and I ended up staying 60 years. It was in the Irish Army that I got my first rap on the knuckles for my socialist sympathies. When I started going on about the difference between the officers' pay and ours, I was told to apply for a discharge. "Why should I?" I asked in all innocence. "Because you'll get it," the officer said. I think he was trying to tell me something.

I got a job on a building site after that. I became a shop steward and stood up for the rights of the workers. "Why do you sack a man every week?" I asked the foreman one day.

"It keeps the job going," he told me.

"I'm a shop steward," I said then, "and you won't last long yourself." He didn't. I saw to that.

I didn't regard myself as anything special as a trade unionist. My only ambition was to stop the hiring and firing that went on willy-nilly and negotiate decent site conditions – things our own society takes for granted but which earned me the name of subversive. It was illegal to apply for a wage increase in those days. I led a march against this system and got two months in the clink for my pains. When I was released, the foreman told me I wasn't welcome in the job any more, but the other workers went on strike on my behalf and I was reinstated.

That was really the beginning of it all for me. I went to prison fighting a ban on May Day marches and was also jailed fighting the imposition of an arms programme that has subsequently bankrupted Britain. I have been called a "fermenter of discontent", but I am not unhappy with this label. Once the BBC slapped a ban on broadcasting my voice because I told a Tory MP that his party spent most of their time bonking their secretaries.

My play *The Begrudgers* suggests one remedy for Britain's ills would be to close down the House of Commons and replace it with a reasonably honest computer. Any takers? It also suggests that the House of Lords is the only concrete proof of life after death.

I also composed an open letter to the people of Brighton in which I said, "Margaret Thatcher and Neil Kinnock have no mandate for their unholy alliance in the Gulf. Unfortunately we live under an elected dictatorship. A small committee of grey men in even greyer suits meets and decides the issues of peace and war. We have no say in whether we live or die. All power corrupts and absolute power corrupts absolutely. People's power is the only answer."

On another occasion I submitted the following letter to *The Irish Post*: "A trial of war criminals was held here today. In the dock were Saddam Hussein, George Bush, John Major and Neil Kinnock. Charged as accessories were Douglas Hurd, Gerald Kaufmann and Paddy Ashdown. All were found guilty of the mass murder of innocent people. Charles Haughey is out on bail pending extradition."

In the sixties I was granted a place at Sussex University, which is probably the strangest thing that ever happened to me – or any other brickie for that matter. The event was picked up by the media and attracted a bit of fanfare. I was even interviewed by William Hardcastle on *World At One*. He was a former newsman with the *Daily Mail*, a man guaranteed to shake several kinds of shit out of you. "So you have decided to quit the dole, Mr Behan," he began by saying. "You've decided to be so good as to leave your houseboat for four years and live off the taxpayer. And then when you're finished I presume you'll become a teacher and continue to pour your anarchic gospel into more young ears."

"All I'm getting for my family is £14 a week," I replied. "I understand you are receiving in excess of £600 a week from the same taxpayer." He wasn't too pleased with the direction the interview was taking but it was live so he couldn't edit me out.

I found the University enchanting. It was a culture shock to me to see middle-aged women swishing by me in long skirts instead of hairy-arsed bricklayers in sweat-stained shirts. Sweet-scented creatures in Levis and long hair invited me to smoke dope with them and listen to 'The Beach Boys'. Needless to say, I didn't need much persuasion. I could imagine Brendan laughing his arse off at the whole charade. It would be like the final treachery to him. But who was he to talk? He had his Luggala and I could have my Sussex.

In my first test I scored ten out of ten, which wasn't bad for an untutored lad from Russell Street, but it wasn't long before the old rebel in me came alive. I was encouraged by some students to join their campaign against sit-down exams and I rallied to the cause.

In more recent times, I've tried to start an organisation called SID, which stands for Shut It Down, and refers to the House of Commons, the longest running farce since Agatha Christie's *The Mousetrap*. I wrote to the Speaker of the House of Commons two years ago and told her I would be chaining myself to the railings outside the building in support of SID. I asked for her permission in carrying on the good work begun by Guy Fawkes but she wasn't forthcoming. Instead she told me to beware of the long arm of the law if I contemplated such an action. This disappointed me. I reminded her that I was a kind of male suffragette, telling her where women would be if they hadn't chained themselves to similar railings in times past.

In the end, I abandoned this plan and settled for the more civilised stratagem of picketing the building wearing my SID T-shirt. The police reassured me that provided I walked at a reasonable pace, I would not be arrested, so we were all happy. But unfortunately, two years on, the House of Commons still stands and very few people have heard of SID.

Like Brendan, I have always been a man of the people. When I was working on a building site on London's South Bank in 1951, I was offered a job in the office instead, with a pay hike thrown in, but I turned it down. I knew where I belonged. On another occasion I refused to allow the Queen to visit a building site I was working on because she didn't have a union card. You have to be consistent about these things, don't you? I mean if you start making exceptions for Buckingham Palace, where will it all end?

People have tried to blackball me over the years for my union activities. A reporter called Henry Fielding interviewed Ma in the sixties and tried to put words into her mouth about me. "Didn't you have a lot of trouble with Brian as a child?" he asked, trying to make some trite connection between my politics and juvenile delinquency. "Oh yes I did," Ma said, to shut him up. That was during the dummy run for a television broadcast, when he asked her the same question on the live programme, he expected her to give the same answer. Instead she piped up, "Not at all. He was one of the best boys I ever reared. I hear he's causing a lot of strikes in England and more power to his elbow. Sure the working man never got anything without fighting for it, did he?"

I was never more proud of Ma than at that moment. Once again, the lowly Behans had outfoxed the might of the BBC. Brendan said famously that he didn't turn to drink; rather it turned to him. Well I feel the same about writing. I never craved the kind of attention he did. I always saw my primary avocation as a political activist. To this day I'm more proud of securing better conditions for labouring men in Britain than writing a hit play.

When I wrote my memoirs *With Breast Expanded*, it was primarily meant to be a polemic against social injustice rather than an overtly literary enterprise. (With such a daft title as that, the miracle is that it got recognised as anything at all.) It was intended to be a diatribe against poverty, against religious and sexual repression, against the plight of the Irish in Britain – the great Brendan themes, if you like. I felt then, as I feel now, that the world is crawling with fence-sitters and knee-benders, and I wanted to put that on record. I wanted to let the world know that when you start bending the knee at all it gets easier and easier to bend it further, and before you know where you are you're on the ground, with little or no redress against the people who put you there.

It was a book that denounced the status quo – and those who lost their own status in the process. I felt I had a right to speak about such matters, having suffered under the yoke of John Bull while fighting for the rights of my fellow immigrants. I didn't take up a gun to do this, as Brendan did, but rather a placard – and maybe I had more of an effect than he did in the long run as a result. A new Anglo-Irish Agreement was signed in April 1998 through negotiation rather than at the barrel of a gun, and a similar eventuality took place in 1922 when Michael Collins forsook violence for the ballot box. Alas, for him it was too late, but the point stands.

Similarly, when I wrote *Mother of All the Behans*, I did so with some reluctance. Some-writers would make a drum out of the skin of their mother's arse the better to sound their own praises, but I preferred to tell Ma's story rather than my own in that little book. In fact I asked Maeve Binchy to write it for me, but she refused. In the first draft, admittedly, my own voice came through, but Tony Whittome, my editor at Hutchinson, put me right when he said, "I don't really want you in this book at all; it's your mother's story." The book is her valentine, with only gentle nudgings from me.

When people ask me why I wrote about her rather than Da, I reply, "Because she was a much stronger person than he was." In fact if there wasn't a Kathleen Behan, there might well not have been a Brendan. And obviously I don't just mean that in the biological sense. He took his whole world view from her, as we all did.

All I want is a bit of fair play in the world. A few years ago a man called Derry Mainwaring Knight got seven years in prison for conning £216,000 from wealthy Christians. I wanted to write a biography of him in protest at that sentence. It seemed somewhat harsh to me being delivered not long after a youth who mugged old ladies got 18 months and walked from the court laughing and a rapist of a six-year-old girl got just three years. My family always stood up for what they believed in through thick and thin and I was determined I wasn't going to be any different.

Ma could fight her way out of a barrel full of tigers. A baker sold me a loaf once that was rock hard. It was bought with our last sixpence so obviously action had to be taken. When she asked the baker to take it back, however, he said no. So what did she do? She hit him across the face with it, that's what. I was getting on-the-job training for my communism.

I represented the ordinary people, the ones who drank their subs in pubs, who worked without fear or favour until they dropped. People who had no pensions or sick pay, no three weeks sunning themselves in the Algarve or two-car garages in the suburbs. People who never knew what was coming tomorrow, who never knew what a golden handshake was, or even a silver one. Who had to accept dismissal without rhyme or reason, who marched to the beat of a fat cat's drum. People whose only guarantee in life was two hours notice on a Friday.

My present position is the one I've held for a long time now. I spent much of my youth searching for an organisation that would bring happiness to society, but I finally came to realise that all organisations, almost by definition, are corrupt. Because their primary ambition is to perpetuate themselves – at any cost. At the moment I believe that no movement comprising more than one person is totally trustworthy. Any organisation worth its salt should be able to hold its AGM in a phone booth.

I inherited my rebellious spirit from Ma and Da. Ma never let her bone go to the dog, and Da spearheaded the 1936 strike of house-painters and decorators that all but starved us. There was a lock-out for nine months but he wouldn't even go back after that because of his principles. "You can't eat principles," Ma said to him. True enough, though none of us quite starved.

But you shouldn't take yourself too seriously. The principal of the London College of Printing, where I used to lecture, asked me one day if I was a terrorist. "Only on Sundays," I replied. Do you think that sounds like one of Brendan's lines? Maybe it does, but the question is, who got it from whom? Part of Brendan's problem was the fact that he was embraced by the affluence of the Guinness family. Once that happens you're done for. Bernard Levin claims Brendan was destroyed by the fashionable people that picked him up and then dropped him. It's a moot point. I met some of these fashionable people at a party Brendan invited me to. It was peopled by wall-to-wall gobshites: the idle rich bored out of their tiny minds.

At one stage an American woman came up to me and asked me to beat up her husband. The rest of the night I spent trying to get into a loo crowded with dopeheads sniffing cocaine through £20 notes. There were lots of wannabes as well: all those poor lost souls looking over your shoulder to see if there was some celebrity in the room that they could be seen with so they could shine in his or her reflected glory. When I told them I dug ditches for a living they beat a hasty retreat.

One fat MP who had dashed straight from Parliament so that he could guzzle drink stood beside me. "All power corrupts," I said to him, "and absolute power corrupts absolutely."

"Nonsense old boy," he harumphed, chewing on a biscuit. "All power is lovely and – absolute power is absolutely delicious." When I said I was in favour of direct democracy, he laughed out loud.

Were these the kind of people Brendan was courting and being courted by? I found it hard to believe he could fall for the whole charade. But the attraction of being noticed is a deep and human trait. It begins with seeing your name in print and ends with the ultimate sell-out. Vanity thy name is writer, we might say. In fact I'm guilty of it myself. Ironically, it was my left-wing activities that later resulted in Brendan being barred from the English mainland. He was anxious to come to England to further his writing career and asked the Home Office to lift the old deportation order against him. However, they were advised not to lift it on the grounds that I was "agitating public discontent". Brendan never knew this but I doubt if it would have bothered him. A life in England could have prolonged his life or it could have even shortened it. Who knows? Either way, I know he would have approved of my actions, even if he couldn't embody them in his own life.

The fact is, he was never a joiner. I told him the Communist Party was always there for him if he was interested, but of course he never was. His attempts to lead any kind of delegations were doomed to failure – even delegations of his own. Brendan told me he liked smoking expensive cigars with Castro because it made him feel both bourgeois and radical at the same time. I don't know if he was winding me up or not when he said that. You could never be sure with that man. Another time he gave out yards to me for leaving the Communist Party. "You fucking renegade!" he said. He was sitting between two millionairesses in a Rolls Royce at the time. It was priceless. It gave smoked-salmon socialism a whole new dimension.

The Communist Party sent me to Bulgaria once and I led the life of Reilly. I was wined and dined in a hotel in Sofia and then brought out to the mountains to live in a house that had been owned by a tobacco millionaire but was now a kind of retirement home for weary Stalinists. I had a butler, a maid and a cook. The latter was a large burly man who informed me that he had strangled the leading Fascist in his village with his bare hands. Outside my house sat an old lady breaking stones, with a steady drizzle running down her back. When I pointed this out to my security guard, all he said was, "That's her job."

I was reminded of the old story about the man breaking stones in Kerry when a rich man passes by on a horse. "Can you tell me sir," says the stone-breaker, "who won the election?" The rich man looks down at him and says, "It's equal to you who won, my good man, for either way you'll still be breaking those stones tomorrow."

It wasn't long before I got fed up of this lifestyle. After a few weeks I left the hills and asked the security man to drive me through the plains. He drove like billio, with peasants having to jump for their lives as we thundered through remote villages. We stopped in a place where we ate grapes, drank wine and had *al fresco* meals in a beach-house. The sea was as level as a billiard table, the water so warm you could take a bath in it. But all this meant nothing to me. We were cut off from reality not only by the guards but also a barbed wire fence. It all seemed so dead, so pointless. Was this how the very rich lived – barren empty lives with not a breath of humanity to touch them?

I saw a hospital with state-of-the-art services for the hierarchy and just outside it a stinking hole where the masses tended their wounds: it was hardly palatable to my communist way of thinking. To me it seemed distinctly Orwellian. In this society, some seemed definitely more equal than others. I couldn't even enjoy it from a decadent point of view. The only emotion I was left with was boredom. To have money and do nothing seemed like a death sentence to me.

On a television show one time I found myself in the company of four millionaires. "If every rich man in the world died tomorrow," I said, "I would feel nothing, but if every binman stopped work for a week I would be eaten alive by rats tearing into mountains of rubbish."

When I went to Moscow I couldn't believe the contrast between the living conditions of the poor and the party bosses. I stayed in the Hotel Metropole just off Gorki Street. I ate only the best, my belly bursting with grub while outside the ordinary citizens queued for food for hours, often winding up with nothing in the end. I said to my delegates that the inequality was worse than anything I had ever experienced in the West, but they didn't want to know. They were too busy stuffing their gobs.

In New York nobody cared if you lived or died, but at least nobody bored you with high-sounding pap about helping their fellow man. And at least in New York there was always the possibility of getting up off your arse and improving your lot. But not here. This was dead grinding poverty with no remission. What does all this say about me? Probably that I'm a communist who likes to flirt with the well-to-do occasionally.

One night, for instance, I was at a performance of the Bolshoi Ballet and when it ended there was an explosive round of applause – not for the ballet dancers, but somebody in the audience. Had my fame preceded me, I wondered. But no, my hopes were dashed when I saw Stalin taking a bow in a box above me. I was also ferried round China in a limo when I was over there with the British Communist Party. However, I have to admit the experience left me rather cold. I was nostalgic for my old bicycle, if you must know. Worse was to transpire. I was expelled from the Communist Party for opposing the invasion of Hungary, and also for protesting against living conditions in China.

I was also thrown out of the Anarchist Party. That was an unprecedented experience because their manifesto, by definition, doesn't have any mechanism for expulsion. It was a very Irish situation – a kind of Catch 23. Since then I have been known to debunk communism in its various forms, but I have also defended it by saying that becoming a communist is still one of the best ways I know of meeting middle class women. So it can't be all bad. You might think this all sounds contradictory, but which of us isn't a mass of contradictions?

Brendan met Princess Margaret at the premiere of *The Hostage* and she put her arm around him. I said to him, "How do you square that with your republicanism?"

"We must leave room for a little humbug in life," he told me.

Hemingway used to say, "I mix with shits nor lose the common touch." Brendan identified with that. He was most at home with the stock from which we both had sprung. Sometimes people saw him decked out in a suit and accused him of being a counter-jumper or a poacher turned gamekeeper, but he never had that crisis of identity. He may have enjoyed hobnobbing with the gentry now and again but nobody who knew him well ever thought there was any danger he would become seduced by the aroma of gentility.

Francis Stuart quoted Eric Bloy's statement: "The enemy of the good is not the bad, but the respectable," and Brendan, when he wrote of himself, "I belong among the down-and-outs" was expressing much the same feeling.

All of us Behans have travelled different roads to similar goals. Seamus fought Hitler, while Rory became a Free Stater. My forte was mobilising the industrially deprived or victimised. Brendan approved of this in principle but union activity would have bored him in the long run. He gave a speech to the painter's union one night in which he denounced the capitalists for "driving along the Stillorgan Road in their brothel wagons killing the children of the poor".

It was rousing stuff but it meant nothing to his audience. A hundred faces looked up at him open-mouthed and he wrung his hands in despair. That was the beginning and end of his brilliant career as an orator. "It's not about poetry, Brendan," I told him, "it's about hard graft." But he didn't want to hear this. He simply decided to shift gear and continue doing things his way, allowing me to be the chip off the old block in this particular department. "If you fight for the liberty of a small country you're an anarchist," Brendan claimed, "but if you do it for a big one you're a patriot." That was how the semantic dice was loaded, and why he tried to crack it with his own endeavours.

Brendan wasn't violent by nature Beatrice often said, "Anyone he ever clocked deserved it". He said himself that he was a pacifist. If we look at his military careeer with the IRA it was a series of false starts. Not only was the explosives mission to Liverpool a non-event, but even the bullet he fired at de Courcey Square failed to reach its destination. There were orders to shoot him on sight after this incident, but Da interceded for him and got this edict lifted.

It was a gesture Brendan never properly thanked the old lad for, relations between them being somewhat strained at this time. Later on, Brendan told the Governor of the prison that he hadn't intended to do the detectives an injury at all, but was merely trying to wrest the rifle from the arms of another man. This contravenes his other story of berating himself for missing his target from a short distance. With Brendan there were always many angles, and sometimes you feel he wasn't even sure what happened himself because he had told the story so many different ways.

He always enjoyed the aura of danger that surrounded him, and he also liked to exaggerate it, particularly in his last years when he would pathetically goad Da into telling anyone who came to the house about his republican involvement. He was like a toothless dog bemoaning the loss of his fangs, if he ever had them. C A Joyce, the governor of the borstal where he spent most of his behind-bars time, said he was a model prisoner and looked like he wouldn't harm a fly. Brendan apologised to Joyce once for swearing in his presence: hardly the sort of behaviour expected from a convicted gunman.

Sean Kavanagh, the Governor of Mountjoy when Brendan was there, underlined that appraisal, as did Eoin O'Mahoney, when he dubbed Brendan "a spiritual lovechild of the Irish Revolution". J Bowyer Bell put this in a slightly more formal context when he said, "Whatever his other virtues, the IRA found that Behan's military talents were at best unorthodox, and his capacity to discipline negligible. Abroad he may have seemed the typical Irish rebel, but within the IRA he was the antithesis of what a volunteer should be. No-one could ever manage to dislike him, but there must have been those who thought the IRA was better off with him in prison and out of harm's way."

He had a complicated attitude to killing for an ideology. If he was alive today he'd be all for the peace process. He would have much preferred a happy Ireland than a united graveyard. He was never proud of his violent acts, but he saw political violence as a necessary evil. He liked to quote George Bernard Shaw: "A perambulator hasn't much chance of tactics against a furniture van." He said he disparaged the violence in Ernest Hemingway's books because Hemingway seemed to be "childishly pleased" about it, but I'm sure Hemingway would have felt the opposite to be the case.

In Hemingway's books, violence is usually depicted in a tense and ominous argot, whereas with Brendan there are kinds of Rabelaisian overtones to it, and of course the old bravado. Harry Cohn once said of Errol Flynn that he was only happy when he was fighting or fucking. Brendan was a bit the same. In prison he could do neither, or at least not in the way he might have liked. I don't think he was as highly sexed as his sailor friend Peter Arthurs suggests, but his penchant for violence never abated.

For a time he did it for his country and afterward carried on his own private wars in every bar he frequented. He became a rebel without a cause – or maybe a rebel with a thousand causes, which could well boil down to the same thing. In a letter he wrote to the editor of the *New Statesman* in late 1962, Brendan complimented me on leading "English, Irish, Scotch, Welsh and negroes in the struggles of London building workers". We had had our differences in the past and it was reassuring for me to have this testimonial from him in print.

The biggest strike I ever organised was the one at Shell Oil opposite Waterloo Station. It subsequently came to be called 'The Battle of Waterloo'. The McAlpine family closed the site, dismissing three and a half thousand men in the process. It was a pitiful situation so we decided to take drastic action. We decided to 'black Mac' even without union backing. It proved a wise move, and resulted in me being hailed as a hero of sorts. "Let's put a human wall around the site," I urged, "so not even a mouse can squeeze through." We did too. I ended up, doing time in Wandsworth prison for my troubles, but I had made my point.

Brendan visited me in the course of the strike, parading himself round to see all the picketers, congratulating them on the fight and handing out money to all and sundry. Then he marched in the gate and roundly abused the scabs working inside. He drove round the site reciting a poem that went down very well with the picketers. It went like this:

> *He who works hard,*
> *And does his best,*
> *Will get the sack,*
> *Just like the rest.*
> *So brothers as you,*
> *Paint that wall,*
> *Take your time,*
> *And fuck them all.*

As we looked out at the mass sacking of 3,500 men, it seemed very apt. Then he got up on his soapbox. It was a sunny September afternoon and the workers lay scattered round us like confetti as they ate their sandwiches from lunchboxes. His voice boomed out as he sought to encourage them to stand up for their rights. "What do you imagine that old McAlpine does when he gets home at night?" he asked, "sit and pick his toenails? No, he works out more ways to make a profit, more ways to put blood on bricks!"

Afterwards we went for a drink and he told me he was proud of what I was doing. "We don't see much of each other," he said to me, "but I'm behind you. We came from the same egg." He meant it too. A

blow struck anywhere against any oppression or injustice had his full
support. On the other hand, he felt a bit out of things with the rest of
the strike committee. Large, strong and manly, they were completely
different from the people he had become used to drinking with. These
were men you didn't fool around with. For a while he tried pressing
them to drink with him, but they politely refused. He stood silent and
worried: he was losing contact with the very people he admired.

But suddenly he smiled. A street musician had come into the pub
with his flute. Brendan stuffed the old man's hat with coins and notes.
Then, taking up the flute, he dipped it in a pint of cider and slowly
began playing and dancing. Out into the street he went, begging from
the passing crowds. To the old man's delight he filled the hat several
times over. The song he sang was suitably self-deprecatory:

> *Oh the working class*
> *Can kiss my arse*
> *I have a foreman's*
> *Job at last.*

This was Brendan at his most loveable: trying to reach out through a
clown's mask into the hearts of humanity.

❖

Brendan once imprisoned the entire police force of the Aran Islands,
and if that sounds daring even for him, I better explain that such a
force consisted of just two men. He locked them up and threw the keys,
down a cliff. A friend assisted him in his anarchic endeavours. "We
didn't do this without some provocation," he explained afterwards,
"because they had come to arrest us for singing a song in the village
street."

He wanted to see Beatrice some years after this incident when she
was holidaying in Aran but because he was prohibited from ever setting foot on the islands he had to be smuggled aboard a trawler so the
rendezvous could be organised.

❖   ❖   ❖

He liked to tell the story of an American woman who went into a Dublin library and asked to see a book on Irish guerrillas. "Gorillas in Ireland," the intellectually-challenged librarian mused, "Divil a one I ever
saw. Sure the climate here isn't at all suitable for those sorts of beasts."

❖   ❖   ❖

Another yarn he enjoyed was one featuring an aunt of ours. It appears she went down to the GPO during the 1916 Rising to see her husband, who was inside doing his bit for his country. Shells from a gunboat on the Liffey were falling all around the place and she was implored to go home. She refused, so her husband eventually came over to a sand-bagged window and shouted out, "Go away, Maggie!"

"I will," she said, "but what I wanted to know was are you going to work in the morning?"

❖   ❖   ❖

Brendan was approached by a man who claimed to have been in the same IRA brigade as him. He was suspicious of the man's credentials and told him in no uncertain terms, "The only brigade you would be fit for is the fire brigade."

❖   ❖   ❖

Brendan loved the following two stories. The first is where two blokes are in a pub and one says to the other, "Where were you in 1916?"

The other replies, "I wasn't born till 1921."

The first goes, "Excuses, excuses!"

The other one he liked has two pub patriots getting into an argy-bargy after one too many pints. "What year did you die for Ireland?" the first fellow asks. When the other gaffer puts a date on his death, he says, "No, that can't be right. You're far too young to have died for Ireland." Brendan loved telling these two stories probably because he had a bit of that absurdity in himself.

❖   ❖   ❖

In *The Hostage* he wrote that he wondered what he would do if a warder came up to him and said, "Here you are; sing two bars of *God Save The King* an I'll give you this piece of roundsteak."

"Would I take it? Mary Joseph, he'd be a lucky man that I didn't take the head and all off him."

❖   ❖   ❖

When berated for not having a steady girlfriend, he replied to his accuser that it was equally un-Marxist to reproach a man for not having a regular date as it would be attack him for not having a motorcar.

❖   ❖   ❖

Former *Irish Times* editor Robert Smyllie once remarked, presciently to Brendan, "You'll kill yourself more with the drink than you will with the IRA."

❖ ❖ ❖

There was a gambling racket operating round Sean McDermott in the twenties. The people involved in it stopped at nothing to get money. When the police proved powerless to stop them, the IRA decided to step in. Brendan took it upon himself to achieve this, going into one of the gambling dens one night armed with a gun. He burst into the room and grabbed as much money as he could from a table. "I'm taking this money," he said, "for the cause of the Republic." As he was going out the door, though, one of the gamblers who knew of his reputation, shouted at him, "You're an effin' liar, Behan. The only cause you're interested in is the cause of Arthur Guinness."

❖ ❖ ❖

When he was asked what he would most like to witness during his stay in Spain, he replied promptly, "Franco's effin' funeral!"

❖ ❖ ❖

He claimed he didn't want to be a politician because he had only one face. "Politicians who call upon people to sacrifice themselves for their country are dangerous," he declared. "They are entitled to six ounces of lead between the eyes. Not in the brain, because they have no brain."

❖ ❖ ❖

When he was still a young man, Ma brought him out to see the lavish Guinness residence in Luggala. After they got there, a member of the Guinness family, aware of his political affiliations, said to Brendan, "What's a socialist like you doing out here?" Undaunted, Brendan replied, "Learning to fulfil my ambition to be a rich Red."

❖ ❖ ❖

Though Brendan referred to himself more than once as a "working class snob", he didn't have much time for champagne socialists. "Half of them," he said, "wouldn't know the difference between communism and rheumatism."

❖ ❖ ❖

The reason he carried gelignite as an IRA man, he claimed, was because dynamite wasn't safe. Work that out yourself!

❖   ❖   ❖

Like Brendan, I have also had some experience of guns, at least on the
receiving end. In December 1970, when I was having a snooze after
reading a book called *Religion and the Rise of Capitalism*, five bullets
ripped through the teak frame of my houseboat, penetrated a food cup-
board and whistled across the galley at ankle height. One of the bullets
hit a grapefruit. I tried to look on the bright side: myself and my female
companion were alive, even though we would have to go shopping for
an extra grapefruit. But I was left with the nagging question: who would
want to fire five bullets at such a decent skin as yours truly?

A Chief Superintendent came down to the boat the day after and
said his detectives were busy hunting the would-be assassin. I was
wondering why he spoke so loudly until I saw there was a television
camera behind him.

Ma was on the boat at the time and she thought the shooting was
done by some man who was resentful of the fact that I had his girlfriend on board. (I was a bit wild in those days.) She asked me why I
brought so many women onto the boat. "It's a home for distressed
women," I told her. She thought for a moment and then said, "Well if
they're not distressed when they arrive, they surely will be by the time
they leave!"

❖   ❖   ❖

After the IRA blew up a statue in the Phoenix Park, Brendan was
amused. Was this what the struggle was reduced to – blowing up a
piece of marble? He wrote a satirical poem about the incident. It went
like this:

> Neath the horse's prick
> A dynamite stick
> Some gallant hero did place.
> For the cause of our land
> With a light in his hand
> Bravely the foe he did face.
> Then without showing fear
> He kept himself clear
> Expecting to blow up the pair.
> But he nearly went crackers
> All he got was the knackers
> And made the poor stallion a mare.

This is the way
Our heroes today
Are challenging England's might.
With a stab in the back
And a midnight attack
On a horse that can't even shite!

❖   ❖   ❖

Considering this book is called *The Brothers Behan*, I would like to finish the chapter by relating another rebel's confession to you. It concerns my half-brother Sean and myself. When we were in our teens we formed the rather fanciful notion that we were going to become rich selling turf door-to-door. Don't ask me how we imagined this would be a goldmine, we just did. There was going to be no doubt about it.

We decided we'd buy a horse and cart, load the turf onto it, and hey presto, we'd be instant millionaires. Things, however, didn't quite work out like that. The first thing we did was approach a man we knew (his name was Murphy) who agreed to give us a loan. With this we bought a horse – though she didn't look much like one. She was more akin to a cross between an elephant and a giraffe. We christened her Polly. Polly must have thought she'd fallen into the hands of madmen.

We'd bought the cart before we bought her, with the result that we couldn't get her to fit between the shafts no matter how hard we tried. We finally decided to leave them pointing to heaven, But that didn't help much and every few yards she would skip like a circus pony. On the street people jeered at us, their advice ranging from, "Take it to the knackers" and "Get down and milk it" to "Let's make the next dance a waltz".

We eventually decided to buy another pony to fit the cart, but the second one wasn't much better. He had dodgy legs, and when he ran he threw them out sideways, which made him look for all the world like the leader of a black and white minstrel show. The man who sold him to us was called Dunphy. He had a wide-brimmed hat and under it a huge yellow scarf. He kept his trousers hooked up over his boots. He asked Sean and myself if we would take a glass of porter with him and we said yes. When we got to the pub we were amazed at how generous he was. Throwing down a bundle of notes, he asked if we seriously thought he was worried about a paltry twenty. That did the trick for Sean. Ten drinks later he had our own twenty quid for his steed.

We stabled him in a food emporium, asking the stable manager for his advice on the amount of food a horse needs. After a moment's silence to commemorate the advent of looneys he replied, "Half a stone

of whole oats three times a day and a bale of hay of a night." We did
that and by the end of the week the two nags were leaping out of their
skins, the extra grub and lack of work making them very playful. Like
Members of Parliament they were victims of a dependency culture and
refused to be yoked for honest toil. To all Sean's entreaties Polly, who
was still with us, turned a great big bottom and let fly with her enor-
mous hooves. "Stop mollycoddling her," said the stable manager.

Pushing Sean out of the way he confronted Polly with a whip about
twenty feet long. He threw up the whip in a commanding fashion and
ordered Polly to leave her nice warm bed. Unfortunately for him the
whip got caught up in the rafters and Polly bit him across the back
with her great yellow teeth. Sean and myself were secretly delighted
that justice was done. With the help of two Corporation dustmen we
eventually succeeded in driving our equine vampiress back to idleness.

It was time for Plan B. Sean said, "Let's hire a barge and we won't
need the nags at all." I said OK so we loaded the boat up at Robertstown
near the Bog of Allen. Then we set sail for Guinness harbour. On the
way I noticed either the water was getting deeper or we were shrinking. Sean, who had by now taken on the role of ship's captain, was
sporting a sou'wester and a hooked pipe. "We'll go through like a dose
of salts," he said, and seizing the tiller he made for the entrance. Bad
choice. A sudden gust of wind threw us to one side and we hit the wall
with a thunderous crack. The barge stopped and began to sink. "By
God," said Captain Sean, "there'll be a porter famine in the midlands
tonight."

Murphy, our backer, was almost gone mad with worry and was
using most unseasonable language. Frothing away, he brandished a
claim for the Port & Docks for the sum of £300 being due for harbour
clearance. Crestfallen we told him we were finished. "What about the
nags?" Sean asked. We owed a month of a food bill on them by now,
but in a few choice words Murphy told us what we could do with the
pair of them. "Public shame is what the fella needs," Sean whispered
to me. But how could we bring that about? Luckily Sean had an idea.

The following morning was Christmas Day. "Right," said Sean, "let's
take the horses out for a little walk." We headed out for Rathgar with
Murphy, who had bought a turkey and was carrying it under his oxter.
When we got to a Georgian Square, Sean said, "This is the place. Through
here." So up the gravel we went. Loosening the tethers we watched the
nags wander across the well-kept lawn. Murphy had a glass in his hand
and he raised it for a toast. But then his eye met the reproachful gaze of
Polly. Struck quite dumb, he dropped the glass to the ground in fright.
Polly, imagining this gesture to be hostile on his part, turned a con-
temptuous rump and with two blows of her hooves shattered a nearby
window. She daintily picked her way through the broken glass and,

seizing the turkey off Murphy, made off down the garden. Neither Sean nor I waited to see what happened next but headed for the boat to Kilburn.

Chapter 10

Always the Bitther Word!

He-seemed to me to be half-angel, half-beast. On the one hand a very handsome little man with a delicate feel and hands and a quick intuitive mind, on the other a beast with a crooked mouth that spat poison at people.

John Montague

"There are 733 pubs in Dublin," the *Washington Post* journalist Walter Hackett wrote the day after Brendan died, "and he was barred from roughly 725 of them." That was because he didn't just go to bars to drink: he went to perform. They were his theatre. Here it was that the jumble of sensations that was his brain secreted themselves in such wonderful and manic whimsy, but also where his mood swings could equally be deemed schizoid.

Drunk or sober he copped a vibe in milliseconds, and if things weren't going his way the bearhug of a moment ago could become an uppercut to an unlikely recipient. Flann O'Brien said he was his own best play. If somebody had captured him live and unleashed – if he lived in the age of the camcorder – maybe any one of his nights in McDaids, The White Horse Bar, The Palace or The Catacombs could be a play all of its own, a one-man show to blot out even the hype created by his other creations.

Joan Littlewood understood this when she said to the cast members of *The Hostage*, "Live with Brendan and you'll know how to play it." She even considered taking them on a pubcrawl with him. If such a scenario unfolded it would have been interesting to see who was the last man or woman standing.

Max Sylvester said he had a tongue that could curl hair. Insults rolled trippingly from it and some of these are unrepeatable even here. He couldn't talk, as Dominic said, unless he had a chip on his tongue. When Brendan lived in Chiswick, the people he stayed with owned a parrot and Brendan unloaded himself of some choice expletives to it every morning as he walked to his bus stop. Pretty soon, Polly had nearly as racy a tongue as he did, and was given to advertising that fact, much to the annoyance of her owners.

He seemed to reserve his most cutting abuse for those he saw as epitomising some hypocritical or snobbish agenda. Telling a friend to fuck off was almost as much a term of endearment as anything else, a kind of signal that you were one of his inner circle. And if you said, "Good morning" to him and he replied, "What's so fucking good about it?" it wouldn't be advisable to take this personally. It was just Brendan being Brendan, a bear with a sore head.

He might have said to the people of Ireland, as the German composer Johannes Brahms once remarked, "If there is anyone here whom I have not insulted, I beg his pardon."

❖

Brendan was at a party in London in the mid-fifties which was also attended by Kingsley Amis. He was talking about having done some painting in Paris when Amis cut in with, "Oh, I didn't know you went in for art, Brendan." Brendan, momentarily taken aback at Amis' ignorance of his day job, growled, "I don't mean painting fucking pictures. I mean serious painting: painting fucking houses." That's an anecdote Da would have been proud to hear.

❖   ❖   ❖

In a letter to the *Evening Herald* printed shortly after Brendan's death, Arthur Flynn wrote that he had "the wit of Shaw, the intellect of Joyce and the crudeness of O'Casey". Maybe the wit wasn't quite as sophisticated as that of Shaw, but it was certainly as pungent and memorable. There were no bourgeois niceties here, no effete nuances or innuendoes. No, Brendan's barbs hit like slugs from a Colt .45, or repeated pummelling to the solar plexus. He had a mouth, as he might have said himself, like a plateful of mortal sins.

❖   ❖   ❖

He was one of those people who got away with murder in life – and you could almost say that literally. He was released from prison prematurely due to an amnesty, but in civilian life too there were many amnesties. His court sentences were light and forgiveness of wronged friends generally forthcoming. Because it was always 'our Brendan', the decent skin who had one too many. The big-hearted bowsie gone temporarily deranged from the curse of drink. Our modern age wouldn't be quite so forgiving, or patient.

❖   ❖   ❖

We were different kinds of people, Brendan and myself. And, as was the case with Dominic, he didn't take too kindly to the idea of me writing books to earn a crust when I should have been building houses, unloading ships or signing my autograph in the nearest unemployment exchange. In fact when Da told Brendan that I was contemplating writing my memoirs, his reaction was, "Memoirs be fucked. You'd get them on the back of a postage stamp and still have room for the Koran." But that was Brendan. He had to grandstand and we understood it in him. He was after all the most famous Behan. And who's to say we weren't piggy-backing on his name in getting our work to the attention of editors?

❖   ❖   ❖

I had, in any case, a much better relationship with Brendan than I had with Dominic, the third writer of the family. When Brendan died, Dominic thought he was the arch-Behan. Then up I stepped, bloody Brian, to spoil his party. Because of this and other reasons, he didn't speak to me for 34 years before he died. If he had lived to be 90, I doubt whether we would have talked. He even told me not to come to his funeral. I went for him bald-headed one night on the Pat Kenny show on RTÉ some years back and I sometimes regret that. I didn't know he had cancer at the time. In retrospect, I think his sickness even made him more aggressive to me. However, I don't feel too guilty about that night. When I was a Trotskyist we learned that you never spare an opponent in an argument. You have to go for his guts.

One man in the Trotskyist movement said he would shoot me if he had a gun. In another instance I was grilled for four hours by a man threatening to rip my eyes out with a docker's hook. Dominic was small beer after that.

When I asked Tim O'Keeffe why he thought Dominic hated me so much, he replied, "Life is an escalator. Dominic is going down and you're going up. It's as simple as that." My first instinct was to refuse to go on *Kenny Live* but Seamus' wife Kitty said to me, "If you don't appear, that little shit will think you're afraid of him." That's why I went on – not to draw blood. But once I got motoring, my worst instincts came out. In a way I suppose were both guilty of bravado. Brendan being dead, we were competing for the empty throne, the heirs apparent. I think I was winding him up a bit for the publicity as well. I knew there's nothing the press like more than two warring brothers. It was like the Cain and Abel syndrome. But if you came right down to it, we were like two bald men fighting over a comb. If it wasn't so tragic it might have been funny.

From the moment I came an to the show, I regret to say, I was out for his blood. If Pat Kenny had told me that war had just broken out in Indonesia, I would probably have said, "I'll wager Dominic is behind that."

Pat asked me how I found Dublin and I replied, "With great difficulty. There was a fog at the airport and we had to circle it. I found
myself wondering if Dominic was the pilot." I went on to call him the
smallest of the Behans, and an ugly little cretin, in contrast to myself,
who was (ahem) described by Ulick O'Connor as the most handsome
member of the family and then I said he was going bald, with nothing
between himself and heaven.

Dominic hit back by saying I was a mean man – mean with money
and mean with the truth. I said that was good coming from Mister
Generosity: he was so mean himself, if he was a ghost he wouldn't give
you a fright. The audience got a giggle out of that and I knew I was on
to something. Even if we didn't kiss and make up by the end of the
show, I was going to get some nice publicity for a book I was launching
that night, my Dublin saga *Kathleen*.

That was another bone of contention for Dom. "Brian wrote that
book first as *Mother of all the Behans*," he announced. "He had to write it
twice to make sure everyone understood it." The score was now one-
all and we were coming up the home stretch. He called me a liar for
saying Ma was friends with James Joyce: a chronological impossibility,
he alleged, considering she was in Goldenbridge until 1904, the year
Joyce left Ireland. We disagreed about when Joyce came back to Dublin
to open a cinema, whereupon Pat, who was by now frantically trying
to referee the bout for under-the-belt punches, intervened. He expressed
sadness that blood wasn't thicker than water. We both looked like chips
off the old block, he said, what a pity we couldn't bury the hatchet.
Sadly, the only place I felt like burying it was in little Dom's neck.

Dominic said that he came to visit me in London in 1957 and that I
instructed my wife to charge him £3.15 for bed & breakfast. "What about
supper?" I asked. "The woman has to make a living, you know."
Dominic didn't get the joke as I went on ranting in Biblical vein, "Did I
not take him in? Did I not give him shelter?"

When we got on to politics, I mentioned Brendan had once said,
"The closest Dominic ever got to republicanism was stabbing fish fingers in the BBC canteen," adding, "the little gobshite should have been
arrested for armed begging!" He went on to call me a Tory sympathiser
because I had said in *The Sunday Times* that Maggie Thatcher was a
great woman and I'd marry her in the morning. Poor Dominic: he must
have left his sense of humour in his other suit. He didn't get the joke. I
was also a communist and a terrorist, he alleged. "If a man can combine all those functions," I countered, "he should be running the bloody
country."

"Anyway," I said, "I'm opposed to labels of any description. I'm
not a can of baked beans and I object to joining anything at all – including my two hands in prayer." I went on to say that I had given Dominic
the words of *McAlpine's Fusiliers*, so if we wanted to talk about who

was a phoney, we should start there. "The nearest he's ever been to a building site," I said, "was when he posed as a hod carrier with a straw hat on his head."

By now Pat Kenny, whose maiden voyage it was on *Kenny Live*, looked distinctly discommoded. Would his ship sink like *The Titanic* now that he had these two mad brothers using his show as a boxing ring? And would it get physical before the night's end? "You have sins on your soul," Dom alleged, and I stuck my shoe out at him. "Oh we're getting religious now are we. What do you mean – the sole of my shoe?" It was all very childish really. If it had happened a half-century earlier, Ma would have given the pair of us respective kicks in the arse and sent us to bed. If he dropped his defences with me we could probably have got on, but that he refused to do. He knew I was baiting him, but refused to acknowledge that fact.

Being ignored is the ultimate insult and Dominic ignored me that night. To be honest with you, I would have preferred it if he stood up and biffed me in the mouth. At least then he would have had to come down from his high horse. I hit hard in life, but I don't mind being hit back. If you dish it out, you have to be prepared to take it. Dominic wasn't and that was his tragedy. Like Brendan, he was his own worst enemy when it came to handling fame – or the lack of it. He had a chip on his shoulder that fed his paranoia, and vice versa. And in time the whole family became targets. Dominic accused me of being stingy on Pat Kenny's show, but neglected to mention that he once invited Ma and Da over to London offering to pick up the tab. He failed to do so, leaving me to pay their fare back home. Like many little men who nurse their grievances, he had a selective memory for things like that. He said I was so mean that I wouldn't even fork out the boat fare to attend the funerals of Brendan or Rory. I did my best to tell him I don't like funerals, but he wouldn't listen. "I may not even attend my own," I declared. And I mightn't.

Dom accused me of being a Provo sympathiser and as a result of this, an indirect murderer of a number of his friends. Whenever I tried to defend myself, he ignored me. He was still suffering from the Frank Delaney sin of 'High Seriousness'. "You take yourself so seriously," I said, "you'd like to set your farts to music." I firmly believe that if he had learned to laugh at himself a bit more, he'd still be alive today. *The Irish Times'* television critic Godfrey Fitzsimons summed up the night by saying, "The Brothers Behan appear to have devised a profitable new double act in which they play Olivia de Havilland and Joan Fontaine in reverse drag." Miriam Lord wrote in the *Irish Independent*: "There is no truth in the rumour that an American television network wanted to buy the exclusive rights to the show in place of the Mike Tyson/Frank Bruno fight."

The *Kenny Live* show, in any case, was Dominic's last hurrah because he died shortly afterwards. I really don't know why he carried such a large grudge against me all his life. I remember hitting him on the head with my fist one time when we were chislers and I deeply regret it now. Could that little incident have started it all? Maybe because he was the youngest he expected special treatment. Instead of that, we bullied him. Then when he grew up he took it out on all of us. Dominic could never live with the fact that he wasn't as famous as Brendan. He resented Brendan having hit shows on Broadway and London at the same time, while he himself foraged for tame recognition from left field.

He also resented Peadar Kearney having written the National Anthem and Da being the subject of *This is Your Life*. Like most insecure men, he wanted all the glory for himself. I put a lot of Dominic's problems down to sexual jealousy. He had married a widowed woman older than himself, while I was living with a woman half his own age. Dominic described me as an "illiterate Tory yuppie with IRA leanings" which is a mouthful, you'll agree. I still haven't figured out how that particular mix could find itself accommodated in the body of one individual, but I'm highly flattered he thought me capable of the achievement.

"Dominic is Brendan with his brains kicked out," I countered. I couldn't resist tweaking his little tail. Dom was stuck in a Stalinist time-warp. He never forgave me for a series of articles I did for the *Irish Press* denouncing communist bureaucrats I had witnessed at first hand in China, living the life of Reilly while the peasants starved around them. Dom's main problem is that he was obsessed by his image. He wanted to be seen as an intellectual on false credentials, which would give him the right to look down on me and my paltry literary efforts. He was so bloody uptight about what he represented he nearly met himself coming back.

Brendan never knew that kind of self-importance, thank the Lord God, and neither did I. Dominic acted like the big shot of the family whereas he was really small beer, and for Brendan it was the other way around. If they could have swapped identities, maybe both of them would have lived longer. As it was, each was trapped in the poisoned juggernaut of their own delusions. Brendan needed to wind down and Dominic to chill out. But I knew neither of them ever would, which is probably why I've learned from their mistakes. "The play's the thing," Shakespeare said, but life is important too.

The sad thing is that we had respect for one another's achievements which we never gave ourselves a chance to express. I have always praised Dominic's literary gifts to anybody I knew and anytime I ever heard his name being announced on the radio I felt a glow of pride. I have great respect for his play *Posterity Be Damned* and his other works. And he had a powerful singing voice. It's a pity Dominic didn't accord me the same reverence. He sang at a concert in Brixton for me when I was released from prison, but there his magnanimity ended. He never took me seriously as a writer, which was a bit rich considering he didn't read anything I wrote. How can you rubbish somebody when you haven't read their work?

He warned me not to put him into *Mother of All the Behans* or he would sue me for "obscene literature". Chew on that one, dear reader. After that book was widely praised, he said it was full of lies. (He didn't even read it, but heard it serialised on the radio.) Well if it is it isn't me that's the liar, but Ma, because all the book consists of is transcripts of tape recordings of her voice. So now we're into a different dimension.

Dominic admitted that I had done well for myself, but added, "Paper won't refuse ink." He said I made the Behan name synonomous with conservatism, and did to it what the yuppies did to London culture. He said he didn't hate me, just disliked me intensely – which I thought rather nice of the old bugger, really. "I am in favour of using Dominic as a Public Health Warning," I said in retaliation. "In the same way as you warn the public against AIDS or rabies, so also the dread visage of brother Dom should warn us all against the sin of taking ourselves too seriously and thereby ending up in the madhouse."

Anxious to patch up our troubles, I once told an intermediary to ask Dom what dreadful misfortune befalling me might cause him to talk to me. Would brutal robbery qualify? Or dismemberment? Or being eaten by cannibals? Sadly, Dom replied to my intermediary that none of the above calamities sufficed. So The Long Silence continued. "Don't fight," Ma would say to us, "don't beat each other: the world will beat you both long enough." How right she was, but we didn't listen.

Dominic was out to destroy me. This was partly because he was insecure and partly because he was dying. From my own point of view, I felt it was him or me. It was sad it had to come to that, but there you are. Just as the worst kind of war is a civil war, so the worst kind of squabble is a domestic one. I never expected a reconciliation and I never got one. That never bothered me because I took the trouble to understand Dominic, which is more than he ever did for me. It reminded me of Ma's saying, "If you can survive your own family, you can survive anything."

Dominic, as you probably know, wrote many songs like *Liverpool Lou, Avondale, The Sea Around Us* and *The Patriot Game*. He accused no less than Bob Dylan of stealing the melody of the latter for his polemic, *With God On Our Side*. When Dominic accused me of exploiting the family name on the Pat Kenny show, I replied, "I notice you haven't changed your name to Pilsudski." It was the pot calling the kettle black. That kettle is very black now. But at least we're still going down the mine, still keeping Brendan's name alive by tapping into his lunacies and his complexities. I make no apology for that. He would enjoy it, smiling down from whatever Valhalla he inhabits.

He would want the machine to keep churning, with or without him. He wouldn't deny us our laughter or our tears as we remember the good times or even the nepotism. "Inside of Dominic," he often said, "there's a little Brendan trying to get out." And maybe there's one inside me too. Well maybe it's time to let the genie – or even the monster – out of the bottle.

Funnily enough I saw a horse running the other day by the name of Pilsudski. For a moment I thought it might be Dominic coming back to kick the shit out of me. Actually I've never really worried about people who accuse me of trading on Brendan's name because in many ways I see myself as a far better writer than he was. Or maybe I should just say a far different writer. I don't like comparisons. I never wanted to be the 'other' Behan. I'm me, for better or worse. Aping Brendan is almost as bad as trying to denigrate him.

Ma told me at a very early age, "There's no-one on earth any better than you. As good, maybe, but no better." I've lived all my life by that maxim.

❖

When Dominic's play *Posterity Be Damned* was staged in the Gaiety Theatre in 1960, Brendan made a very poor effort to conceal his dismay that a sibling would dare try to usurp his throne – especially when Dominic had the added temerity to cast aspersions on the IRA in the text. Brendan would have found fault with it whatever the subject matter, but Dominic's iconoclastic vision of the 'Armed Struggle' sits badly with Brendan's ultimately soft-centred one. In fact it was only after pronounced efforts by Ma that he consented to go and see the play at all. When it transferred to London a month later, Brendan became bored at the rehearsal and fell asleep. When he woke up he started abusing the cast, telling them they were making a dog's dinner out of it. Which was funny really because if the play itself was nonsense, how could they make it any worse? Dominic took all this very badly because he had been behind Brendan's leap to fame all the way. As for Brendan, we were all reminded of the story of the day long ago when he pushed Seamus down the stairs and said of Granny English, "She's my Granny – not yours." He might now have said, in a similar vein, "The Gaiety is my theatre – not yours." Or, more appropriately, "London belongs to me".

❖   ❖   ❖

Anthony Burgess, in his autobiography, tells a story about meeting Dominic after Brendan's death. He asks Dominic to say a prayer over

Brendan's grave and Dominic replies, "I'd prefer to fuckin' piss on it."
If this is a true story it reflects a deep and troubled hatred. Ulick
O'Connor says Dominic carried his hate around with him like a port-
able dog that he could unleash at a moment's notice. In fact he threatened to break Ulick's jaw on at least one occasion.

❖   ❖   ❖

Christy Moore sought shelter with Dom when he first went to England. Dominic was glad to put him up, but on his first night there a
strange thing happened. Dominic descended on Christy in the wee
hours, telling him he must leave. "What have I done?" Christy asked,
wide-eyed. "You're sexually molesting my wife Josie," Dominic told
him, "and you must leave now – if not sooner. If you don't, I'll have the
police down on you." Christy fled for his life, being a reasonable man,
but as he was half way down the street he saw Josie running behind
him. "It's all right," she said, "you can come back now. The silly old
fool is asleep."

❖   ❖   ❖

Seamus has a good phrase for Dom: "He pissed on people selectively."

❖   ❖   ❖

Dominic could haunt even in death. On the day of his cremation his
ashes were taken to the Grand Canal, where Brendan wrote *The Auld
Triangle*. As Sean Garland lifted them aloft, however, a sudden gust of
wind came up and blew them all over everybody. The little bastard
didn't know when to stop!

❖   ❖   ❖

Brendan told Bill Kelly, author of *Me Darlin' Dublin's Dead and Gone*,
one night after being refused entry to a pub, "That hungry effer barred
me last week for singin'. He's so miserable that if he owned Switzer-
land he wouldn't give you a slide."

❖   ❖   ❖

Brendan had this to say about the Abbey Theatre company, "It must be
the best-fed company in the whole of Europe. Every time the action
slacks, they eat something. You can't get away with that in revue."

❖   ❖   ❖

When asked if he would be interested in dallying with a pair of ageing prostitutes, Brendan gushed, "The only way I'd touch either of them World War One relics would be if I was wearing a deep sea diver's suit and had a fistful of tetanus shots in my pocket for probable rust infection."

❖　　❖　　❖

Brendan was out fishing with fellow writer John Ryan in the latter's yacht one day, but was unimpressed with its speed. "The only thing you can catch from this," he complained, "is a feckin' submarine."

❖　　❖　　❖

An Irish beggar is in London and he's just spotted a rich man in a Merc. He taps on the window of the car and when it rolls down he says, "Any chance of a few bob, Guv?" The man starts to drive away saying, "'Neither a borrower nor a lender be': Shakespeare". And the beggar says, "Fuck off: Behan!"

❖　　❖　　❖

Dudley Sutton played the homosexual in a New York version of *The Hostage* in the sixties. Brendan came in to the theatre halfway through the performance and shouted up at the stage, "Sutton's a bloody queen!" Whereupon Sutton who had forecast something of the like being roared at him, and therefore had a riposte ready, out-heckled his heckler with, "That's Brendan Behan and I know his sister Les Behan."

❖　　❖　　❖

When the literary critic David Nathan came to Dublin in the early sixties to read *Richard's Cork Leg*, Brendan invited him to stay with himself and Beatrice. As Nathan thumbed through the manuscript, he expressed a wish to bring it over to London with him for further scrutiny. Brendan, however, demurred. "It's my only copy, old son and I can't allow anyone, even your good self, to take it up in an aeroplane with you, for fear the plane might go down into the Irish Sea on its way to England. I would deeply regret your passing, of course, but I have to admit my main sorrow, like all self-respecting writers, would be for my text."

❖　　❖　　❖

Anthony Cronin read the obituary of Cyril Connolly to him one Sunday morning from a British newspaper. The closing passage was: "The gardens of the west are closed, and there is no place now for the writer to wander." Brendan looked disgruntled at this and fumed, "Arrah sweet and holy Jaysus, would you mind telling me what fucking gardens of the west did you or I ever wander in?"

❖   ❖   ❖

Brendan said to Séamus de Búrca one day, about the republican movement, "Do you know what I was wondering, Jimmy? If we got the Six Counties back, what will we do all them fuckin' Catholics?"

❖   ❖   ❖

He crossed swords many times with Ernest Blythe, the sometime Managing Director of the Abbey. Blythe rejected some of his works with sarcastic comments. Brendan later commented to Séamus de Búrca. "The only thing I ever had in common with Blythe was that I could tell him to fuck off in Irish."

❖   ❖   ❖

He was at a party one night and clearly not enjoying himself, even though he had a glass in his hand. Bewildered at this turn of events, the hostess came over to him and seeing the bored look in his eyes, said, "Haven't you met any interesting people?"

"Not yet," he rasped back at her, "but then I've only been here five hours."

❖   ❖   ❖

Upon arriving in New York in the early-sixties he was asked if he would consider giving a lecture to the Women's Christian Temperance Union. "Maybe if they didn't look so miserable I might," he said. "I don't think anyone is going to drop the H-bomb just yet."

❖   ❖   ❖

Dominic said to him one day, "I was just thinking."

"Well stop at once!" Brendan shot back. "The unfamiliar exercise will do your brain an injury."

❖   ❖   ❖

After *Borstal Boy* had just been staged in New York, Brendan met an emigrant the following day on the street.

"I saw your play," the disgruntled emigrant pined. "It's a disgrace and a slander on the Irish people. You have no right to put prostitutes in your play. Everybody knows there is not a prostitute in Ireland.

"And what part of Ireland do you come from?" Brendan enquired.

"I come from Drumsna," said the man.

"Drumsna," said Brendan, "you're so fuckin' poor in Drumsna you couldn't keep a snipe, never mind a prostitute."

❧   ❧   ❧

This is how he described the company he tended to meet in bars, "Hard chaws, ex-convicts, chancers and tramps who'd lift the froth off your pint if you didn't keep your nose well in over the edge of the glass."

❧   ❧   ❧

Even when he liked somebody, his flattery tended to be tainted with a barbed undercurrent. He said of our cousin Jimmy Burke, with whom he got on well, "He's the only one of the Burkes who can write." And then added venomously, "I mean his *name*."

❧   ❧   ❧

When he went to Hollywood, he found it almost as corrupt as the publishing industry. "It's a quagmire crawling with Judas Iscariots," he said, "eagerly waiting to crucify me on high."

❧   ❧   ❧

He said this of a bar he disliked, "The drink in that pub isn't fit for washing hearses."

❧   ❧   ❧

When an acquaintance offered him some advice on a painting job, he dispensed with his suggestion by saying, "Fuck off. I wouldn't give you the job of white-washing a lavatory."

❧   ❧   ❧

He interrupted a production of *Borstal Boy* with this fairly characteristic outburst, "Yiz are makin' a muck of me play." It's easy to understand his frustration. He was such an accomplished performer himself, he could spot falseness at a hundred paces. A man who could in another guise have had a career treading the boards, his final theatre wasn't the Abbey or the Gate but rather McDaids. Here the world and his wife had backstage passes to see him perform. The downside for him was that there was no admission price and no applause. There was no script either, but that wasn't a problem: he had a hundred of them inside his head.

❖   ❖   ❖

When asked if he ever gave a painting exhibition, he said, "Only one: a sign the window of a café in Paris designed to attract the attention of English speaking tourists. It went like this:

> Come in you Anglo-Saxon swine
> and drink of my Algerian wine
> 'Twill turn your eyeballs black and blue
> and darn well good enough for you.

"At least I got paid for it," he said. "But I ran out of the place before the patron could get my handiwork translated."

❖   ❖   ❖

When Ma was pestering him with incessant phone calls to a Hollywood hotel at which he was staying, he grunted, "She'd give a headache to an effin' aspirin."

❖   ❖   ❖

An arch exponent of the age-old Irish tradition of slagging, he hit an acquaintance with this barb, "I hear there's someone dead belongin' to you. It wouldn't be yourself by any chance, would it?"

❖   ❖   ❖

He hated the would-be trendies of Greenwich Village, the hippier-than-thou brigade with their moaning and their guitar-twanging and their Mona Lisa hairdos. They were all over the place and he didn't even rule out his own family becoming infected with the strain. "I know the BBC have corrupted some members of my family," he said, "and I shouldn't be surprised to see my mother arrive in the Village with her hair hanging down to her ankles carrying a mandolin."

❖   ❖   ❖

And his view of folk singers? "They should all be taken out and shot.

There has to be better ways to line coffins." Folk sessions weren't much better, he felt, saying, "I think they burn the chairs at these because apparently they don't feel that a chair is a proper place to sit when listening to one of those groaners."

❖   ❖   ❖

He was drinking in The White Horse Bar one night when a fan asked him for an autographed copy of *Borstal Boy*. "Certainly," he replied. "Buy the effin' thing and I'll autograph it for you for nothing. How the bleedin' hell do you think I'm goin' to live if I give a copy free to every moocher in Ireland?"

❖   ❖   ❖

This was his view of culchies, "They put years on me. They're about as talkative as a tomb."

❖   ❖   ❖

He hadn't much respect for actors either. During his time in the States, he was offered a small part in a film being cast by a Columbia Pictures mogul, but declined, saying, "I'm a not an actor – or anything else connected to that bird-brained ilk incapable of earning an honest living."

❖   ❖   ❖

After a judge banned him from attending the St Patrick's Day Parade in New York in 1961 he said, "I now have a new theory of what the snakes did when St Patrick banished them from Ireland: they swam over to America and became judges."

❖   ❖   ❖

Paddy Bolger, one of Brendan's friends in the *Irish Press*, recalls being in a police squad car one night when they passed a three-sheets-in-the-wind Brendan hitching a lift at College Street. "That was Brendan Behan you just passed," Bolger said to the policeman driving the car, only to get the reply, "Why didn't you tell me sooner and I'd have run the bastard down!"

❖   ❖   ❖

He never saw a situation so bad, he said, that a policeman couldn't make it worse. None of the breed he had ever met, he contended, would be able to catch a virgin in a nunnery. Nor could one of them organise a piss-up in the proverbial brewery.

❖   ❖   ❖

He wanted to be a policeman himself as a child, he quipped, but they wouldn't let him after they found out our parents were married.

❖   ❖   ❖

Brendan was on a painting job in Harcourt Street in the early-fifties when a wicked thirst assailed him and he decided to drop into a neigh-bouring watering-hole for a quick one. However, once inside the door who did he see but his own chargehand. Thinking quickly, he realised that the latter man had as much to hide as he had himself so he said to him (with typical refinement), "You bollox you – caught in the fuckin' act. Be the holy Jaysus, if you dare to inform on me, I'll have you cas-trated." Needless to say, the misdemeanour went unpunished.

❖   ❖   ❖

One of Brendan's favourite jokes was the following:
    Q. How do you get 600 MPs into the back of a Mini?
    A. Make one of them Prime Minister and watch the rest vanish up his arse.

❖   ❖   ❖

When he was in the Bridewell as a result of shooting at a policeman, a charwoman asked him what he had done. After he told her, she went on, "Oh Jesus help your poor mother."
    "Fuck my mother," said Brendan, "it's me that's in danger of being hanged!"

❖   ❖   ❖

When *The Hostage* was playing in Paris in the 1959 International Thea-tre Festival, Brendan coined a piece of doggerel. It was on a balmy spring night as he was walking back to his hotel with journalist David Nathan. He passed a poster advertising an exhibition devoted to the foreign writers who lived in Paris in the thirties and roared out, unre-hearsed:

    I absolutely must decline
    To dance in the streets for Gertrude Stein

And as for Alice B Toklas
I'd rather eat a box of fuckin' choclas

❖   ❖   ❖

Brendan loved Ma deeply but he blamed Da for leaving her alone every night for twenty years as he proceeded to get drunk in pubs. In this Da was no better or worse than many men of his time – and certainly not in the same league as Brendan with Beatrice. Brendan threatened to kill Da one time but Ma told him to stop his foolishness. She said Da wasn't a bad man, only foolish with drink. Brendan often stuffed £100 notes into Ma's skirt, but not a light would he give to Da.

❖   ❖   ❖

When Eamonn Andrews did a *This Is Your Life* show for Da, Brendan was livid that it wasn't himself that was being honoured.

People said Andrews wanted Da on the show because he was afraid to tackle Brendan head on. Maybe so, but let's not forget Andrews did that famous interview with Brendan some years before. Still, it was a different Brendan now, fame and drink having made him into a much more unpredictable animal. Andrews' decision was probably wise in view of what happened after the show. "Why did you want to inter-view that old bollox anyway?" Brendan said to Andrews. I told him to ease off, that I admired Da, but there was no stopping him. He was pissed as it was, but then some girls arrived with nips and Brendan invited them to leave the bottle. Andrews then introduced the pair of us to RTÉ's spiritual advisor and Brendan ran amok. "How the hell can Fr Flat Hat lecture a television mast?" he wanted to know. I thought for a moment there was going to be a digging match. I watched Andrews' face get red as a beetroot as he clenched his fist. I took him by the arm and said, "Remember, Eamonn, we're all from the one family" (He was married to our cousin Grainne Burke by this time). That seemed to appease him, but only just.

❖   ❖   ❖

One day leaving a pub he bumped into a woman laden down with parcels, sending them scattering all over the pavement. He did his best to retrieve them, but the lady remained irked.

"I'd have you know," she barked, "that my husband is a detective and if he was here, he'd take ye."

"I don't doubt that," Brendan replied gamely, "if he took you, he'd take anything."

Chapter 11

Women of no Standing

I wonder why dreams must be broken idylls lost and love forgotten.
The transience of life has always exasperated me.

Beatrice Behan

Like most of my compatriots, I've had a vexed attitude to women throughout my life. A character in one of my plays says that he wanted sex without children and all religion gave him was children without sex. That attitude says a lot about the generation in which Da grew up. Indeed, the character is partly based on him. "The Blessed Virgin conceived without sinning," he said, "but I wanted to sin without conceiving."

Five nippers later he was still cursing the lack of birth control facilities. "That must make me an Immaculate fuckin' Conception," Brendan said to me when we talked about this. "Jaysus, it's the first time I can remember being compared to the Blessed Lady in a while. The oul' fella should be havin' us all assumed into heaven one of these days. Jaysus – I'm the Mother o' Jaysus!" Da worked hard and played hard. He spent most of his evenings in the pub, which was the done thing for most men of that generation and that class. Ma felt hard done by, but she understood why it was happening. He supported her, and to that extent she left him to his own devices in the evenings.

In the case of Brendan and Beatrice, much the same applied. Both Ma and Beatrice knew that they couldn't change their men, so they might as well grin and bare it. That was long before the strident, anti-male brand of feminism reared its ugly head. And before you start calling me a male chauvinist pig, let me tell you I agree 100 per cent with the precepts behind Women's Lib. What bothers me is the way it has been hijacked by predatory opportunists with elastic consciences and greedy minds.

For the past 15 years I've been trying to get a society called Male Liberation off the ground, but so far haven't met with much success. Maybe I should try and get Camille Paglia on board. I brought out the Male Liberation Handbook some years ago and argued in it that feminism was fine if equality was its goal but not if women wanted domination out of it. In that book I also said that extra-marital affairs stimulate marriages instead of ruining them. If a bloke lives to be 80, I argued, you can't reasonably expect him to stay with the same woman for 60 of these years – and vice versa. If you wanted to stay friends with someone, I argued, don't marry them, because there's nothing like marriage for turning two reasonably decent people into a cross between Stalin and Hitler.

The sex war, I said in the book, was much more dangerous than the class war. All an employer wanted to do, I argued, was exploit you between the hours of 8 and 5 o'clock, but with the wife, the battle is 24 hours a day, every day of the year. I advocated sex for men to be put on the National Health, and 'Houses of Pleasure' to be heavily subsidised to alleviate the situation. To those who say to me, "You can't legalise prostitution." I reply, "We've already done so – it's called matrimony." I felt such measures were urgently needed.

If a man married for cheap sex, I argued, he lived in the shadow of the doss-house, whereas if he paid for it outside the home, it could knock him back up to 60 nicker a week. And that was in the seventies, when 60 nicker was actually worth something. The idea I advocated was 'Sex Sam'. This was a variation of 'Meals on Wheels', but instead of a lady bringing a sick person food, she would bring him sexual re-lief. To me it all made perfect sense, but somehow it didn't take off. Personally I blame Maggie Thatcher for not running with the scheme. It could have been the making of the Tory Party.

"Sexual appetite," I said, "was largely composed of curiosity, and how the hell could you be curious about someone you had lived with for 20 or 30 years?" It would drive anyone to jump out of a 34th floor window. Monogamy was monotony. I advocated the setting up of these 'Houses of Pleasure' by Town and County Councils, to be funded by the local rate-payers. "I can't afford a mistress," was my plea, "and even if I could, I'd be afraid of getting some disease from her. I also said I'd be afraid she might turn into an animal even worse than a wife – in other words, someone who'd try and take me for every penny."

My basic argument was that most women just wanted a kitchen and two kids and bugger the man. Or rather not bugger him. They spent most of their time either filing their nails or filing depositions. The kind of man they most wanted, as Brother Brendan said of Ameri-can women, was one with "a will of his own – preferably made out in their favour".

As a result of my anger in this regard, I once told my wife I was going to deny her the pleasure of my body in bed. It was my own kind of DIY protest at the status quo. Unfortunately, the stratagem proved foolhardy as she didn't seem to notice. I wonder if she was trying to tell me something. I was reminded of the man who said to his wife, "I'm giving up sex for Lent," and she replied, "I thought that was *last* year."

They have you every way, don't they? I now view marriage in a more positive light. For one thing married men live longer than single men. Some people say it only seems that way. Maybe they have a point. Single women, on the other hand, outlive married ones, so maybe marriage isn't a good idea for women. Which makes it rather awkward for us men looking for wives. Maybe we should just marry other men and it would solve all our problems. You can love another man just as easily as a woman, you know.

I have for a long time now been a target of right-wing feminists and hopefully will continue to be one for a long time to come. I have nothing to fear from them or indeed learn from them. I've often been accused of being sexist. That's a word that has lost all meaning nowadays. Pretty soon we'll be called sexist for blowing our noses in a politically incorrect fashion. If women get a bad rap in my plays, so do men. I write it like I see it. The idea that women somehow or other are images of the Virgin Mary without a single bad bone in their bodies and that all men are bastards is horseshit.

Beckett put a woman in a bin for two hours on the stage and got the Nobel Prize for his troubles. Why do I have to be the whipping boy for somebody with a large chip on their shoulder? And Sam: how do you manage the trick of burying a woman up to her diddies in shit and still get the femmies to love you? Shay Healy said I was in danger of being dubbed a male chauvinist pig when he interviewed me on his show *Nighthawks*, but as I often say, today's male chauvinist pig is tomorrow's meat. We're an endangered species.

My own history with women was rather complicated. The Christian Brothers in Artane brought me up to believe you weren't allowed to touch them or terrible things would happen to you, but the women themselves seemed to have different ideas. They started by resisting my advances, as Oscar Wilde said, and ended by blocking my retreat. I never really fancied myself as a Don Juan, but two women thought me good enough to marry, so I must be doing something right. I now live in Brighton with my second wife. My first one threw me out because she said my sexual deviations weren't to be tolerated. I'm a much more chastened soul these days, a fact my present wife will vouch for. A veritable pope of conformity, you might say. I'm twenty years her senior, but am still determined to outlive her. Everytime she coughs I make a note of it. I have a swim at Brighton Beach every morning to stave off old age and I think it's working.

But back to Brendan.

Peter Sheridan collaborated with me on my play *Mother of All The Behans* which enjoyed some success and I had a fruitful relationship with him. However, he annoyed me a few years ago when he suggested that some of Brendan's wild behaviour could have been the result of being sexually abused as a boy by our uncle Paddy. This was a preposterous allegation. It's true we slept six to a bed in Russell Street, but that was normal for the time and I can assure you nothing untoward went on – or off. Paddy was a little runt of a fella and if he had done anything to Brendan he would have been torn limb from limb by the rest of us, if not Brendan himself. In any case, with six in the bed, you'd think we'd have noticed, wouldn't you? (Paddy, by the way, never married. It wasn't that he had anything against marrying, mind you – except for the fact that you had to do it with a woman.)

Having said all that, however, I don't think Brendan loved Beatrice as much as he did another man: Arthur Guinness. My father used the pub as a form of contraception for 40 years. He was like a lot of Irishmen in that, subduing of his sexual urges in the gargle. And you could say the same about Brendan. He confessed to Beatrice that he wasn't the great lover she might have been expecting. How could he have been with all that stout in him?

Since he died, many people have come up with scandalous stories about him. Valerie Danby-Smith, whom he's alleged to have impregnated shortly before Blanaid was born to Beatrice, has been having a go at him. Ms Danby-Smith, as you may know, was an Irish lass who was employed by *The Irish Times* to go out to Spain in 1959 to interview one Ernest Hemingway. She did that and they got on so well together he invited her over to his home in Idaho to be his personal secretary. There was even talk of a romance between them. Anyway, after Papa topped himself, Valerie started dating his son Gregory and they eventually married. They are now divorced.

In a 1980 book written by Dundalk sailor and wannabee actor Peter Arthurs, there was a lot of ink spilt on the fact that Brendan, in addition to having had a four-year homosexual relationship with Arthurs, also had an affair with Valerie. The man was busy, you will agree. In 1997 Michael O'Sullivan wrote a biography of Brendan where he took the story a stage further. Brendan, he alleged, impregnated Valerie. The child was christened Brendan, so now it appears we have a Brendan Hemingway running round the place. The plot, as they say, thickens.

Arthurs says Brendan slept with him for four years. Well he slept with me for fourteen. Sorry about that, Pete! I hasten to add that nothing unsavoury transpired in those years, but considering we were squashed together like sardines with other siblings head to toe, it might have been difficult to get an orgy going. Some writers have suggested Brendan's alleged homosexuality resulted from being locked up with other men for extended periods of time. That's hardly a new theory. The jury is still out on whether prisons turn people into homosexuals, but we all know how ridiculous it was to punish people for homosexuality by locking them up with other men in a cell. Brendan used to say that was like locking an alcoholic up in a brewery.

I've been in prison myself so I know what he meant. After being denied female company for a prolonged period of time, you could con-

ceivably find yourself looking longingly at a Malayan ape for satisfaction. With this in mind, I once advocated prisons where men and women
could share the one cell. When I mentioned the idea to a married friend
of mine, he said, "If that was brought in, you'd have queues a mile long
trying to get into prisons." I replied, "That only goes to show how boring the average person's sex life must be."

In actual fact they have prisons in Denmark where men and women
associate freely. I would imagine the incidence of homosexual sex is
much less there than elsewhere, which must go some way towards
showing that this kind of orientation can be environmental rather than
genetic.

"All of us are ambisextrous," Brendan said to me one day. "There's
only one sex, and that's the female one. All of us men are just deformed
women. Otherwise, why do we have tits?" Another time he was asked
if he was a practising homosexual. "I didn't know you had to practise," he said. Brendan took himself, and his sexuality, much less seriously than the academic historians who were to follow him. Of course,
he had a high sex drive – like many Irish writers. Look at Joyce, half
blind from the pox and the biggest whoremaster that ever walked. He
probably contracted it from the Dublin brassers – those women the
Catholic Church told us never existed.

Like all good – and bad – Catholics, Brendan never lost his sense of
sin, and he felt original sin was more likely to have come from the pair
on the ground than the apple on the tree. But he didn't think there was
anything worse about Adam and Steve committing that sin rather than
Adam and Eve. When Brendan was asked if he was gay, he replied,
"Well if I had to choose between Michelangelo's David and Whistler's
mother, who was as ugly as the back of a bus, there'd be no fuckin'
contest."

Anyway, where would he have got the time for all that stuff? We're
told he slept with a man for four years and also his wife at the same
time. He managed to father a son in America as well as a daughter at
home in Dublin. No wonder he gave up writing. There should be a
monument erected to such a man because he'd be someone who could
bull a cow from three fields away.

John Ryan said he would get up on the back of the Drimnagh bus.
I don't know about that but everything he did in life he ended up over-
doing, so I'm open to theories on that score. Ryan believed that, for
Brendan, homosexuality was simply another "tasty morsel on the smor-
gasbord of the bohemian running buffet"…whereas for Arthurs it was
more the main course. I prefer to see it as, if anything, the dessert.

Michael O'Sullivan and Peter Arthurs have blamed Brendan for
not coming out of the closet, as it were. Maybe he didn't, but he was
always very respectful of homosexuals in any conversation I had with
him. There was a scandal in the fifties about a High Court judge who

was gay and I made a crack about him being as bent as a hoop to Brendan. "If you dropped a half crown in Howth," I said, "you wouldn't dare bend down till you kicked it into Raheny if yer man was about." Brendan obviously didn't like that joke. He thought I was being laddish about an orientation that was as natural to him as my heterosexual urge. He went as red as a beetroot and laid into me.

It all meant nothing to me then, but I understand it in hindsight. Poor Brendan. Like Wilde, he missed the sexual revolution – the only one that really changes people's lives. If he were living today the public couldn't care less what he did with his libido provided he didn't frighten the horses in the street. I have to confess I'm rather bored by this whole subject. Brendan had a strained foreskin and had to have an operation for it in America. Afterwards, it's my view he was quite unequipped for sex of any sort. Case closed.

Brendan loved Celia, my first wife, very much. She was a buxom, handsome girl, very sensual. A Yorkshire pagan in fact: everything that Beatrice wasn't. I had married her at sixteen. Brendan used to grab her and not let go. She called him 'Andy Pandy' and said he was worse than Da when he got hold of her. She said he had more hands going over her body than an octopus. I often wondered if he might have been better suited to a wife like this than Beatrice. When I said as much to him he just shrugged his shoulders. "If, if if," he laughed. "If my aunt had balls she'd be playing for Dublin."

In a letter he wrote to the editor of the *New Statesman* in late 1962, Brendan described Celia as "a lovely English girl that knows how to keep herself attractive in a way that was unknown in the days of my childhood in the Dublin slums". What surprises most people about Brendan is the fact that he married a woman who was his polar opposite. And, even more surprisingly, that their marriage lasted until he died.

Mary Manning said of him, "He was the average Irishman who prefers the company of men and pub-life to the hearthstone, and has no use for women except as begetters of children." That wasn't a true picture. Contrary to popular conception, the relationship between Brendan and Beatrice wasn't always like living over the San Andreas fault. Brendan said with extraordinary ordinariness, "It happens that Beatrice and I like each other very much, and when I'm on the wagon we go out and talk and laugh like so many other couples." For many, it was hard to imagine a man who looked as if he was born with a snake in both of his fists while a hurricane was blowing (to borrow Bob Dylan's phrase) could be content marrying the demure daughter of a well-to-do artist and bringing her breakfast in bed in their leafy Dublin 4 residence. But that's exactly what happened.

Before Beatrice, Brendan hadn't evinced much interest in women. He was a man's man who looked as if he would have expected his girlfriend, or friendgirl, to match him in drink if she was to stand any chance. He was a man whose idea of passion would be taking a cigarette out of his mouth before he kissed a woman.

But then relationships don't happen because people look right for each other on paper. If they did, computers would be able to create happy marriages. They happen because of chemistry. Beatrice was impressed with Brendan's charm. She knew the dangers, so she wasn't going into the relationship blindfolded. Her father warned her about Brendan's drinking habits (which he was hardly qualified to do as he suffered a similar weakness for the drop himself) and also his prison record. "Dates", Brendan claimed, "were only for the police" – so a night out with Beatrice really consisted of roughly the same rituals as a night out without her. She was allowed to watch him perform, in other words. There would be no flowers, no 'Moon in June' sonnets, no midnight serenades. The kind of relationship, which only a very independent (or crazy) lass could countenance. He made it clear, in any case, that he didn't want to grow old sitting by the fire in his cardigan and slippers.

But Beatrice had an old head on young shoulders and she knew what she wanted. She had been dating a civil servant but was tired of him. Brendan had colour, he had electricity. OK, so their nights together wouldn't consist of eating chocolate eclairs in the foyer of the Abbey Theatre, but she felt she could hack it with him even if he was an incorrigible chauvinist.

She was impressed with his literary promise and his fund of stories, and she probably felt she could save him from himself with her stabilising influence. She might even rescue her 'laughing boy' from his wild ways with a cuddle and a coddle. She might make staying in for a night a suddenly attractive notion. Even alcoholics were known to reform in life if they had a goal. His writing could be his salvation, and she would give him the ideal environment in which to practise it. Literary Dublin was of course gobsmacked when they started 'walking out' together. We weren't talking Romeo and Juliet here, but rather a tentative liaison between a retiring botanist-cum-Board-of-Works clerk and a bellicose ex-con who was wired to the moon. Optimists said it would be a marriage made in heaven, whereas the more cautious said "so is thunder and lightning". And both, in their way, were right.

Most people doubted the marriage would go the proverbial distance. They pointed to her sweetness versus his ebullience, her refinement versus his obnoxiousness, her liking for the finer things of life – like painting – and his penchant for hanging out with lowlifes. As she said herself, however, she would have been terminally bored by a straitlaced individual. And she was fiercely entertained by her husband, as anyone who came to know him had to be. She also envied his ability to hold court in front of large gatherings of people, which would have been like Chinese torture to her diffident sensibility.

The big question was whether he would climb to her level or drag her down to his. Or maybe they would just go in different directions, with him descending further and further into the mire while she played the Florence Nightingale figure from the sidelines. Beatrice saw the inner beauty in Brendan. She saw him as a diamond in the rough, a man haunted by demons for which he was only half responsible. She also put up with what she called his "few auld flings", even when one of these was reputed to have resulted in a baby.

Beatrice lived with a dormant volcano. What made the marriage work was the fact that she knew how to gauge that volcano's moods and keep it dormant, either by indulging Brendan or coaxing him away from temptation. Pre-dating an age of feminism, she was content to do his bidding because she loved him. It's hard to imagine any other woman in Ireland putting up with what she did, or indeed any woman staying with the powder keg that was Brendan for as long as she did. Considering the sea-changes in his moods, a walk-out on either of their parts would have been on the cards from the beginning.

What they shared, on the other hand, was a great sensitivity to life and an openness to adventure. Beatrice was able to experience such adventures without any artificial stimulants, but they would have been inconceivable for Brendan without drink. This was the X-factor built into any equation for him, whether he was swimming in the nude at Kilmurvey Harbour in Aran or chewing the fat with Harpo Marx in the Algonquin Hotel in New York.

Beatrice took him warts and all, and there were more than a few of those. But forewarned was forearmed. She had few dreams, so how could those dreams be punctured? Before Brendan, she had lived with her father, another man who over-drank, so she knew it could be an addiction. Cecil Salkeld's gentle tipsiness was like somebody from the Total Abstinence Association in comparison to Brendan's wild escapades. He warned Beatrice what to expect and she took it on board. She was, after all, in for the long haul. And if that meant picking Brendan out of ditches as many times as linking his arm to ceremonial functions, so be it. Love would find a way.

On the other hand, the three great passions of his life were writing, drinking and patriotism, with women coming a very distant fourth, so that hardly boded well for the bashful artist from Morehampton Road. Brendan was also a chauvinist, and got away with murder in his every-day (mis)behaviour with Beatrice. In many ways he treated her like a skivvy. When they went travelling, it was she who carried the bags. She was like his porter and secretary rolled into one. And if he was being toasted by the literati, or the glitterati, she had to disappear into the woodwork. Not that she would have wanted it any other way, but even if she did, it wouldn't have been feasible.

Brendan's philosophy of marriage was that a woman was there to administer to a man's wishes and then bid a hasty adieu when she wasn't needed any more. If Ma had been married to a man like that, she would have had his guts for garters within a week. Beatrice sacrificed her career – some would say her life – for Brendan. She took up her cross and followed him. If he was happy, she was happy. If he was sober, she was happier still. And when he was working hard and the money rolling in, well that was very heaven.

She asked for little out of life beyond her husband's wit and tenderness, and though such oases of comfort were sandwiched in between all the bad times, they seemed somehow enough for her. One might have expected Beatrice to have given Brendan an appreciation of the good in unlikely souls, but it actually worked the other way round. "No matter how horrible somebody appears," he said to her, "they have some redeeming qualities." It was an expression, and an attitude that stayed with her. It also helped her to relate better to some of the dodgy characters Brendan brought home with him to Anglesea Road when he was on the way down.

Sadly, some of these wretches had no redeeming qualities at all. But the door of *Cúig* remained open to stragglers, hobos, bohemian poets and the un-housed. There was always room at the inn. Like Brendan, Beatrice was socialist in her sympathies and never turned anyone away from her door, from heroes to hobos – or those seeking reflected or refracted glory from breaking bread with the shakers and movers of the Irish literary scene.

She was used and abused by many of the latter, as Brendan was, but she never became soured by that fact, merely cautious. Her main priority was always to protect Brendan rather than feel sorry for herself. Many people, when they try to analyse Brendan, fall into the trap of looking for the secret key to his personality, some hitherto unexplored X-factor. But there isn't one. What you saw was what you got, for good or ill.

We should be weary of anyone who tries to sum him up because not even his wife could do that. She was as continually surprised by his behaviour as the rest of us were – including maybe even himself. He could be a gurrier one minute, a sensitive poet the next. I'm not sure I could have lived with him for any long stretch in his adult years, and I take my hat off to Beatrice for taking him as she found him. I'm sure there were many times in her life when she wondered to herself why the hell she hadn't married her civil servant friend after all.

Beatrice only spent one-eighth of her life with Brendan, but it was these eight years that defined her, and about which she never stopped talking or thinking. That's hardly surprising considering the amount of living both of them crammed into those years. Maybe they knew their time together was limited. Life with Brendan had perks, to be sure, but they came with a big price tags. The 'Brendan Voyage' led her to lands she could never have seen as anyone else's wife, and gave her introductions to more celebrities than you could shake a stick at.

Beatrice was an emotional woman, but she suffered so much with Brendan, a lot of that emotion was burned out of her. She became his watchdog and his nurse rather than his wife, and approached every evening out with due caution. When was he going to blow up? Who was he going to insult? Would they be poor again like they had been before he made it? And – the old question – would he drink himself to death before he was 40?

Living out of a suitcase wasn't much fun either, especially when your roots were in the home country. It was all very well to sit at a table opposite the likes of James Thurber and Harpo Marx, but people like these were carrots Brendan dangled in front of her head and then withdrew again, because he couldn't be trusted to behave himself with any of them, no matter how much he respected them or their work. That's why Beatrice's priorities shifted as time went on. Her ambition became not so much to have a great time any more as simply to have peace. Forget adventure: a day without a crisis was a good day.

The celebrity workload also took its toll. Beatrice told his promoters once, fearing another binge was imminent, "This is a human being you have here. It isn't a machine. You can't expect a man to travel 300 miles today to stand up and give a funny speech and then travel 300 miles again tomorrow to do the same thing." But the sad fact is that they *did*. And what's more, he obliged. Meanwhile, Beatrice was left to try and pick up the pieces of her wrecked domestic routines – and Brendan's ravaged liver. She never blamed him for his alcoholism, though. In this she was before her time. She agreed with Sr Stanislaus' definition of alcoholics as "wounded people".

After Brendan died, Beatrice's phone stopped ringing. The constant turmoil of living in his shadow was replaced by a new problem now: loneliness. It might have been hard to live with Brendan but it was infinitely harder trying to live without him. Just as Brendan's 'friends' deserted him when his celebrity status collapsed, so Beatrice's deserted her when he died. Pretty soon it became abundantly clear to her that she had been indulged all those years purely because she was married to an icon rather than anything she represented in herself. And that was a bitter pill to have to swallow.

A friend of mine suggested to me recently that Beatrice committed suicide. I wouldn't like to say either way, but it's a possibility. Though Brendan was an incorrigible chauvinist, the story goes that he walked out of a church one day when the parish priest declared that women were forbidden to go into public bars: this I could well believe. From Beatrice's point of view, though, that anecdote was ironic. "When Brendan struck a blow for sexual equality," she said to me, "it's hardly surprising drink was involved." And yet they went the distance, despite his insults to her, his violence, his language, his mad drinking sprees and even his infidelities. Why? Because of one simple fact: he never said he didn't love her any more, and somehow that was enough for her, even at the worst of times.

Like me in Artane, she kept her heart up. Together they saw the "two days". One of these days was awash with mirth and sunshine, the other a descent into a near Dante-esque inferno of the soul as Brendan continued to indulge his wanderlust. And, perhaps, his lust. While Beatrice kept house and counted the bills she couldn't pay because of his philandering. The fact that she tolerated such a lifestyle was a tribute both to her patience and her soulful calmness: the two qualities that had attracted him to her in the first place.

In actual fact it wasn't that simple. Beatrice might well have said they saw the 22 days, because nothing was ever black and white in this marriage. Brendan misbehaved almost constantly after he became famous, so her excitement at meeting celebrities and visiting exotic lands was always tarnished by this perennial fear. Alternatively, when he was a struggling writer in the early days of their marriage he drank relatively little – at least by his standards. But at that time there were other problems, such as money. So it wasn't a simple curve that went up and down. Like most of our lives, it was more akin to a very vicious circle, inset with occasional hoops of delight.

Many people imagine that Beatrice was a wealthy widow, but nothing could be further from the truth. The fact is that when Brendan died, he owed people books. In death as in life he left Beatrice clutching a handful of bills.

Caitlin Thomas experienced a somewhat similar situation to Beatrice. Both women were like paupers sitting on dilatory goldmines, forced to continue the paid-on-Friday-broke-on-Monday lifestyles of their dead spouses. There weren't even any manuscripts to sell. As Beatrice said, "So many publisher's have offered me fabulous sums for Brendan's love letters, thinking they must be saleable and passionate. But the true fact is, there aren't any!" Did he refuse to write them due to a lack of the romantic spirit or a fear some opportunist would rifle his writing cabinet when he was dead and grow rich out of the proceeds? I'll leave you to come to a conclusion on that one.

❖

Beatrice knew a woman who had ten children, but who seemed to spend all her spare time in the bookies. "How does she feed them?" she asked Brendan. "Docket stew," came the brisk reply.

❖   ❖   ❖

Beatrice was never partial to alcohol, but one night she became merry at a function as a result of mixing the different wines she was presented. Her hardly sober husband went ballistic at this eventuality, castigating her with being out of control.

❖　　❖　　❖

Beatrice left the key in the door of their Anglesea Street house one night so that Brendan would find it easy to come in even if he had had imbibed one too many. The condition in which he arrived home, however, was so extreme that even turning the aforesaid key proved beyond him. Instead, he managed to kick in a side door to gain entrance. Beatrice's reaction was typical of all the time they spent together. "It didn't matter," she commented indifferently, "we needed a new side door anyway."

❖　　❖　　❖

He was up at 4 am on the day of his wedding, getting down to some serious drinking in the Markets and not looking forward to meeting the priest, whom he referred to as 'The Druid'. The Druid put some hard questions to him, saying things like, "I believe you were ex-communicated from the Church for being in the IRA." Brendan was unfazed by this onslaught. "They wouldn't talk to me like that in the registry office," he taunted . . . and the priest drew in his horns and performed the ceremony.

❖　　❖　　❖

His proposal of marriage to Beatrice wasn't overly romantic. "Let's shag off together to the south of France and give it a try," he suggested.

❖　　❖　　❖

The following story is probably made-up, but nonetheless . . . Brendan arrived home to Anglesea Road one night with his usual bunch of cronies, even more wasted than usual after an especially heavy bender. One of them shouted out, "Mrs Behan, are you in there?" Beatrice came out and enquired what the problem was. Five men stood there looking at her, finding difficulty standing up, and then one said, "We were just wondering if you could tell us which of us is Brendan so the rest of us can fuck off to our own homes!"

❖　　❖　　❖

Asked what he thought of mixed marriages, he said all marriages were mixed – between men and women.

❖   ❖   ❖

His own wedding day was hardly the stuff of Mills & Boon. There was no ring so he had to get one from a pawn shop. The best man was recruited on the spot – Fine Gael senator Joe Doyle – and Brendan's first words after "I do" were, "Thanks be to Jaysus that's over. Let's go and have a few jars."

❖   ❖   ❖

One day Beatrice was choosing a coat for herself when Brendan walked into the shop and proceeded to waltz round the floor with one of the wax dummies.

"Look Beatrice," he said to her, trying to wean her into his affections, "I'm really respectable."

"I don't care if you're respectable or not," she whispered back, "I just happen to like you."

❖   ❖   ❖

When Beatrice implored him to tone down his riotous lifestyle after their marriage, he rasped at her, "What you want me to be is a fucking suburbanite. Into the office at nine in the morning and the dog along Sandymount Strand after tea."

❖   ❖   ❖

When he was asked why he lived in the 'posh' area of Anglesea Road considering he was a child of the slums, Brendan replied with typical querulousness, "To annoy the neighbours."

Chapter 12

The Quare Fella

I can't remember when I first met Brendan, which is rather like saying I can't remember the first time I was run over by a jet-propelled steam roller.

Alan Bestic

I've done some mad things in my life, like dyeing my hair green for a pop video to raise money to bring my play *The Begrudgers* to London. But this was mild in comparison to the sort of stuff Brendan did.

Maybe it's unfair to call him queer, because he was really the quintessence of the wanton Irish lad. If he was queer, it's the world that's odd, not him. Nevertheless, he got up to some pretty crazy exploits in his life, something to which the following pages testify. Alan Brien said he was "a one-man Beatles quartet, an omelette served up from a mixed bowl of Gilbert Harding, Dylan Thomas and Michael Collins". He was, as he put it himself, "as large as life and twice as mad".

Even as early as *The Confirmation Suit* we can see the rich and varying shades of his character: from the mischievous fun-lover to the sensitive lad who could empathise with the emotional vulnerability of an old woman, and not be afraid to show it "in the spills of rain".

I asked him once what sort of a society he would ideally like to see. "One where the old people are warm of a night," he answered, "and can sleep easily in their beds." He always had a great *grá* for old people, as he did for very young ones, and there can't be too much wrong with a man like that.

The hard-chaw overtones he carried about him weren't as resonant as the thin skin he kept under wraps as often as he could. They say that the feminine outweighs the masculine in most writers and this would seem to be true of Brendan, notwithstanding the caveman antics that became synonymous with him after fame hit. We tend to see him today as primarily a man's man, an individual never more at home than when propping up a bar counter or backslapping a fellow tippler. But when we view his life from a bird's eye perspective it's the women he knew who seem to cast the longer shadow – all the way from Granny English, who doted on him, through Ma, Beatrice, Rae, Carolyn and Joan. These were all guardian angels of sorts to him, all women who saw the little boy lost in him and probably wanted to mother him as a result of that, camouflaged though it was under all those caustic jibes.

And let's not forget that the sister of the man who sentenced him to fourteen years imprisonment gave him a coffee pot for a wedding present a few years afterwards. As John Jordan said, "The roistering, brazen-tongued public entertainer was merely the defensive obverse of the warm-hearted, generous, slightly unsure friend."

Brendan didn't only inherit his republicanism from Ma: he got his nerves from her too. In her later years she was a chronic hypochondriac. She died every year for her last twenty. Brendan hid his nerves well, but they came out when he stuttered. And of course when he was under the weather. In fact they may also have been a reason he was such a heavy drinker.

Colbert Kearney summed up his convolutions when he said, "He was a complex and apparently contradictory person: the shy stammering introvert and the ebullient extrovert, the weekly communicant and the spoiled brat, the universal charmer who would begrudge his brother a penny."

He said to J P Donleavy once, "I'm a great believer in the Irish principle that more is better than less. And that if variety is the spice of life, then why not have plenty of that as well?" His whole life was a kind of coda to those premises.

I always felt a bit in awe of him. From his early days he could cut you up with his tongue or his fists, but I always knew there was more to him than this easy belligerence. Underneath his ebullience he was a quivering mass of too much feeling. Feelings that were deep and raw and violent . . . and liable to explode at the slightest provocation. Then like a stallion he couldn't bear to be bridled by anyone.

In the main we were afraid of him. It wasn't just that he could be cruel and biting: he had an unpleasant habit of putting his finger right on the truth. So when you had a conversation with him it was like walking in a minefield.

"Brendan, love, take care of yourself," Ma would plead whenever she saw trouble coming. She was convinced he was mad. Not mad in the loony sense, but mad with spirit and too much feeling that knew no bounds. Mad in the sense of having all-too-deep perceptions, of second sight almost. Mad in the sense that one minute he could be prickly and truculent and impossible to communicate with, and the next cuddly and loveable as a teddy bear. He was always our Granny's darling boy, but to the rest of us he was like a set trap. If he was a bomb he could have blown up half Dublin.

He was a clown and a braggart, a court jester and a pillock, a sinner and a saint. Irascible on the surface, at least to phonies and what would subsequently be called yuppies, behind all the posturing and the four-lettered words lurked a pussycat all too well aware of where his life was going – or not going.

Colbert Kearney speaks about the day in Leopardstown when he was confronted with a bevy of stuffed shirts and yet had them in stitches within fifteen minutes. That was the point about him. He didn't care if you were landed gentry or something the cat dragged in if he was in form for the crack.

Maybe his biggest sin was the fact that – like most writers – he never really grew up. Kenneth Allsop wisely noted that his appetite for living was even greater than his thirst for drink. But for Brendan, the two were well-nigh mutually exclusive. He would have been just as charismatic as a teetotaller, but (like many excessive tipplers) this was a fact he was too emotionally insecure to realise.

As Cathal Goulding said, "We always expected you'd do something crazy, Behan, even if it was only strangling your mother."

Eamonn Andrews interviewed Brendan for RTÉ in 1960. Or should I say Brendan interviewed Eamonn Andrews, because that's the way it looked a lot of the time. Andrews had a few pat questions prepared to ask him, about Brendan being a naughty boy with the booze and whatever, but Brendan turned them all on their head. He didn't rear up at Andrews but gave enough attitude to let you know the rabble-rousing image he had cultivated (or had cultivated for him) was very much secondary to a learned and erudite man who was totally in control of his life and work – not to mention his interviewer.

Brendan appeared to be more bemused by Andrews' prodding than irked by it, and set about dissembling the Behan myth even as it reached its apogee. He trotted out the old line about fame being nonsense after a month and quoted liberally from various sources as he made his points. He got the title of a Dylan Thomas poem wrong, but what struck you most about the interview was his literary acumen.

The most telling quote of all was from Keats: "God help the poor little famous". Well he wasn't poor, and he certainly wasn't little, but he was just beginning to realise that fame was not quite what he might have expected. For one thing it meant his native Irish became hard on him as a result, but as he pointed out deliciously, the Irish weren't his audience, only his raw material. (Begrudgers beware.)

"In my private life I'm a gloomy sort of person," he said, "nothing at all like my public ministry, if I may so describe it." He had started by telling Andrews he was a nurse and now he was a priest of sorts. It was hardly surprising Andrews accused him of being an inverted snob.

When Andrews asked him if he was embarrassed to have been seen drunk on the Muggeridge show (a bone he didn't let go of lightly), Brendan came into his own, telling him television wasn't the Mass so it didn't really matter to him whether he was drunk on it or not. He even adopted a whimsical attitude to death after Andrews asked him if he feared it. He didn't like the "dyin' lark" at all, he admitted, but poured cold water on the idea that he was heading down that road just yet. Then, as ever, he turned the question on Andrews, telling him he was probably immortal himself because the tin god of television would make him so. The iconoclasm was gentle, but irresistible despite (or maybe because of) that fact.

Andrews took off his gloves not knowing whether he had found out what made Brendan "tick" or not and Brendan probably remained behind in the pub to skull a few more pints.

The publisher Sinbad Vail gave a revelatory glimpse into Brendan when he said, "We saw each other frequently. He always dropped by when he wanted a small loan or drink or food. I don't recall talking much about writing. He used to ramble on, sing Irish songs, tell dirty jokes and try to get off with a very pretty American girl who was helping me."

Peter Arthurs put it a different way, "Brendan possessed the all time rib-and-gristle appendages of the instant clownsman – a gnome with a multi-functional face."

And here's Anthony Cronin's estimation of him, "You could not have a better companion in a day's idleness than Brendan. He was a kaleidoscopic entertainment, but he was also fecund in serious ideas. He had a line in bemused wonderment about the activities of the world, which was only partly an affectation, for he was genuinely naïve in certain ways, and genuinely full of questionings. And he knew too when to drop the act and show himself capable of intimacy. The salt which makes a penury palatable he had in abundance."

After yet another drunken display of singing, fisticuffs and/or crawling across the floor on all fours in some demented anecdotal display, pub-owners didn't know whether to put him in a taxi, an ambulance, a black Maria or a straitjacket.

He was a rogue to the core, but like most rogues, the only person he really did damage to was himself. Abusing your mates is something of a cottage industry in Ireland, and not to be confused with our old friend begrudgery. So also are ubiquitous expletives. And that gnawing tendency to see a cloud hooked on to every silver lining.

He had his problems, did the Quare Fellow, but he rarely moaned about them. His zest for life in the raw was insurmountable, and his fierce need for someone to share it with fuelled all those Rabelaisian nights and hellacious mornings-after. He was a far more intelligent man than he ever let on to anyone. In fact, dare I say it, he was something of an intellectual in his way. But no doubt he would have regarded that tag as an insult. It would have made him a eunuch in the harem – like the critics. And that would have been a crueller death to him than cirrhosis of the liver.

❖

His friend J P Donleavy was out the first time Brendan called to his home in Kilcoole, so Brendan let himself in by unlatching a window. He sat in the splendour of Donleavy's residence for a while, but soon grew bored and decided he would go for a drink. The only problem was that the pub was a mile away and he had no wheels. He decided he would take the unprecedented measure of walking to it, but when he went down the road it started to bucket rain and it wasn't long before his shoes (which he always kept unlaced, for some reason) were running with water. Back he went to Donleavy's house where he espied no less than 21 pairs of shoes. He helped himself to about a dozen pairs, which he put into a suitcase and then started off down the road again. Every time the ones he had on him showed signs of wetness, he kicked them off him into the nearest field and put on a dry new pair. He repeated this action an indeterminate amount of times until he came to the pub in a dry state. There he partook his fill and waited for the weather to clear before embarking on the journey home.

Donleavy came back in the meantime and got to wondering where all his shoes had gone. After a while, Brendan ambled merrily in the gate and Donleavy asked where his shoes were. Brendan explained to him what he had done, finishing off by saying, "You'll have no bother finding them. Your first pair is just there over the fence and the rest of them every 50 yards or so up to the pub."

❖   ❖   ❖

This is how Brendan contrasted his upbringing with that of some of the more refined acquaintances of his youth, "It was suspected that some of them took piano lessons and dancing lessons while we of the North Circular Road took anything we could lay our hands on which was not nailed down."

❖   ❖   ❖

Brendan had great admiration for Noel Browne as a politician, so much so that he wanted to canvas for him during the latter's 1959 election campaign. Having Brendan fighting your cause, however, wasn't necessarily going to garner votes, as he well knew. He thought about the predicament for a while and then hit upon an ingenious solution. "I'll tell you what I'll do," he said, thoroughly pleased with himself, "I'll canvas for the other fella. That'll be enough to win the election for Browne."

❖   ❖   ❖

He fled from hospital once against his doctor's orders. When asked about his medical condition, replied, "I'm only staying alive to save funeral expenses."

❖   ❖   ❖

Brendan was sitting in a pub in Ballsbridge one night when a pretty nurse walked in and started collecting money for under-privileged children. Brendan gave her what change he had and then asked her what age was the oldest child her organisation took in. "About twelve," she replied. Brendan sighed disappointedly and said, "Oh well, that rules me out."

❖   ❖   ❖

Brendan was singing bawdy songs in a pub when an anally-retentive lady complained to the management about him. His response was to tell the pub-owner she was a prostitute – which he believed – and she was thrown out instead of him.

❖   ❖   ❖

The sign-writing he did in France was never what you might call professional, but it had his indelible stamp on it – particularly the time he wrote on the wall of a Left Bank pub: "This is the best fucking bar in Paris".

❖   ❖   ❖

J P Donleavy remembers somebody complimenting Brendan on a new suit he wore one time and Brendan reacted as only he could: he walked out onto the street and rolled round in it in a gutter until it looked sufficiently creased and ragged that he felt comfortable in it.

❖   ❖   ❖

He was at a party with the writer Ben Kiely when a handsome man passed by, Brendan said to Kiely, "Given the choice, who would you prefer to shag: him or Eleanor Roosevelt?"

❖   ❖   ❖

The establishment at the Algonquin Hotel raised their eyebrows when he came down to dinner one night looking slovenly in an open-necked shirt. They informed Mr Behan that this wasn't kosher, that he would have to dress in something more befitting his station. When Brendan heard this injunction he disappeared upstairs. When he came down again he was dressed impeccably in a spanking new shirt and tie. There was only one thing wrong: he had no shoes or socks on him!

❖   ❖   ❖

A typical piece of Behanesque apparel, he said, was "a Brooks Brothers suit with two buttons off and a big fucking booze stain on the front".

❖   ❖   ❖

When Brendan first went to London, he got a job with a street repair gang. On his first day he noticed a group of workers in a hole singing "Happy birthday" beside a foreman.
"Is it the foreman's birthday?" he enquired.
"No," he was told. "It's the third anniversary of the hole."

❖   ❖   ❖

When he was on his way to court with his former IRA friend Eamonn Martin he was nervous of what sentence he might get, being up for assaulting a policeman. As they passed the Liffey he said to Martin, "Look, I'm a fine swimmer. Why don't you jump into the river and pretend to be drowning and I'll jump in and save you. When we get to court they'll ask us why we're wet and you can tell them I'm a hero and maybe they'll let me off." Martin baulked at the suggestion but Brendan still got a light sentence – as ever.

❖   ❖   ❖

Cathal Goulding said that shortly before Brendan died he arrived home to Beatrice accompanied by four prostitutes and their pimps. It was about 3 am when he knocked on the door. Beatrice let him in and did what any mannerly Irish housewife would do if their husband arrived home in the middle of the night with four prostitutes: she made them tea and sandwiches.

❖   ❖   ❖

He once had a cat that he taught to give an IRA salute, standing on its hind legs.

❖   ❖   ❖

Brendan was in the company of a Jewish friend in Paris in the forties when the pair of them met an anti-Semitic gendarme. He wouldn't shut up boasting about the Nazis and all the Jews they put in concentration camps. When Brendan couldn't take any more he got an idea. He looked at the gendarme's handcuffs and said, "How do these work?" He put one on his hand to show Brendan. As soon as he had it on, Brendan grabbed his other hand and pushed it against a railing, handcuffing the gendarme to it. Then off he went with the gendarme roaring behind him.

❖   ❖   ❖

His eating habits were as unpredictable as everything else about him. His friend John Ryan claimed that he sometimes put his food into a "galvanised bathtub". In this bathtub one was likely to see an entire chicken floating around, or a sheep's head.

❖   ❖   ❖

The actor Arthur Shields went to the toilet in the Abbey Theatre and emerged with a pair of Brendan's socks. Expressing surprise at the discovery, he asked Brendan how they'd been left inside. "Anytime I'm in the company of Abbey actors," Brendan explained, "a fit of claustrophobia overcomes me. My only relief is to take off my socks, drop my feet in the toilet bowl and then flush the thing."

❖   ❖   ❖

He was in the Blue Lion pub in Parnell Street one day when the owner said to him, "You owe me ten shillings. You broke a glass the last time you were here."

"God bless us and save us," said Brendan. "It must have been a very dear glass if it cost ten shillings. Tell us, was it Waterford glass or something?"

The man went on to explain to him that it was a pane of glass he had broken . . . in the course of trying to shove a man's head through it.

❖   ❖   ❖

A taxi driver asked him why he never buttoned up his shirt fully. "I can't get one to fit me anywhere," he replied. "If it buttons at the neck, it comes down to me ankles."

❖   ❖   ❖

He had a fondness for old people that didn't only extend to Granny English. One day he called for our Aunt Maggie and told her he was bringing her out for the day.

"Oh Brendan," she said. "I'm too shabby. Look at the cut of me."

"To hell with poverty," he told her, "we'll kill a chicken."

❖   ❖   ❖

According to John Ryan, Brendan bought the Bailey Bar by accident in 1955, having gone to the auction to purchase an electric toaster.

❖   ❖   ❖

After he threw his clothes in a heap on the floor one night after he had undressed to go to bed, I asked him why he hadn't used the hook on the wall to hang them up. "I did hang them up," he barked back, "I hung them up on the floor where they can't fall off."

❖   ❖   ❖

He did a month's hard labour once for assaulting a policeman. His defence before being sent to Mountjoy Prison wasn't very convincing. "The sight of police uniforms upset me," he announced.

❖   ❖   ❖

Brendan was cantankerous from a young age. Ma brought us out to the Bull Wall as nippers one day and he got lost. When she went looking for him, she found him in a hole in the long grass with only his head sticking out. Da went to great trouble pulling him out but all that he got in the way of thanks from little Bengy was, "Are yis blind or what? Is it that you want to get rid of me?" He was eight years old at the time – and just about revving up for an incendiary future.

❖   ❖   ❖

One day, Francis MacManus said Brendan arrived into his offices in Radio Éireann with a gash on his chest oozing blood "behind the remnants of a belly-open shirt". On his way into town he had passed over Leeson Street Bridge and after seeing a few young people cavorting in the canal, decided to join them. However, when he dived in, the edge of an old rusty bucket cut into his chest. Only very reluctantly did he allow MacManus to apply an anaesthetic to it.

❖   ❖   ❖

Another day he arrived in "with his mop of hair shiny and stiff like a gorgon's wig of hissing angry snakes". On his way down Granby Row (an area he termed "Matt Talbot country") he had seen a man varnishing a door. He asked him for his union card and when the man failed to produce one, Brendan threw the can of varnish up into the air. As MacManus put it, "What goes up must come down" and it did: on Brendan's own head! He later called it "Matt Talbot's revenge" as he related the yarn to MacManus, hardly able to speak for laughing at his own stupidity as the varnish lay matted into his hair.

❖   ❖   ❖

Brendan warned Micheal O'hAodha not to let anyone see his early writings because they were sprinkled with expletives – a rarity in those days, even in hyphenated form, as O'hAodha pointed out in an article in *The Irish Times* on 22 March 1974. When he became famous, however, he was less circumspect and wont to boast that he once earned his living in France by writing pornography. O'hAodha was inclined to doubt this. The competition in that particular field, he noted, would probably have been too keen even for the bold Brendan.

❖   ❖   ❖

In a pub one day with the author Richard Fleischer he tucked his hand up into the sleeve of his jacket for fun.

"What happened to your hand, Brendan?" asked one of the other customers.

"It's gone," he replied, "I must have left it somewhere."

❖   ❖   ❖

When *The Hostage* was being premiered in London, Brendan got up to his usual antics during rehearsals. Unable to sit still, he kept leaping out of his seat to inform the cast that they were doing it all wrong. After repeated attempts to get him to shut up, he got worse and worse. He started singing then, and roaring lines from the script before the cast had a chance to say them. One of the actors asked the manager of the theatre to get rid of him. The manager replied, "How can I? He's the *author*!"

❖   ❖   ❖

When Eamonn Andrews was doing the *This Is Your Life* show for Da, he rang up Brendan and asked him would he appear on it. Brendan thought he was going to be the guest of honour and he jumped at the chance. "Would a duck swim?" he said. But then Andrews explained that he was only going to be a guest and he went half mad. He eventually agreed to take part, but he brought a crowd of lowlifes with him and they got footless and nearly wrecked the BBC after the show. Andrews wasn't too impressed. (As for myself, I got £84 for saying "Hello Dad" so I was quite happy with myself. For that kind of money, I'd say hello to the Devil himself – with a long spoon or a short one.)

❖   ❖   ❖

A merciless prankster all his life, when a neighbour in Russell Street annoyed him one day in his youth, he got his revenge by putting sacks over the windows of her room so that when she woke up she thought she was blind.

❖   ❖   ❖

After he was arrested on the possession of explosives charge, he said he wanted prisoner-of-war status if he was sent to jail. Asked for his profession at his trial, he replied, "Housepainter – the same as Hitler."

❖   ❖   ❖

In his house-painting days, Sheila Greene observed, you would often see him atop a high ladder, spitting down on people he didn't like, and shouting ribald remarks to those he did. Another time when he was painting the Gaiety he dropped a can of paint down onto the head of a young lad he thought had notions of grandeur.

❖   ❖   ❖

When he was doing his apprenticeship, he was just as feisty. In fact his foreman had to bring him home to Ma once because he was spending half the day jig-acting round the place with his imitations and he had all the other workers in convulsions. He was a pantomime – but an expensive one if he was performing on your time. The foreman said to Ma, "Brendan will have to make up his mind if he wants to be an actor or a painter." And I don't think he ever did.

❖   ❖   ❖

Nobody could ever accuse Brendan of dedication to his chosen craft of house-painting. He liked to arrive late at a venue, waste as much of the bosses' time as possible, skive off for a drink (or drinks) at every available opportunity, and try to extract the maximum amount of money from the least labour. Even when he was painting, he never stopped talking to his colleagues. And that was about anything but painting. His ideal day would have been work from 1 to 2, with an hour off for lunch.

❖   ❖   ❖

During one painting job, he fell asleep the morning after yet another heavy drinking session. As he was waking up, he overheard the foreman say behind him, "Sleep on, Behan, sleep on, for while you're asleep ye have a job, but as soon as ye wake, ye're sacked." He kindly took the foreman's advice and went back to the Land of Nod, content in the knowledge that, even if he was out of a job, at least he was being paid for his present snooze.

❖   ❖   ❖

Lest you were in any doubt that Brendan was ever a contender for 'Painter of the Month Award', let me advise you of a letter written by one D Blakely, who was the Principal Keeper of St John's Point Lighthouse in County Down in 1950. Mr Blakely was so underwhelmed by Brendan's dedication to the cause of duty and penned this missive to the chief engineer at the Irish Lights Office to record his dissatisfaction:

> Sir, I have to report painter B Behan absent from his work all day yesterday and not returning to his station until 1.25 this morning. No work was carried out by him yesterday. I also have to report that his attitude here is one of careless indifference with no respect for Commissioner's property or stores. He is wilfully wasting materials, opening drums and tins by blows from a heavy hammer, and spilling the contents out. There are also drums of whitewash opened and exposed to the weather, and dirty paintbrushes lying all around the station. He doesn't clean up any of the mess, just stamps through everything. His language is also filthy, and he has ruined the surface of one wall by burning it. He mixes putty and paint with his bare hands and wipes off nothing. The spare house, which was clean and ready for painters, has been turned into a filthy shambles inside a week. Empty stinking milk bottles, articles of food, coal, ashes and other debris litter the floor of the place, which is now in a scandalous condition of dirt.

Mr Blakely ended this tirade by saying, "I invite any official of the Irish Lights to inspect this station and verify these statements. He is the worst specimen I have met in 30 years service and I urge his dismissal from the job now before good material is rendered useless and the place ruined."

❖   ❖   ❖

Comic performer Niall Toibin got to know Brendan well when they used to meet in and around Searson's pub, near where both lived for a time. In fact Brendan and Beatrice once occupied a flat in Herbert Street which had just been vacated by Toibin. Anytime afterwards when Brendan met him on the street he would say something along the lines of, "Hey bollocky, come here – you never paid your electricity bill." Or, "There's a letter from so-and-so waitin' for you. Why don't you tell them to write to your new address and not be botherin' me with your fuckin' problems."

❖   ❖   ❖

Another time, Brendan was at a charity rugby match at Dalymount Park when he saw Tony O'Reilly leaving the dressing-room. He said to him, according to reports, "I was going to send Beatrice in after you, but when I saw what was on show in the shower, Jaysus, I thought I'd never get her back again." Toibin says this probably never happened, not only because he doubts there were any showers in Dalymount at the time, but even if there were, O'Reilly would hardly have used them!

❖   ❖   ❖

The actor Gabriel Byrne tells a story about being on the 50B bus one time when a passenger got on who caused something of a commotion. He was dressed in a sports coat that was too small for him, and trousers that were too big – and dirty. He had no socks on him and his shoes were scuffed. He broke into song for the bemused audience of passengers, and when he got off, the bus driver threw his eyes to heaven. The man saluted the departing bus with some Gaelic phrase as the rain teemed down on him, appearing oblivious to it all. And the name of this strange but fascinating man? Who else – Brendan Behan on his way out to our gloryhole in the Crumlin sticks.

❖   ❖   ❖

One day Ma went down to Brendan's school to complain about him misbehaving at home. She didn't get far with his teacher Sister Monica, however.

"Do you realise," the kindly nun said in upbraiding tones, "that you are raising a genius?"

"Genius or not," Ma barked back at the nun, "he can be a bold lump when he likes."

❖   ❖   ❖

Brendan's friend Mick McCarthy tells the story of the time Brendan got two tickets to see Yehudi Menuhin, the violinist, who was playing in the Mansion House. They were complimentaries from the *Irish Press* but he was no more interested in Menuhin than the man in the moon so he tried to sell them to a Protestant friend of his, Jeffrey Farmer. Brendan and Mick waited for Farmer in McDaids but he never turned up so they just had a few pints instead. The pair of them ended up going to the show anyway, just to use up the tickets.

Everyone was terrified of how Brendan was going to behave. He had no shirt on him and his pullover was pulled up over his navel. His hair was flying in about 44 different directions as well. When they got inside they found themselves sitting just behind the Diplomatic Corps . . . and President Eamon de Valera. That was enough to make Brendan explode. "Holy divine sufferin' Jaysus." he said, "Do you see that scrawny cunt Dev. That bastard kept me locked up below in The Curragh for four fuckin' years." Mick tried to tell him to cool down, that everyone could hear him, but that only made him raise his voice. "Cool me bollox," he said. "you didn't spend four years in The Curragh, did you? What the fuck gives you the right to tell me what to talk about or not talk about."

Then he fell asleep and started to snore like a horse. Everyone was horrified. Mick gave him a few thumps to try and wake him up but it was no use. Then Menuhin came out and started playing. Mick gave Brendan an unmerciful dig in the stomach and he gave a few snorts and started to wake up. "Let's get the fuck out of here," he said. "That's only a bollox of a fiddle player." The whole row of people had to stand to let them out. Everyone was delighted to see them go. In fact the newspaper people were so relieved that when they got to the front door of the Mansion House, loads of them started pushing money on him.

They must have pressed about £50 into his shirt. He never had it so good. They decided to go back to McDaids and have a few more pints. When they got there, who was there but Ma. "Where were you?" she said to Brendan. "Watching a fiddle player who couldn't play fuck," Brendan told her. Then the three of them proceeded to get drunk in earnest!

❖   ❖   ❖

You could never be sure what Brendan would come out with. He was leaving a pub one day in London just as three house-painters strolled in. Going up to the middle one, he said, "Listen here, I told you before: stop having it off with my Granny." All three were bewildered until they recognised who he was. Then relief descended. "It's that mad Paddy," said one of them. I think he meant it as a compliment.

❖ ❖ ♣

Brendan had an uneasy relationship with J P Donleavy. When Donleavy was writing *The Ginger Man*, Brendan saw the work in progress and made some changes. Donleavy was furious at his insolence and told him so; it was only years later he realised Brendan's observations on his manuscript were all too relevant. Anyway, Donleavy and Brendan were in Davy Byrne's pub once when Brendan insulted Donleavy. Donleavy then asked him outside. The other drinkers were curious as to how things would pan out, but when they got outside Brendan offered Donleavy his hand. "Why should the pair of us be out and here beat the bejesus out of each other," he said, "for the satisfaction of eejits like them inside. Fuck the ignorant bunch back in there who wouldn't know a present participle from a hole in their buried mother's coffins. Come on, the two of us will go somewhere and have a drink, and we'll tell the story round that both of us were so fast at getting our of the way of each other's fists, neither of us could land a punch." Somehow, the story was believed.

❖ ❖ ♣

Brendan's friend Sheila Bradshaw recalls seeing him one day as she was on her way into a shop. He didn't salute her from afar, or roar hello as was his wont, so she knew he was up to his tricks. When he got into the shop he threw himself on the floor and started begging from the rest of the customers. He said he had ten starving children at home and they were driving him mad with their screeching. He wasn't looking for money for food for them, he stressed, but for drink for himself. Then he pretended to suddenly see Bradshaw. When he did, he told all the other people in the queue that she was the greatest drunk in Dublin and that he was fine now that he had seen her because she would bring him out with her and they'd both get pissed together.

❖ ❖ ♣

Brendan was cat-sitting for his friends Desmond and Beverly MacNamara one night, but got a fit of hunger (not unusual for him) and ate the meat that was left for the cats. When he heard the MacNamaras coming home, he grabbed the cats and pushed their mouths into the melted dripping in the pan where he had cooked the meat. The cats started screeching as Beverley came up the stairs, but Brendan remained poker-faced. When asked if he had fed them, he said. "Jaysus, can't you see the bastards lickin' their chops? Some people are never satisfied."

❖   ❖   ❖

Des MacNamara was a sculptor by trade and made a bust of Brendan in the fifties, as you probably know. On the day it was to be done Brendan had a massive hangover and promptly fell asleep just as MacNamara was about to get to work.

A supine position not being exactly ideal for an about-to-be-busted head, he propped Brendan up with a few volumes of an old encyclopaedia and proceeded to work. The only problem was Brendan's stubble. MacNamara had to shave him to get the outline of his face, and he even slept through that. When it was finished, Brendan woke up and himself and Des went for a drop of the craythur across the road. Brendan later told me it was one of the most enjoyable day's work he ever did, and he was seriously considering taking up bust-posing while sleeping off hangovers as a way of life. Anyway, the said bust was sold for a not-to-be-sniffed-at £2,800 by Sotheby's in 1992. What a pity he never got to see any of that lolly after working so hard for it.

❖   ❖   ❖

A plaque was eventually put beside the front door of our old house in Kildare Street in 1977. The day was given the big treatment and a huge crowd turned up to witness its unveiling. There was a carnival atmosphere. The Transport Union Band even came along, taking up residence on a small platform in the front garden. The band struck up, bunting blew in the breeze and the crowd sang *The Auld Triangle*. Eventually the dramatic moment came when the curtain was drawn back and Brendan's plaque was revealed for the first time. A huge cheer went up from the crowd but then a little woman at the back (isn't there always a little woman at the back?) looked up at it and said, "I'll tell ye one thing for nothin'. Ye'd have a hard job sellin' your house with that thing over your hall door."

❖   ❖   ❖

He always preferred a swim to a bath. "Anyone who would sit in a tubful of water for hours has to be some class of an eejit," he said. "Stewing in me own mud is not my idea of a good wash."

❖   ❖   ❖

"It's like the Sacrament of Penance. Whenever I'm asked if I've been to

Confession recently I say, 'that's only for sinners'."

❖   ❖   ❖

Our cousin Colbert Kearney claims that Brendan went off to France one year with nothing more than a toothbrush in his top pocket.

❖   ❖   ❖

Another time Brendan fed a horse a bottle of whiskey. The horse died and was buried on a beach. A day in the life of your average playwright.

❖   ❖   ❖

Brendan could never exactly be called dainty in his eating habits. He was asleep once in the back room of a pub off Parliament Street working off a hangover. Waking up suddenly, he saw Major Louis Carter, the then-editor of the *Evening Mail* about to tuck into a plateful of stew. "Ah, lunchtime!" he beamed, plunging his hand into the plate for a handful of the stew. Carter was understandably dismayed. "Good loving Jesus," Brendan roared, "don't say he objects to me eating a bit of his dinner."

❖   ❖   ❖

His failure to develop a liking for games probably went back to the influence of Granny English. She had this to say of soccer, "Who in their right mind would pay twelve and sixpence to see a crowd of eejits kick a ball away from them and then run after it?" This was a woman who believed whiskey was good for – among other things – sunstroke.

❖   ❖   ❖   ❖

If we take Brendan at his word that he was born in a bottle and grew up in a glass, it was Granny English who poured him from that bottle into the glass, setting him off on the road to alcoholism.

It was probably sitting at her bedside imbibing the Black Stuff that he learned all those epithets that are scattered liberally throughout his work. Maxims like: "An empty sack won't stand." "You can stay in bed all day if you get the name of being an early riser." "What can you expect from a pig but a grunt?" "We never died a winter yet, and the devil out of hell couldn't kill us in the summer."

He had many others. He referred to Dominic and myself (and no, we weren't flattered) as 'The Brothers Grimm'. He cursed enemies with,

"fuck you and all your uncles in America". If somebody broke wind
he'd say, "it's a poor arse that never rejoices". After he spat he'd say,
"get out and walk".

❖   ❖   ❖   ❖

Maybe his favourite of all was that profoundly simple maxim: "It's a
queer world, God knows, but the best we have to be going on with."

Chapter 13

Borstal Boy

I served a sentence for attempting to murder two policemen – but by Jaysus, they weren't charged with a prior attempt to murder me.

Brendan Behan

B rendan was imprisoned in no less than four different countries in his short life. Also, as I mentioned already, Da's first sight of him was when he himself was locked up. For a man who loved his freedom so much, though, Brendan took to incarceration with alarming resignation. He described borstal as "the poor man's public school" and such it definitely was for him, since it was here he first began to write – and read – in earnest. Prison was also a place that forced him to stay off the drink, and he always boasted about the fact that he never put pen to paper under the influence. Neither would it take a genius to notice that most of his more serious fiction and drama concerned itself with characters in captivity, be they thinly-disguised versions of himself or people he had heard about.

In most ways he found prison a salutary experience, despite the obvious discomforts and deprivations. The most unpleasant fact about it, he joked, wasn't so much being locked up as "the other Irish patriots in along with you". His fellow inmates saw the situation differently, however. One of them, Maurice Richardson said, "I can't think of anyone I would rather share a cell with than Brendan . . . in spite of the noise." (That final reservation speaks volumes.)

I was actually on guard duty in The Curragh camp, where Brendan was imprisoned after the Glasnevin shooting, and often wondered what might have happened if our paths crossed. Maybe he would have seen me as a Judas, I don't know. I let my imagination run on the subject in a play I wrote, envisaging a scenario where he says to me, "So you'll pull the trigger on me, will you, if I make a break for it?" and I reply, "I'm an economic conscript. It was either the army or a stretch in jail for me. Anyway, if I don't shoot you, somebody else would. Would you not prefer it to be kept in the family?" I sometimes laugh to myself thinking of what Brendan's reaction would be to these lines if he's reading them wherever he is now.

Much of Brendan's contentment in borstal was down to C A Joyce.

Joyce was Governor of Hollesley Bay Borstal in Suffolk, and ran it along lines that were far ahead of their time. He had seen enough recidivism to convince him that lawbreaking was a spiral that could only be broken by rehabilitation, which was one of the reasons he took such a special interest in Brendan. He was like a kindly schoolmaster of the Mr Chips variety and operated on the basis of mutual respect between inmates and warders rather than a master-slave relationship. He also organised leisure activities like rugby and drama and gave the prisoners much more freedom than they were used to. Surprisingly – or maybe not so – they were less inclined to try and escape even though escape was easier than it would have been anywhere else at that time. If this was reverse psychology, it worked a dream with Brendan, who always had, and always would have, a problem with authority.

Brendan hated anyone in a uniform, and that went all the way from a bus conductor to a High Court judge. But the distinctions were blurred here and he thrived on it. It was a far cry from what Oscar Wilde had suffered in Reading Gaol. It may not have been Butlins Holiday Camp, but the library facilities gave him the opportunity to build on the literary lore Da had instilled in us all as kids. Brendan didn't have much time to listen to him round the hearth, but there wasn't much choice here.

He told me he buried himself so much in books he even forgot he was in a cell. There was no faster way for time to pass than when you lost yourself in someone else's life, or wrote about your own. He discovered sensitivities in himself he didn't know he possessed, and started to exploit them. In a funny way, prison freed him. Meeting Cyril Alfred Joyce, for Brendan, was almost as good as meeting James Joyce. "I have no complexes and no inhibitions," he said to Joyce when they first met, about nothing in particular. Joyce told him he'd take him as he found him, and he did.

He gave him a working environment that was as beneficial to Brendan as somewhere like Annaghmakerrig would be to a budding writer today. He had expected Brendan to be a hard-chaw and was amazed by his gentleness and honesty. The pair of them had a relationship that gave Brendan an ideal springboard for his craft. Almost single-handedly Joyce took him from the world to the word.

There's an argument to be made for the fact that he did his best work in prison because here he was freed from any distractions, particularly the obvious one of drink. From this point of view it was even more beneficial than hospital for him. He could escape from hospital, or have drink smuggled in to him, but in prison all he could do was write. It was here also he got his raw material, soaking up all his borstal experiences like a sponge.

He claimed his neuroses were the "nails and saucepans by which I get my living", but so also was prison life, which impinges to some extent on all his major works, be it in the form of literal recall, stage-craft or ideology. Reggie Kray said *Borstal Boy* was the finest book on prison life ever written. In *Confessions of an Irish Rebel*, Brendan wrote, "The crinkle in my belly would straighten out in this kip without the aid of porter."

One also has to say that, either for this reason or a multiplicity of others, Brendan was a fairly model prisoner. Recently-released papers have borne this out, and indeed it was apparent from his own writings, where early insolence was beaten out of him and seems to have been replaced with an acceptance of his lot. He may have written republican slogans on his walls, and carried a gung-ho attitude about the place with him, but by and large he was content inside himself. Borstal may not have been a five-star hotel, and nobody enjoys the daily Dickensian grind, or the humiliation of slopping in and out, but a beans-and-bacon lifestyle can have its pleasures too and Brendan adapted to the prison regimen with remarkable elan.

In fact he was much more cantankerous in what we might call the free world, for want of a better term. Not only did borstal deprive him of the destructive, personality-altering effects of drink and provide him with a commodious writing environment, it also introduced him to a motley crew of characters whom he enjoyed, and was enjoyed by. The resounding impact *Borstal Boy* leaves on the reader is one of innocence and mirth. These aren't ground-down men, but rather jocularly bantering ones most of the time, making a virtue of necessity and enjoying what few luxuries that come their way to the hilt.

Robust conversation is the most obvious one of these. In fact Brendan appears to be having such a good time throughout much of this book, one is betimes tempted to think he got himself arrested deliberately to become a guest of Her Majesty. Even more ironically, borstal also gave him respect for the British who had put him there. With Ma's milk he had been given blanket dismissals of the 'Auld Enemy', but in the chokey he met many without prejudice or a political agenda.

If you think about it, our whole history has these sorts of ironies. Dev was born in America after all, and Michael Collins in London. And Patrick Pearse was English. In Borstal, as Brian Inglis wrote, Brendan learned to separate the English from that detested abstraction: England. Thereafter he was cosmopolitan in his sympathies.

Gay Byrne said in a book some time ago that when he was growing up he got a lot of anti-English propaganda at school, as we all did, but at home it was leavened. Then he went to work with Granada and he found the British were very kind to him. Some Irish people, he says, have the attitude of "Oh, he has a good word to say about perfidious Albion, therefore he must be a West Brit." I know what he means. That's one of the problems with Ireland, the sense that people feel you have to be either/or. And that's one of the reasons I despair sometimes about peace in the North.

In the end there are only people, no matter where you were born. And you don't have to die to prove you love your country. Try living for it. The Beaverbrook Press actually wrote of Brendan, "Though born an Irishman, he remained an Englishman all his life." He regarded this as high praise if taken in context. He said to J P Donleavy, "Let me tell you about the Orangeman. There's no better human being on earth, if it came to a choice between me own and one of them, I'd have the latter on my side any day."

"After his stint in borstal," as Rae Jeffs said, "Brendan realised his parents hadn't been totally truthful with him when they castigated all British people as demons. He still disliked them *en masse*, but not individually. And that confused him." It's difficult to imagine him allowing any of his plays to be staged in London, or himself to be interviewed by somebody like Malcolm Muggeridge on television unless he had developed that cosmopolitanism.

It's interesting to note that when Ma first met Joan Littlewood, Brendan's mentor and theatrical co-pilot, she said to her, "It was your lot who killed Kevin Barry."

"Leave the girl alone," Brendan bristled at her. "She knows nothing about those things." And then he added, "There are plenty of Irish bastards too." I think this might have been the only time in Ireland's political history where a sometime republican guerrilla found himself defending a British person to the woman who had bred that very republicanism in him almost from the day he first drew breath.

Such cosmopolitanism also saved him from the responsibility of having to write solely for what he looked on as the craw-thumper readership. And of course the shleveens. The Horse Protestants were another matter, and the *nouveau riche* Angsters. "England has a great influence over the Irish," he said. "On account of my success in the West End my popularity has risen at home. The people here are a pack of shawneens. They follow blindly whatever the English press says." This was an amazing statement for a man to make about a nation that locked him up for over one-fifth of his life. "If England sneezes," he said, "Ireland reaches for its handkerchief."

"The Old Lady said no to *The Quare Fellow* first time round," he said, speaking of the Abbey Theatre as he paraphrased Denis Johnston, "but when it broke box office records in London they soon revised their opinion. That's this fucking country in a nutshell. The Abbey wouldn't know a good play if it jumped up and bit it on the nose."

How right he was. In fact it's still going on today. You have only to look at what happened to the late-lamented Dermot Morgan's *Father Ted* series. It was rejected by RTÉ but then it became a hit with Channel 4, after which RTÉ, in their wisdom, decided they wanted to screen it.

It's easy for us now to look back at Brendan's English career and say, "It's obvious why he succeeded over there – he had all that vivacity." Maybe so, but you have to look at the situation in perspective. This was the fifties after all, unlike today where the English people not only respect the Irish person's penchant for the *craic*, but actually stage their stag parties over in Ireland to ape it. Forty years ago, different circumstances applied.

We were regarded as the poor relations of John Bull then. Added to which, their theatre was trapped in every other kind of straitjacket. What we now call 'kitchen sink drama' hadn't yet arrived in British theatre, which preferred to busy itself with a weekly round of life-denying period dramas. These operated on the principle that the 'New Wave' movement pioneered by the likes of Brecht and Pirandello hadn't yet happened. Beckett's *Waiting for Godot* had been staged in Paris in 1953 and would become the most famous play of its time, but three years later it still hadn't been picked up by the West End.

Alan Simpson had it right when he said, "An Englishman likes everything cut and dried. He likes his funny plays to be funny and his tragic plays to be tragic. In Ireland we see tragedy and comedy marching hand in hand." John Osborne's grim and grittily realistic *Look Back in Anger* was just about to change all that, and Brendan was lucky enough to be able to capitalise on that sea-change. But he didn't sneak in under Osborne's coat-tails: he had his own distinctive voice. It wasn't so much 'look back in anger' as 'look back in blood, sweat and tears' and, of course, laughter.

"If there's any vice the Irish really abhor," Brendan told Alan Bestic, "it's success. They think it's a mortal sin the size of a cartwheel." Bestic saw the truth of that statement when one of Brendan's begrudgers said after he died, "Sure what did he ever write anyway?" Bestic replied, "He wrote *Borstal Boy*, a fine and worthy book." The begrudger replied, "Sure that was only an autobiography!" Bestic loved the "only" bit. In another way, Brendan was carrying on exactly the way our grandparents – who wanted us to burn everything English except their coal – would have wanted, because he was taking all its money.

The country he tried to blow up was now, metaphorically, blowing him up. "John Bull is feeding the hand that bit him," he said to me with some glee, "and isn't it only manners for a Behan to accept their generosity graciously." Whether this was tongue-in-cheek or, to use his own expression, "tongue-in-gums", it seemed to me to be a peculiarly Irish form of logic. If you can't beat 'em join 'em – or let them put your name in lights.

From the ages of 16 to 23, Brendan spent most of his life in the nick. These were years he should have spent courting and dancing and making love. Instead he found himself swept up in the net of some very funny fish, all interned like himself by the Special Branch. Maybe the most controversial of these was one Neal Verschoyle Gould.

Gould's people were rich, with estates in Donegal, but he became a communist. He spent some time in Russia but was expelled by Stalin and came back to Ireland to launch a peasant's revolt against the powers-that-be. With Joe O'Connor and Sean Daly, two of Brendan's IRA buddies, Gould lit two tar barrels in Dundalk and declared the revolution on. It was all a bit of a farce as far as Brendan was concerned and he forswore his allegiance to the revolt, despite the protestations of Ma, who worshipped the ground Gould walked on.

Gould was expelled from the Irish Worker's League after this and drifted back to Russia again. Something of a Jesus Christ figure by now, dressed up in corduroy trousers, hobnailed boots and a peaked cap, he taught Brendan Russian and ran classes in Marxism. These were so successful some of the more rigid IRA men tried to throw him back over the wire to the authorities as a result. The prisoners with Brendan were split along two main lines: the traditional IRA who were antiEnglish to the core and what we might call the left-wingers like Brendan who supported the United Nations' war against Hitler.

This split later on became the split between the official and Provisional IRA. Brendan said to me, "It's only the Belfast Brigade of the IRA that take the national movement seriously any longer." Some of the IRA men who came to our house would sing the German army song:

> To the Rhine, to the Rhine,
> To the German Rhine I go,
> To join our battle line.
> Our hearts are strong,
> Our faith is true,
> We are faithful German land, to you.

I often wondered what would have happened if the Germans had invaded Ireland. The threat was very real. In fact the Americans and the British were hastily equipping the Irish Army with Bren guns and Springfield rifles, hoping they would at least offer token resistance if such a thing transpired. If the Germans won, which they undoubtedly would have, Brendan and his friends would have ended up in a different kind of prison camp, i.e. one with a gas oven attached.

Gerry Adams' uncle was interned with Brendan. Like Reggie Kray Adams once told me he thought *Borstal Boy* was the best book ever written on prison life. I think so too. Brendan writes it almost like a *Boy's Own* adventure story. It's like a patchwork quilt of impressions, with no self-pity at all. Brendan writes about people like himself, people whose mothers scraped and borrowed, who lived in slums and did the pawn. It's this kind of shared experience that comes out in *The Hostage* as well.

The character of Leslie is very much the type of lad Brendan would have met in borstal and that's why Brendan's sympathies are very much with him. The fact that he's English, and facing death at the hands of the IRA, is beside the point. The play was never meant to be a polemic. It was a human story. In war, all nationalities were victims, Brendan was saying. There were no winners on any side of the fence.

What got to him most about borstal was the loneliness. If unease with one's own company is a tell-tale sign of depression then Brendan was a very depressed individual indeed. He used people in the same way as he used drink: to get him away from the pressure of his own mind. And that's why the solitary confinement of a prison cell was the greatest punishment that could be bestowed on him. Hard labour in a chain gang would have been easier for him to bear. In *Borstal Boy* there's a passage where he says he would even have welcomed a beating from the warders rather than to have to spend an evening totally alone. I don't think anybody could have expressed the true dread of solitude more graphically than this.

Borstal Boy has a very strange ending. After praising the Wicklow hills that form a protective arm around Dublin Bay, Brendan comes down the gangway to a greeting from an immigration official. "*Céad míle fáilte sa bhaile romhat*," says the official, and Brendan replies, "*Go raibh maith agat*." ("A hundred thousand welcomes to you." "Thanks.") Then the official says: "*Caithfidh go bhfuil sé go hiontach bheith saor*." ("It must be wonderful to be free.") To which Brendan replies enigmatically, "*Caithfidh go bhuil*." ("It must.")

The distancing of himself from the emotion, as if he doesn't know his own mind, or is seeing himself from an external perspective, leaves the book dangling on a precipice. You're left wondering, where will he go from here? Is his release a beginning or an end? And will he be able to accommodate himself to it, this man who was always restless in the big wide world, but somehow at home and comfortable in confinement? "Freedom," as Brian Keenan put it in *An Evil Cradling*, "comes slowly at first."

It was when Mountjoy's old triangle stopped going jingle jangle that Brendan's real confinement began. There would be no amnesty from his own inner demons, no early parole and no remission. You couldn't take off your personality like an old suit and leave it hanging in a wardrobe. No, you were stuck with it like a second skin, all the way from The Waterloo pub to McDaids and The Catacombs and beyond. Such a personality was the invisible ball and chain that stuck to him when things were going well and going badly, when he was married and when he was single, when he was making bombs or making love. It was the personality prison redeemed him from, but only for a time.

"Stone walls do not a prison make," Pope wrote, "nor iron bars a

cage." Brendan was about to emerge into a new cage, or many different
ones, in a phase of his life that would take him from earning a pittance
for his journalism and part-time painting to being a man who could
name his price. But we all know what happened to Midas.

When Brendan got out of prison for the second time he was 24. He
had spent the best – or rather worst – part of the previous eight years
behind bars and was determined to make up for lost time quickly. That's
why he sought the limelight so much, as a kind of over-compensation
for what he looked on as so many wasted years. His premature release
from prison was, as things worked out, not so much the commutation
of a veritable life sentence as the beginning of a death sentence. It put
temptation his way, leaving him at the mercy of an even worse enemy
than confinement: himself.

❖

When Brendan was in The Curragh he went sick one day and the doctor prescribed a daily bottle of stout for him. This was a very popular
decision with Brendan. He saved up the bottles for a few weeks in chamber pots, and, as Séamus de Búrca tells us in his book *Brendan Behan: A
Memoir*, after the mould had settled on top of the brew, he went on a
"vociferous, marvellous binge all to himself".

❖   ❖   ❖

The story that really bothered Brendan in prison was the one about the
butcher who murdered his brother and filleted his body so carefully no
parts of it were ever found. When he recovered from the shock, he joked
that the corpse was sold as fresh pork to the Jesuit Fathers in Tullabeg!

❖   ❖   ❖

Brendan knew a prisoner called Bernard Kirwin who was sentenced to
death. On the day before his execution, Kirwin put a cup of water on
the back of his hand and it didn't even shake. "That's the hand of a
man who's going to be hanged in ten minutes," he said.

"He must be very brave," said one of other prisoners.

"No," said Brendan, "he must be very mad."

❖   ❖   ❖

Brendan did a fortnight in Mountjoy once for scuffling with a Garda at
the door of the Theatre Royal. When notified of his release he asked the
Governor of the prison for permission to stay on another week. "I'm
trying to finish *War and Peace*," he explained.

❖   ❖   ❖

One of Brendan's stints in prison came about after he was caught helping a fellow IRA man escape from Leyhill prison in Surrey. His job was to make sure a Park Ranger in the vicinity of the prison wouldn't do anything to hamper the escape, so he had to keep pretty close to him. It was a task he handled with some relish. As he explained afterwards, "He was a decent man, a quiet, reasonable Irishman who, even though he was employed by The British Imperial Majesty, never spoke a word against us. And the only effin' thing I did to convince him of our good intentions was to hold a .45 revolver to his head all the time. Cocked."

❖   ❖   ❖

We might bear in mind the fact that the man Brendan shot at in De Courcey Square said he could have killed Brendan immediately if he returned fire, but didn't wish to, perhaps realising that this was no ordinary, or callous, assassin.

It's also interesting that Paddy Donegan, the man Brendan was sentenced for shooting at, later became one of his drinking buddies. Brendan never moaned about his sentence. He said his big crime wasn't shooting at the guards, but missing them. He said he deserved a year in jail for every yard he missed them by. Da agreed. He said Brendan's sentence should have been double because he missed. But then in another mood he said in the Special Criminal Court, "That boy is as innocent as a new-born lamb so he should be let out. He's been blind since bloody birth and couldn't hit a cow's arse with a banjo." (Rory claimed he wouldn't even have been able to hit his own parish.)

❖   ❖   ❖

Brendan was never over the moon about prison food during the years he spent incarcerated there. One day he said crankily to the warder, "Are we gettin' food with our meals today?"

❖   ❖   ❖

When C A Joyce asked him for a promise that he would desist from 'the armed struggle' in future, Brendan gave him a muted guarantee in a reference to the Second World War, which had just broken out. "I promise not to do anything until we have done with this bastard Hitler," he crooned, "and after that I can always consider it again, can't I?"

❖   ❖   ❖

When he first got to Borstal, the warden told him he would be allowed
Three Nuns cigarettes: none yesterday, none today and none tomorrow.

❖   ❖   ❖

According to Terrance Dicks, author of *A Riot of Irish Writers*, Behan
was amazed when he was issued with a pair of pyjamas when in Borstal . . . because he·had never worn any before.

❖   ❖   ❖

He lost faith in prison doctors after hearing of one who prescribed two
aspirins for an inmate with a broken leg.

❖   ❖   ❖

Considering the fact that Brendan's first prison sentence was reduced
because he was so young, and his Granny's last one because she was
too old, Dominic found himself wondering what age a person must be
in Britain's quirky legal system to get a life sentence.

❖   ❖   ❖

He was well aware that prison did much more to help his career than
hinder it, because of the wealth of experiences he amassed when inside. This was evident the day Ben Kiely said casually that if the cost of
living got any worse, he'd end up in the debtor's prison. Brendan looked
taken aback and said, "Don't take from me the one advantage I have in
the book business."

❖   ❖   ❖

When Brendan was arrested in 1947 for breaking the deportation order
against him, Eoin O'Mahoney, the well-known lawyer, flew to England
to defend him. O'Mahoney's nickname was 'The Pope', and he sent a
telegram to Brendan to the prison advising him of his imminent arrival
and signing it by that name at the end of it. "How well do you know
the Pope?" the bewildered Governor of the prison enquired upon re-
ceipt of the telegram. "Fairly well," the bad Catholic told him.

Chapter 14

Hold your Hour and have Another

I envied Brendan as I would a millionaire, as he poured thousands and thousands of words down the sink, threw away hundreds of television and radio programmes unseen and unheard in some pub. Such a waste of genius there was, never recorded, all gone now with the windy belch of ten thousand pints of stout.

Anthony Butler

"The Irish are a very moral race," John Braine wrote in his novel *The Crying Game*, "booze and brawling are their only vices." They were certainly our Brendan's most obvious problems – and to many, his most loveable ones, at least if you weren't on the receiving end.

According to legend, he was born with a bottle of whiskey in his hand. Well, not exactly. In fact he was the elderly age of six before he partook of a drop of the hard stuff. This was at the behest of our beloved Granny English, a woman who pontificated on life from the comfort of her bed as she gave him his first taste of money, theatre and comic abandon.

Brendan, as you probably know, was the kind of man to get a panic attack when he saw somebody wearing a pioneer pin. There were people he admired who didn't drink, but they were admired very definitely despite that fact. Equally, there were heavy drinkers he didn't like, but not many. Non-drinkers were people he found it hard to trust. It was like a club you belonged to, almost a freemasonry.

"Yeats can have his fuckin' castle and Joyce his tower," he said to me, "I'm happy in McDaids. We don't talk crap about literature here. We talk about who's goin' to buy the next fuckin' pint."

He liked to boast (or rather confess) that he had a sense of humour that would cause him to burst out laughing at a funeral, provided it wasn't his own. Actually he could nearly have managed the latter feat as well. Maybe this isn't surprising considering he had his first taste of Guinness at the funerals Granny English took him to. She had a lot to answer for, because Brendan was drunk on life long before alcohol passed his tender lips. If it never did, who knows? He might never have missed it. The irony was that it took away his love of life more than it contributed to it and finally even took away his life itself. The miracle was that he didn't go sooner. But then he was made of sterner stuff than most mortals.

Nobody will ever fully know why he drank so much. Was it, as he said himself, because he simply liked the bloody stuff, or did he need it for the Dutch courage to get up to his antics? Or was it a physiological dependency, or a habit that went back to his early childhood, or a social activity that went out of control due to his increased fame and fortune, or a lifestyle imposed on him by his craic-hungry disciples? Or did he repair to the ale-house simply to ease the pain of staring at a blank page?

Maybe it was any one of these reasons, or a little of all of them. Whatever it was, it started as an activity he practised innocently, but by the end of his life he was drinking whenever, wherever, whatever and with whomever he liked. Or, worse again, he drank alone. Dominic described him as a gentle bully, incoherent in sobriety and only loquacious on the dangerous side of a bar counter.

As was the case with Dylan Thomas, he seemed to over-drink in order to deliberately get himself out of control. Paul Ferris, in his biography of Thomas, writes:

"Perhaps (Thomas) drank from the start for the pleasure of being rescued afterwards. It is said that some rebellious adolescents reveal their true motives by their habit of being incontinent when drunk: they behave like babies so they call to be looked after. Thomas in his cups certainly wet and soiled himself more than once. In one instance, when he was 23, an older woman who mothered him had to clean him up after a drinking bout that ended in collapse."

Like Thomas, Brendan too was spoiled as a child, and there's an argument to be made for the fact that he remained one all his life. Beatrice was also cast very much in the mould of Caitlin Thomas – the 'little lady' back home who held the fort while the Other Half gallivanted, disgraced himself, blew money . . . and then ran home contrite and remorseful.

Brendan was a sheep in wolf's clothing, an occasionally violent and obnoxious man, but beneath all the bluster and braggadocio a terminally sensitive and vulnerable sensibility that was more sinned against than sinning. Like many alcoholics, he used the booze as a crutch for an insecure personality, such insecurity turning into its opposite when the drink worked its perverse magic on him. Most of the kind acts he performed in his life (and even the entertaining ones) he did while sober. Neither was it a case of *in vino veritas*. Alcohol released a raging bull inside him, but that bull wasn't his essence: it was a role he played like any theatrical creation, a role that eventually meshed into his real identity until even he couldn't see the difference. The man became the image.

His alcoholism was part genetic, part circumstantial and probably partly due to his diabetes. Whatever, his behaviour over the 40 years he was on the planet would seem to copperfasten the clichéd image of an Irishman as "a mechanism for converting Guinness into urine".

He was a man of the people drowning his gaieties as well as his sorrows in alcohol, his life one long and winding pubcrawl punctuated – intermittently – by creative endeavours.

It's all too easy to see him as a pathetic figure, but he wasn't – at least not in the early years. The drink hadn't quite blunted his writing then, or made his friends make themselves scarce when they saw him coming. Even then, however, he had a kind of shop-soiled grandeur that could melt all but the hardest heart – especially when he broke into song, which was most of the time.

He was, in any case, a man who was both made and unmade by alcohol, and though the last few years of his life make grim reading as a result of the terrible toll the drink took on him, we shouldn't forget that he could be fiercely funny under the influence. If only he knew when to stop, or to tell the difference between those drinking friends of his who were interested in his welfare and those who used him both for free beer and somewhat less than salubrious entertainment. His failure to make that distinction meant that for the last few years of his life he was like a haemophiliac in a razor factory.

"He was always more interesting without drink," Beatrice claimed, saying she once saw him entertain Tennessee Williams for an hour in New York on soda water. Seamus Kelly echoed that when he said that some of the best parties he was at with Brendan were when he was sober. Most of his best work was done when he was stone sober as well. "I never gargle on the job," he insisted. "Water is the formula for writing."

It's probably fair to say that Brendan was baited to over-drink, just as he was baited into violent acts, by voyeurs and hangers-on. But at a certain stage of his life, he needed little encouragement, his own iden-tity of Brendan Behan all but buried under that of *Brendan Behan*. His friend Max Sylvester said, "I could always stop Brendan drinking by walking out on him. He required an audience."

Unfortunately, this wasn't always an option. Dermot Healy has a saying that for every exhibitionist there's a voyeur and that certainly was true in Brendan's case. Most times he wanted to perform there was an audience at hand. And if there wasn't, it didn't take him long to whip one up. I don't think Brendan could have developed his talent as he did in any city but Dublin. In fact it might have been built with him in mind. I've always thought of it as the oral capital of the universe: it's language preserved in aspic.

Dublin is also a place that's produced three Nobel Prize-winners for literature. I don't know of any city of a comparable size anywhere in the world with that distinction. Not only that, but just think about the fact that Brendan, James Joyce and Sean O'Casey came from within 50 yards of one another. Brendan was from Russell Street, O'Casey from the North Circular Road and Joyce lived in Fitzgibbon Street for a time. It's an astonishing thought. Having said that, however, it's also important to add that Dublin is probably the worst city in the world in which to fight alcoholism, particularly if you're a writer.

Ben Kiely told a friend he was on holiday one time and in a walk between O'Connell Bridge and The White Horse Bar, which is a distance of less than 75 yards, no less than 14 people invited him to have a drink. In Brendan's case, you could probably have quadrupled that figure. So what chance had he to stay on the wagon even if he had the kind of willpower he so sorely lacked?

There were too many after-hours haunts – and a kind of gung-ho attitude to excessive drinking that fed into Brendan's adolescent ideas of what exactly constituted macho conduct. A man was more a man with a pint in his hand than a pen, and sometimes it was as if he used the one to almost apologise for the other. Hugh Leonard claims Brendan hid his erudition as if it were something to be ashamed of. Whether this is true or not, he certainly wore his learning softly.

The headlines of newspapers from the late fifties to his death tell his story in microcosm, if one was looking for a porthole into how he spent his days and his money. Most of the money went to publicans, but not a little to wigged men behind benches as well.

Here's a brief sample of such headlines: "Behan Arrested In Toronto" (1961). "Behan Battled, Bailed Out, Bounced" (1961). "Behan Guilty, Fined $200" (1961). "Behan Injury Caused By Fall" (1962). "Behan's Binge Lands Him In Jail Bail, $500" (1961). "Brendan Behan Fined 40s. For Being Disorderly" (1959). "Behan Fined £30 On Assault Charges" (1961). "Behan Hospitalised" (1961). "Behan Injured" (1963). "Warrant Out For Behan" (1961). "Writer fined £2 on Drunk Charge" (1959). "The Quare Fella says 'I Was Drunk'" (1956). "'Drunk? Sure I'd Had A Bottle' Says The Quare TV Man" (1956). "I'm the Fella Who Interrupts" (1961).

A lot of these experiences, I'll wager, came out of anger at himself. Because he knew he wasn't doing the kind of writing he should have been doing. Writers will use any excuse to avoid writing when they don't feel disposed to it, and Brendan was no exception in this regard. Instead of sitting at his desk and gazing at a blank page, it was easier to go to a pub and punch up the proprietor if he was refused service – or even if he wasn't. This was his way of putting a stain on the silence, to use an expression of Sam Beckett's.

By this stage of his life his notoriety status continued to advance. He occasionally tinkered round with *Richard's Cork Leg*, but he was aware that its episodic nature warred against its chances of embellishing the Behan legend in any marked degree. It must have been tortuous for him to try and get the words out of his characters and onto the page considering his own character, by now, had superseded any he could conceivably create in a play.

It was veritably impossible for him to avoid the trap of one spilling over onto the other. Maybe an actor could have managed it, or a musician, because these careers are carried out in public anyway, but a writer needs his privacy to work, and it was a long time since Brendan had had that. Apart from his colourful pronouncements on everything from the weather to the colour of Harpo Marx's hair, his drinking sprees made him fair game for any cub journalist short of a filler.

Even more significantly, when he wasn't drinking, that fact merited a mention, as in his interview with *The San Diego Union* which carried this headline: "Irish Playwright Avoids Gargle: Brendan Behan Captivates Tijuana Gathering". And there were frequent magazine articles emphasising similar patterns, one from John Wain as far back as 1959 in *The New York Times* saying it all: "The Artist As A Young Delinquent".

The drinking also meant he went through money like it was going out of fashion, which was why Beatrice often wondered why their lifestyle didn't seem to match their income. Nobody will ever know how much Brendan spent either on himself or others. There was no better man to buy a round.

This again, of course, is in the Irish culture. I remember when I was writing *Mother Of All The Behans* with Ma, she'd get bored in the house every now and then and suggest we go to the pub. No sooner would we be in the door than she'd say to all and sundry, "This is my son home from England: he'll buy you all a drink." I had to pull her aside more than once and stop her at that lark. Considering the capacity of the average Irish drinker, I'd have been bankrupt in no time. There's this perennial perception among Irish people that when anybody emigrates and then comes home, they're going to be loaded. In Brendan's case, needless to say, that was more true than in my own, but even when he had the money, he was never too drunk to know he was being exploited for free beer. The sad thing was that after a certain amount of time, he even stopped caring about that.

In November 1959, when he was in New York, he appeared on Ed Morrow's television show *Small World*. Jackie Gleason was on the panel so the formula looked good for a ribald interchange. Brendan, however, arrived into the studio in an advanced state of drunkenness. With Malcolm Muggeridge all those years before, the drink had made him genial, but now it caused him to be belligerent. Gleason's attitude didn't help either. He seemed more content to bait this renegade Irishman than sympathise with him or seek to understand him. The pair of them

engaged in an argument about what constituted comedy but it degen-
erated into a kind of pub argument rather than a studio debate.
Brendan's eyes were half closed as he strained to make his points while
Gleason played him like a violin for the cheap laugh.

But guess who came out best? Once again Brendan was deemed to
have disgraced his country (and himself) abroad. It was a long time
since he had traded jolly banter with zealous reporters after disem-
barking from his plane at New York with Beatrice. He was on his own
now, live and unleashed, and his fuse was becoming steadily shorter.
Needless to say, after his heated outbursts, neither Gleason nor his co-
horts were exactly queuing up to sign him up for another appearance.
On the contrary, the phone lines were so jammed with complaints it
was a minor miracle he didn't shut the station down.

He was a great man for the chaser, but the chasers ended up chas-
ing him. He might have got away with one or two of these on a daily
basis even with his diabetes, but as the man said, "there's no such thing
as a small whiskey". And Brendan was never short of an excuse to up
the ante. It didn't matter if he was elated or depressed, he still needed
someone to share the emotion with. And of course like most post-colo-
nial Irishmen, he liked the idea of the forbidden fruit. Why else are
there cattle stampedes to all our bar counters at closing time every night
– even in 1998. I have, of course, been in countries where people drink
more than the Irish, but not as obviously. We like to make a song and
dance about our drinking – literally.

Brendan was the classic example of this. Ever since Granny English
dragged him into his first snug. William Faulkner said that a man
shouldn't fool with booze until he's 50 – but after that he's a fool if he
doesn't. Brendan's problem was that he started fooling with it from
such a young age that he never made a conscious decision about it.

He didn't wake up one morning and say, "I'm going to be a heavy
drinker." It was simply an activity that was an endemic part of his life
for as far back as he could remember. The fact that he didn't consciously
take it up meant that it was all that more difficult to consciously re-
nounce. Asking him to give it up, as his long-suffering doctors repeat-
edly did, was like asking him to give up food. Or maybe that's a bad
analogy considering he ate to live rather than lived to eat. One remembers his famous quotation, "When I was growing up, being drunk was
not regarded as a disgrace. To have enough to eat was regarded as an
achievement and drunkenness a victory."

Why did he drink? Well, as a character says in Elmore Leonard's
Unknown Man No. 89, "I'm an alcoholic. I got drunk yesterday and the
day before, and I thought I'd probably keep going a few more days.
Why I started drinking, I don't know. Maybe because my car needs
new shock absorbers. Or it was King Farouk's birthday. The reason
doesn't matter, does it?" Which pretty much describes it. The character

goes on to say: "I had fun drinking, I'll admit it. At least I had fun for about ten or twelve years. But once I realised I was thinking about the next drink while I still had one in front of me, once I started making up excuses to get drunk every time I went out, I was in more trouble than I realised. You know what happens after that? Drinking not to feel good but just to feel normal, to get your nerves under control." That was Brendan too. When he wasn't drinking he was like a junkie on cold turkey. Short ones didn't even bring him up after a while: they just brought him back from a minus position on the number line to zero.

The alcoholic novelist Charles Bukowski put it a different way, "If something bad happens, you drink in an attempt to forget; if something good happens you drink in order to celebrate; and if nothing happens you drink to make something happen."

Dublin's pub culture, as I say, was partly responsible for this. The Fitzwilliam Street basement The Catacombs was a place that came as close to a *demi-monde* as Dublin could provide, but Brendan visited many another. And there seemed to be always room at the inn for this Wandering Aenghus. Every second house was a safe one for our re-invented freedom fighter; all he had to do was appear and patrons would genuflect. He was famous after all, wasn't he? And that was enough for many.

I used, in England, to hear stories of his 'accidents' and hospitalisations through these years. I didn't know what game he was playing at, or how long he'd be able to continue playing it. I envied him for a while and then I felt sorry for him. It got to the stage where you never knew how sick he was. News of his problems always provided hot copy for editors. "Rumours of my death have been greatly exaggerated," he'd say upon being released (or having discharged himself) from hospital. So you sort of became immune to it all. It was just Brendan being Brendan. He seemed to be living on a different plane to the rest of us mortals, or to have the kind of liver that re-creates itself after each binge.

He was always going to be on a losing ticket trying to stay sober because his profile was quintessentially public. Wherever he went, his reputation preceded him – for good or ill. Niall Toibin remembers sitting with him in a pub one time when he was on soda water and lime and one of his cronies came over and slapped him on the back saying, "Ah, the hard Brendan – never a fucking dull moment." There was always the sense that he was buckling under to the twee brigade by jacking in the hard stuff. No matter how hard he wanted to, his pride, if not a dreadful thirst, seemed destined to drive him back onto it at the slightest provocation. He always wanted to hold his hour and have another.

On rare occasions when he went off the sauce, parasites anxious for some light relief would spike his orange juice, or whatever, and watch

the catharsis of mood take place. But it would be short-lived and usually followed by the inevitable truculence. The dramatic effect drink
had on Brendan, the speed at which it brought his spirits up and down,
was more akin to the effects of drugs than alcohol. Watching it was like
watching a junkie with a syringe. It was that intense, that instant.

Colbert Kearney describes him having his first pint after coming
out of prison, "It was like a sick man getting a blood transfusion just in
the nick of time before he died."

Other times he was smuggled into bars to do his performing seal
act whether he felt like it or not. The prevailing logic seemed to hold
that since he had projected himself onto the literary stratosphere by
being a performer rather than a card-carrying artiste therefore the world
and his wife had a right to push the philistine button whenever it saw
fit. Just to make sure Bengy would never get too big for his boots, or
forget where he came from. Not that there was any danger of that. But
just as he gave up writing poetry when he became famous, and started,
God preserve us, to even dress respectably, there was a hard core of
foul-weather friends who seemed to have a vested interest in seeing
him reduced to their own diurnal level. One of these was the man who
smuggled the bottle of brandy that probably killed him into Meath
Hospital in March 1964.

Brian Fallon, of *The Irish Times*, described him as a man "at odds
with his milieu and, yet unable to break away from it. A man with deep
cracks and fissures in his psyche, always torn between histrionic self-
projection and an almost paralysing shyness". If this is true, then he
evinced the schizoid qualities of many alcoholics exploiting the cathar-
tic properties of the booze while being exploited by its kamikaze un-
dertones. No doubt diabetes accelerated his premature demise, but even
if it weren't for this he probably couldn't have lasted much longer anyway. And even if he had, his best work was probably behind him.

Like all alcoholics, he needed a crutch, and he found it in inventing
new reasons for why he drank, like abusive critics or the failing juices
of inspiration. Combined with such moroseness went the phenomenon
of Brendan claiming he could write the socks off all his contemporaries
when he was in his prime. Or, maybe more tellingly, recycling half-
baked IRA stories that generally owed more to his writer's imagination than hard fact. The reality was that the jig was up on his writing
just as it was on his health – and his involvement with the IRA, as he
well knew, was always tenuous and perhaps best forgotten.

He came to see me one night in London. Bounding up the stairs he
shouted. "Why must you live like an effin' monk? Come on out like a
man and have a jar." I started to get mad, but behind his bluster he
looked so unsure and anxious that I couldn't keep it up. I tried to understand him instead. I knew life was a feast or a famine for him, that
there were no grey areas. I knew he wasn't capable of entertaining the

idea that a Behan could actually have a good time house-hatching.

In the classic tradition of hard Irish drinkers, Brendan was either on the sauce or off it. None of this "I'll have one or two" business for him. No, like most card-carrying alcoholics, he took his drinking seriously. It was almost like a religion. There was no question of cutting down or compromising. You were either 'on' it or 'off' it. He didn't believe in half-measures inside the doors of a pub or outside them. Nothing succeeded like excess.

"I'm goin' to a party," he rasped. "If you want to stay in here at the fuckin' funeral that's fine by me. So what's it to be?" He looked at me as if he was going to tear my head off if I said no. He was a different man to the one who praised my union efforts all those years ago. That seriousness was gone now. He was turning into a parody of himself.

Was this what big brothers were for – leading you into temptation when you wanted to spend a night in? Suddenly, I knew how Malcolm Muggeridge must have felt that night all those years ago.

What do you do if your brother accuses you of being a stick-in-the-mud? Do you tell him what to do with himself? Do you mutter vague noises about the fact that he's killing himself with his lifestyle and that you'd prefer to stay living for a while yet, thank you very much? If I had been more courageous – and my brother's keeper – I might have done any of these things or all of them. God knows I wanted to. I wanted to say no. If I did, I might have been the one person on earth who refused to go for a pint with Brendan Behan and lived to tell the tale. But I didn't. I fell in behind him like so many did before, allowing him to lead me to the Promised Land of the pub. We were brothers after all, weren't we?

So out I went to a sea of brandy. There was nothing hugely bad in the evening, but a part of me couldn't enter into it. I felt he was giving a performance in the pub. He wasn't like the brother I grew up with. It was as if he felt he needed to be witty and insightful and all of those things. I could have been talking to a product. I didn't want this showmanship, this posey flamboyance. But I didn't have the heart to tell him. I wasn't sure if he would have been able to take it. So I just slurped my brandy and sang dumb. Once again I was the straight man for his sit-down comedy routines. Except they were already beginning to fall flat.

The conversation between us took place in fits and starts. He enquired about my life but didn't really listen to the answers. When I asked him about his own life he fobbed me off with a quip or a wave of the hand as he ordered another round. I wasn't having much fun, and neither was he, but he wouldn't admit it. He kept going to the counter for another one before I had time to finish the last but there was no point in telling him that. He was drinking fast to cover up the fact that we had nothing in common anymore. "Will you slow down for Jesus' sake," I said to him at one point, but he just laughed in my face. "You need to stop takin' yourself so seriously," he said, pushing another one on me. I drank it, and another and another, and pretty soon the room began to swim and suddenly it didn't seem to matter that we were going fast in different directions. It was like being in a warm bath with the water round your neck.

We talked more shop but now it was easier because the drink was doing the work for us, making the most inane drivel we could dredge up sound interesting. He started repeating things he had said to journalists as if they were spontaneous and I pretended not to notice, or care. Then he started quoting snatches from his books. As I sat listening to him, for the first time I got the sensation that he had more of his career behind him than to come.

I watched his eyes becoming glazed over. He was looking at me and not looking at me. I tried to get close to him every now and again with a personal question but there was no way through that brick wall he had erected between us. He was playing 'The Writer Who Made It' and I was supposed to be the goggly-eyed kid brother kissing the hem of his garment. But already I saw the diminishing returns setting in.

"Is being famous all it's cracked up to be?" I asked him. For a second the defences came down and his brow furrowed. But then he let out a big guffaw. "It's the most brilliant fuckin' thing in the world until you get fed up of it," he said, "and then it's the most fuckin' boring thing in the world." He looked round him to see if anybody was listening to him but they were all too busy in their own corners.

It wasn't like Ireland where your conversation became everybody's conversation, where all the drinkers were wrapped into one celebratory ball and there was no such thing as a private snug. If it had been an Irish pub I think he would have ended up crawling across the floor doing imitations of The Old Woman of Beare with a shawl round his head, or breaking into song. He was more reticent here, more unsure of himself, which surprised me. Was he changing from the man who had made such inglorious exhibitions of himself so often in the past? It was a while now since he had had a hit play here. Was he already becoming yesterday's man?

Everytime he went up to the bar I quaked a little more in my boots. I've always been wary of free drink. From my experience of people who buy it for me, their manners rarely live up to their generosity. They think buying you a skinful gives them a licence to insult you. Or, even worse, bore you. Which was another reason I told him to slow down. But every time I opened my mouth he told me to shut up. "Who the fuck is talkin' about money?" he said. "I'm loaded." And to prove the point he pulled a wad of notes from his pocket that would choke a horse.

During one silence he gave me a hard look and asked me why he wasn't in the writer's group going to Moscow. I knew this was a sore point with him so I pretended to know nothing about it. In actual fact the delegation had been handpicked by the Irish Committee of the Communist Party, whose members were terrified of an eccentric anarchist like Brendan ranting and raving on the Moscow streets. It cut him to the quick that lesser writers were going and not him. He hated the fact that political people thought him unstable and dangerous. I told him I thought he would have made a great ambassador to Russia and China but there was nothing I could do about it. Inside myself, though, I felt ashamed. Here I was on the Executive Committee of the Party, allowing them to treat my brother like shit.

I started talking about nationalism to change the subject. I told Brendan I thought he was in a time warp. "Religious nationalism," I said, "is a nightmarish net from which I'm trying to escape." "Are you accusing me of that?" he said, jumping up. "Joyce said you had to be a nationalist before you could be an internationalist. I'm afraid you're turning into a West Brit, you fuckin' turncoat!"

Heads started to turn as he raised his voice and a man at the counter told him to keep it down. "Go fuck yourself," Brendan said to him, "I'm sure no one else would." It looked as if they were squaring up for a fight, but nothing happened. Brendan would have been on for a dust-up, but I pleaded with him to cool it, telling him I was known here. "Let's get off the political stuff," I said, "it's not doing either of us any good." He seemed to accept this, or maybe it was just that he was getting groggy with the drink.

I asked him about a recent trip he had taken to Paris but he wouldn't say much about it. I had heard he was running guns aboard a Dutch ship but he remained tightlipped on the topic. All he told me was that he had seen Beckett over there and that he had stayed in a spare room in the Shakespeare bookshop on the Left Bank. Apparently they kept it for writers. "A most civilised custom," he said.

When we got onto Beckett himself, he didn't hold back. He said he admired him as a man, but hated the type of literature he peddled. For Brendan, it was just rambling nonsense adored by those members of the middle class who had no church, chapel or meeting-house. People who had found a new religion for themselves in the theatre.

"Did he say anything to you about your drinking?" I asked. "He did," he replied, "and I said, 'Physician, heal thyself'."

He said he also gave out yards to him for refusing to make love to Joyce's daughter Lucia when she threw herself at him. For Brendan, the refusal to love another human being was a rejection of life itself. There was no way he would have looked that particular gift horse in the mouth. When I asked him what Beckett's reaction to this was, he said Beckett told him he thought *Finnegan's Wake* was actually responsible for Lucia's condition. "Never mind the author, the fuckin' book poxed her!" he said merrily.

We sat in silence and I watched him sinking lower and lower into his seat as the brandy took its toll. "Has success ever gone to your head, Brendan?" I asked him, a daft question that got the answer it deserved. "How could it," he said, "when every second poxbottle is out to do me down." It was a moot point.

As he said that, an old man in a boilersuit poked his head round a pillar. "What are you lookin' at, head?" Brendan said to him. "You're Brendan Behan, aren't you?" the old man asked. "So they tell me," Brendan said, his face cracking into that wide smile that went right along the jawline. The old man didn't know what to say. Maybe he was surprised the so-called wild writer was so accessible. "I saw one of your plays once," he said. "Good man," Brendan replied, "I hope you paid to get in."

The pair of them stood looking at one another and Brendan offered to buy him a pint. At that, two other faces materialised. They must have been Irish, I thought, having a nose for the freebie.

A few minutes later they were all deep in chat. The old man was a brickie from Rathdowney, the other two related to him by marriage. One of them spoke with a cockney accent. Brendan started to talk about the de Courcey Square incident, which I didn't think was a good idea. I tried to kick him under the table to stop but he was either too drunk or too indifferent to notice. He was twice as animated talking to these strangers as he was to me. It wasn't that I was jealous, I had seen the pattern too many times before for that. Anywhere there was an audience to be found, he wanted to be the chief player.

"Didn't you used to be a house-painter once?" the cockney said to him. "That's right, me oul' flower," Brendan replied, "me and Hitler." It was the way he always answered when someone put that to him. "Then the pair of us turned into writers." He took another swig of his pint and then added, "The only difference is, *Mein Kampf* never ran on the West End like *The Hostage* did." That brought a laugh from the three men, but I don't think they knew what they were laughing at.

He bought them another round of drinks and they all started singing together. For some reason, I couldn't work up the enthusiasm to join in. "You're great fuckin' fun altogether tonight," Brendan said to me, "a real fuckin' barrel of laughs." I told him not to mind me, that I wasn't in the party mood. "Maybe you'd prefer to go back to the monastery for vespers," he said. At times like that you didn't know whether to laugh or hit him.

I can't rightly remember the rest of the night. He did a bit more crowing about his plays and the men were more than happy to indulge him as long as he was funding their sups. They were all putting it away like snuff at a wake, their laughter shrieking across the table in a haze of smoke. Brendan did his best to bring me in on the conversation, building up my trade union activities for them, but nobody was really interested, least of all myself. I just wanted to get back to my flat.

"What'll you do when you stop writin'?" one of the men asked him at closing time. "Go back to the paintin', is it?" Brendan laughed so hard at this that he nearly fell over.

We were starting to get some dirty looks from the barman by this stage so I suggested we go. He tried to sing an old ballad, *Bold Robert Emmet* I think it was, but I managed to coax him towards the door before he got into it. He gave bearhugs to the three cronies and scribbled a phone number on the back of an old theatre ticket for them as if they were his long-lost brothers. Meanwhile his real brother stood idly by, wondering how he was going to get this noisy mountain of a man up the road without any more distractions.

"We'll have another one, I think," he said, hardly able to speak now. "A bird never flew on one wing."

"No," I said, "nor on 21 either. You've had enough, Brendan."

"Enough my arse. I'm just warmin' up." He looked at the three men, swaying on his feet. "Listen china," he said to the cockney, "would you like to try somewhere else? I think there's a club up the road." I shook my head at the three of them behind Brendan's back and they got the signal.

The cockney put his arm round him and told him he had to go. "You're a gentleman," he said, "but enough is as good as a feast. The next time we meet you'll have a few on us."

"I will, to be sure," Brendan said, falling onto him, "and a few more again on top of that."

He gave them a military salute as they went off, then slumped back down onto his seat. Trying to get him out of it was like trying to lift an elephant. "I'm tired," he kept saying, "for fuck's sake, can't you let a man kip when he wants to?" As I bundled him to the door, suddenly I knew what it must have been like for Beatrice all those murderous nights that began so auspiciously.

When we got outside he stood against a lamp-post, rocking on the balls of his feet as he tried to light a cigarette, but every time he lit a match the wind blew it out. After a few failed attempts he cursed furiously. Then he threw the whole box into the drain. With an unlit wet butt in his mouth he started to sing, cracking on the high notes. A few people gathered, but nobody seemed to know who he was so they just shrugged their shoulders and walked on.

"Come on Brendan," I said, "I'm freezing my arse off here. Let's go home." His eyes were half closed and he strained to open them. "Home?" he said raucously. "What the fuck do you mean home? Do you call this fuckin' pagan country home now? Have they adopted you entirely?"

I started to walk away and he came after me. I looked over my shoulder just in time to see him tripping on a crack in the pavement. This also occasioned some delicious language. When I picked him up I looked into his eyes but there was nobody home. The funny thing was that I felt stone cold sober myself, and yet I had matched him drink for drink in the pub. Was it true what people said, I wondered, that he didn't have his old capacity anymore because of the diabetes?

"You're in an awful fuckin' hurry," he said as we tottered up the road together, "have you a mot there or what?" "I'm afraid it's the *leaba* for me as soon as I get in the door," I told him. "Be a fuckin' man for Jaysus sake," he said, hoisting up his trousers, which were precariously held up with a piece of rope.

As long as we were in the pub he kept up some semblance of vivacity – probably because there were others there – but as soon as we got back to my flat he conked out on the sofa and started snoring like a pig. After a few minutes I put a blanket over him and went to bed. But I couldn't sleep thinking of what he was turning into.

The next morning he accompanied me to the Labour Exchange, one I shared with John Major. He started roaring about the place being a temple to British imperialism, devoted to the exploitation of the working class. "Blood," he declared, "will flow when labour rises from her knees and declares the broad earth as its own." I didn't know where to look. "This isn't the time or the place, Brendan," I pleaded. But he wouldn't shut up.

We walked outside to Cold Harbour Lane and I looked him straight in the eye. I said to him, "I have to live with these people, Brendan. Could you not go a bit easier on them?" He laughed in my face, not able to think beyond the moment. The next day I feared the manager's wrath as I walked in the door of the Exchange. Instead of that, though, he greeted me with a big smile. "How wonderful it was to see the famous Brendun Beehun in here," he said. Which only goes to prove, if proof were needed, that many people regarded being insulted by Brendan as something to be appreciated rather than regretted.

I don't think Brendan was an alcoholic in the strict sense of the term. You'd be a madman if you didn't agree he was addicted to drink, but what he loved most of all was the atmosphere of pubs. He didn't stash booze away in secret hiding-places at home, or indeed evince much regard for drinking at home, period. He was a great man for the early houses and the late houses or any after-hours haunt, but this was always when other people were present, which leads you to feel it was the company he craved as much as the drink.

J P Donleavy remembers him filling a glass one time with stout, and then drinking a bit out of it to make way for a concoction of port, gin and sherry. . .and then topping it off with poteen. He drank it down almost in one gulp and then keeled over onto the floor like a felled tree, remaining there in an unconscious state until somebody picked him up. That was probably one of his quieter nights.

Sean O'Casey wrote to Dominic asking if there was anything he could do to halt Brendan's decline. "Ireland isn't so well provided," he said, "that we can let our talented destroy themselves as if genius belonged to them alone?" But Dominic could do no more than the rest of us. How can you stop a rocket after it's been launched? All you can do is seek shelter from the fall-out.

My own drinking habits have been markedly different to Brendan's. In fact both he and Dá, as a result of their drunken shenanigans, almost put me off the stuff for life. Brendan, like Humphrey Bogart, believed that the world was three drinks behind him, and perhaps it was, but his excessive intake was hardly the thing to redress the balance.

The point is that Brendan never needed alcohol as much as he thought he did. He was born drunk and he spent the next 40 years drinking himself sober. Now I'm not a pioneer or anything, as you probably know, but neither am I the type of man who thinks it's macho to guzzle eighteen pints of an evening and then go home and beat the wife up.

I'm not saying that description defines Brendan, but the sad fact is that nobody could halt his decline into self-parody in the last four years of his life when he became a hostage to fame. Maybe his main problem was that he didn't leave Ireland forever, like so many of our other writers. He told me many times that he wanted to live in America. He often said that America respected artists but Dublin didn't, and I think he was right in that. But Beatrice kept dragging him back to Ireland. It was her home, after all, and the place she wanted to raise her children, if children came.

And of course a child did come, but the timing couldn't have been worse. When Beatrice became pregnant, Brendan was a loose cannon.

He was living the good life in America, drinking and bed-hopping as if there was no tomorrow. America was like a dream factory to him, and Ireland the country where he had to confront his dementia, and of course Beatrice, the crutch of reality he both loved and hated. Loved because she pulled him out of so many pickles, and of course because she loved him, but hated because she reminded him of the now almost unbearable fact that he was on a one-way trip to Glasnevin cemetery unless he did something to curb his wicked, wicked ways.

He actually decided he was going to leave her at one point. He was gallivanting in America and she was back home in Ireland, pregnant as well as everything else. She travelled over to the States on a pleading mission, confronting Brendan head-on for probably the first time in her life. "You're coming home to Dublin to witness the birth of our child," she told him. Brendan said that wasn't possible. He told her he had another woman now, a woman who was also pregnant by him. This was like another arrow in Beatrice's heart. Then he added cruelly,

"She's younger than you are too." Beatrice exploded at this. "Has this other woman suffered the seas of sorrow I have?" she asked. "Has she spent year in, year out with a drunk? A man who gets into such fits from drink that he isn't even sure who he is?"

Beatrice told Brendan he must have been living in cloud cuckoo land if he really believed any other woman would put up with him for any length of time. Everything would be rosy in the short-term, she said, but it would burn itself out when he got back to his old ways. "You're to stand by your lawful wedded wife," she admonished, "and not your flesh wife" – which was how she referred to his mistress. She added, "I picked you up countless times when nobody else wanted to know. Would you walk out on me now with our first child on the way?" So Brendan went back with her. Home, as it transpired, to die.

"It's all over between Beatrice and me," he told me, shaking like a reed in the wind as he said the dramatic words. But he still went back to Ireland with her – and paid the price, both in terms of his life and art. It bent his nib when he took the coward's way out. Once he stepped on that aeroplane, his fate was sealed.

America was so suitable to Brendan it could have been created with him in mind. It had the love of the big occasion, to be sure, but it was also somewhere he could get lost if he so wished. Dublin ("the largest village in Europe" by his own estimation) never afforded him that luxury – nor indeed did the rest of Ireland. Which isn't to say that this most public of men wanted to retire into his study like other more rarefied scribes, but there's a culture of familiarity in Ireland that can become devastatingly intrusive to somebody like Brendan, who threw himself around a lot. Such a culture can, and usually does, eventually breed contempt. Joyce talked about Dublin paralysing his talent. With Brendan it was more claustrophobia of the spirit. Nobody enjoyed the pub scenes more than he did, but there came a time when the backslapping began to grate.

There's a very thin line between reverence and respect: he only wanted the latter, but that even disappeared when his image became besmirched in Citizen Sean's eyes. When that happened, the dogs in the street seemed to want to crush him, or at least stop him flourishing. The Irish love to see you fall, and the higher you've been before the fall, the more they enjoy it. This isn't to carp, merely a statement of fact. I love my fellow countrymen but I doubt I could have lived my life in Ireland and survived. Like the Mafia, we like to kill our own – from Michael Collins onwards and after we kill them, we then specialise in exhuming their corpses. Look at what happened to Veronica Guerin, a woman who died for her job. We only had to wait two years and a bit before the long knives came out. If this can happen to a latter-day martyr like Guerin, it's hardly surprising it happened with Brendan, who found enemies like a fly finds flypaper.

The higher a monkey goes up a tree, the more of his arse he shows. Brendan knew that. He realised he was a target, and that the stakes were going to get higher the longer he lived. He often told me that he would have loved a year off from his life, a year in which he could disappear and not be known anywhere he went. A year in any country in the world – not necessarily America – where he could just vegetate. If he could do that, he said, the pressure to be Brendan Behan the writer would be totally off his shoulders. Instead he could just be Brendan Behan, private individual, the boy I had grown up with, who was still there if you scratched him hard enough. Who was desperately trying to live with the image of him that was being pedalled by unscrupulous journalists. "A special place in hell is reserved for that breed," he said to me.

"America," Brendan told Beatrice, "was a place where people took you as they found you, not how they wanted you to be." Dublin, in contrast, was a city of "familiarity without friendship, loneliness without solitude".

It may be hard to imagine Brendan ever being lonely, but he was. As I've argued all through this book, his pub antics were usually a compensation for this, as were his appearances on television where he was as drunk as a monkey's uncle. Confident people don't usually need this kind of injection. Mary Manning put it well, "Underneath the bluster, the show-off, the singing and the aimless violence was a shy, shrinking young man with a tolerably strong inferiority complex. Drunk he was the roaring broth of a boy, but sober he was withdrawn. Uncouth, ungainly, with no education except what he picked up for himself, he was gradually forced into the role of buffoon or court jester: he who must sing for his supper."

After he became famous, of course, he could have had as many suppers as he wanted without singing, but he continued that particular activity anyway, especially when he was jarred. And of course the fact that he had money in his pocket made the binges longer. The theatrical director Alan Simpson said much of his problem was the fact that he had the wherewithal to pay for his indulgences with this money. Simpson claimed Brendan was really an author in a housepainter's body. His blue-collar philosophy dictated that he set aside a certain amount of money for drink each week on his painter's salary, but when he was receiving huge advances for his writing, that *modus operandi* no longer applied. Or at least it shouldn't have. Most alcoholics from working class backgrounds develop financial problems with drink at some stage of their lives, but all too often Brendan had a bottomless pocket in this regard, which meant he drank till he fell.

The money was too much of a temptation to someone who had been so long without it and one drink borrowed another. Editors would have had to handcuff him to his typewriter to stop the inevitable foray to the local gin-mill for the stimulation he thought he needed to fire his imagination; if only he had realised the drink was having the opposite effect.

In his last years, giving him an advance to write a book was really just giving him a way to avoid writing a book, because he couldn't resist spending the money on all the wrong things. Publishers weren't to know this, of course, or maybe they didn't care. By now they knew that the name 'Brendan Behan' on a dust jacket sold books, regardless of what was between the covers.

In 1987 I took part in the Four Oaks documentary on Brendan by Alan Miller entitled *A Hungry Feeling*. This has some of the best live footage ever shot of Brendan and also some graphic insights into his fall from grace. With contributions from myself, Beatrice, Rory, Ulick O'Connor and many others, it remains a classic insight into a man who became imprisoned inside the aura he created around himself until it eventually became an albatross that strangled him.

It captures the highs and the lows, the play openings and the arrests, Brendan in high good humour in the pubs and in cantankerous mood with the likes of Jackie Gleason and Ed Murrow. It has him as a skinny young IRA lad who couldn't wait to try and blow up a British ship for his country, and then a broken old man struggling to say a few words to an interviewer about capital punishment shortly before he died. For good or ill, it remains the most vivid visual testament we have to a man who, as Rae Jeffs puts it in one of the interviews, could never really communicate with anyone unless he was rightly sozzled. Carolyn Swift says at one stage that he wasn't wildly original, his main gift being the ability to put down on paper all the gems of wisdom that other Dubbalin men like himself spent their time tossing across bar counters day in day out.

Dominic felt he was too good for *A Hungry Feeling*. He refused to come to Ireland for it, insisting the makers meet him instead in a hotel in London. Here he told them he was famous long before Brendan. He also asked for a fat fee to talk to them in any detail.

The documentary was made in McDaids, where many ructions ensued. The pub was taken over from ten in the morning to midnight. The regulars were kicked out and anyone in any way involved with the film given as much free gargle as they could keep down. Beatrice had a problem with Ulick O'Connor being in it on account of the allegations he made in his biography that Brendan was gay. He was asked to leave the pub by Alan Miller, whereupon he told Miller to fuck off. Miller was ready to put up his fists at this stage, fancying his chances – though Ulick would probably have decked him, being an ex-welterweight champion (and a man who felled no less than the bold Brendan himself on the one occasion they met, after Brendan insulted him). A bloody scene was finally averted by the intervention of Rory as peacemaker, but there were a few dodgy moments during the filming nevertheless.

The makers of the documentary didn't know what they were letting themselves in for, turning a wild family loose in a pub and expecting them to behave like choirboys. At times it more resembled an unused out-take from *The Quiet Man*. In the end, Ulick's contribution to the film was edited severely under Beatrice's instructions. (She threatened to pull out of it altogether if he got centre stage.) It was a bit like the old family feud going on into the next generation, I wonder what Brendan would have made of it. One thing is sure: the idea of making a film based in a pub during real drinking hours would have been enough to get him interested regardless of the tensions (though it would be anybody's guess whether he would have finished his contribution in a vertical position).

I've already talked about my feelings on Brendan's homosexuality, and in view of that you may regard Beatrice's reaction to Ulick as being over-the-top, but you must remember Ulick's book came out in 1970. It was quite a different thing to label somebody as gay in those days, when it was considered to be slanderous, in comparison to today when it would almost add to the mystique of somebody like Brendan. Brendan has often been compared to Oscar Wilde, a man who was persecuted for his sexual peccadilloes. If Wilde were alive today, he'd be thought of in the same way as Stephen Fry. It would be a case of "So what? The guy either has talent or he hasn't." A piece of graffiti I saw recently says it all: "Thirty years ago, homosexuality was condemned. Twenty years ago it was frowned upon. Ten years ago it was disapproved of. Today it's encouraged. I'm getting out before it becomes bloody compulsory."

Rae Jeffs makes an interesting observation in the film. She says that Brendan needed people to stimulate him like an electric charge. He didn't really like himself, she alleged, but hid that fact both from himself and everyone else by always being in company. But you couldn't write books in a pub, so something had to give.

Towards the end of the film, Beatrice talks about the flipside of the years of fame – the threatening phone calls she got in America from Irish-Americans telling her to go back to Dublin and take her "drunken bum" husband with her. She also talks about Brendan hearing himself singing on the radio towards the end and saying pathetically, "Was that me?" as if he couldn't believe he was once able to hit those notes. And she has him comparing himself to other writers who drank themselves to death.

"Scott Fitzgerald was able to write until the day he died," he said to Rae, "what's wrong with me?" The overall picture that emerges is of a man increasingly bewildered by what was happening to him, a man who had refused to listen to the signals of his body for too many years,

a living ghost visiting past haunts in search of succour but not receiving any. We watched the city that gave him birth largely disowning
him as the whole cavalcade collapsed round his ears. Fame distracted
him from his work in almost the same way drink did, Rae Jeffs tells us,
and he handled both equally badly. He made a brief stab at climbing
back on the writing wagon with the tape-recorded books, but he was
far too professional a writer not to know that this wasn't the way to go,
which probably explains why he never got around to editing them, as
he had promised to do.

Beatrice was the comfort zone he always returned to in times of
trouble, but in another sense maybe she would have been better advised to take a harder line with him on the drink when there was still a
chance he could mend his ways. She often said that she understood he
needed up to a dozen pints and a few chasers to slake his thirst, considering his background and constitution. When stricter groundrules were
laid down in later years, he was too addicted to the stuff to even hear
her advice, never mind listen to it.

Brendan felt an operation to stop him drinking would affect his
brain. He always had a terror of going mad. That's why he put an ultimatum to Beatrice. "If you force me into one of those places," he told
her, "I promise you I'll drink myself to death as soon as I get out." This
was the kind of emotional bribery he rained down on her.

"I don't want to come out of hospital like a thick," he said to me.
"That's what operations like that do to you."

"What's the difference?" I said to him, "you're acting like one anyway." I thought he was going to hit me, but instead he just went quiet.
"The difference," he said, "is that this way it's my fuckin' choice."

Beatrice rowed in behind him on this one, surprisingly enough. "I
had no right to commit him," she said, "especially since he had been
locked up so much before. He still had a horror of confinement."

He wouldn't entertain the idea of being interviewed by a psychia-
trist at all. "Anyone who goes to one of that shower needs his head
examined," he quipped, but he was really just whistling in the graveyard.

He knew what had happened to his hero Hemingway: another
would-be macho man laid low when excessive drinking caused him to
be admitted to an institution. Hemingway had had electric shock treatment and never quite recovered. Not only did it fail to alleviate his
depression, but it interfered with his memory too. And memory is one
of a writer's prime tools.

Like 'Hem', Brendan wanted to die with his boots on. Being hospitalised would also remind him too much of his borstal past. With one
difference: in hospital you weren't given a direct 'sentence'. You didn't
know when, if ever, it would end. So Beatrice was very slow to play
this card.

She could have confronted him and precipitated a permanent walk-out on his part, or take him as she found him. She pursued the latter course right to the end, both from love and loyalty – and, I suppose, common sense. Because nobody could change Brendan's mind when he had it made up. The other possibility was for her to leave him, but she couldn't bring herself to do that. "If he got back the success he had in his early years, I might have thought about it," she said, "but you don't kick a man when he's down."

By now he was waking up in the mornings feeling as if he'd been out the night before even when he hadn't. In 1962, a doctor had told him he'd be dead in two years if he kept up the way he was going, so he knew pretty much what was happening. The prediction was right on schedule.

Norman Mailer, who was almost as adrenalised as Brendan, said, "He was like a steam engine, bang bang bang in your ear. He had a need near the end to speak to someone. He wanted to reach you, as if he knew he was going to die. He also brought out stinginess in you – you didn't want to involve yourself. I have a theory that when a person is dying and he can have a conversation with you, he won't die. Behan knew he had his death inside him. He knew that he was ill, but his pride was almost unbearable."

When Mailer was being interviewed by Eugene Kennedy in 1984 about an Irish-American character he put into his novel *Tough Guys Don't Dance*, he exemplified certain traits of Irishmen he had met which must put us in mind of Brendan. "A prime characteristic of Irishmen is loyalty," he said, "they are truly loyal to the point where they could be killed because of it. It is a death loyalty. These Irishmen also usually have a slightly embattled relationship with the Catholic Church. And a certain strain of hypocrisy may show up. In these you will find a kind of sexual Puritanism side-by-side with broth-of-a-boy lust."

Mailer went on to say that when he was growing up he often felt the Irish in Brooklyn were tougher than his fellow Jews. And that they possessed a mad kind of generosity. "You see it in the Irishman who only has ten dollars in his pocket," he said, "and has mouths to feed and bills to pay at home, and yet buys a round of drinks for everybody at the bar." I wonder who he was thinking about when he wrote that?

The most important thing in life, Brendan often insisted, was to remain in a state of good humour. His own humours were either great or dismal, so ecstatic he couldn't stand them (as he said himself) or low enough to be described as dark nights of the soul. So maybe the man who brought him in that famous brandy did him a favour, accelerating the inevitable. Mercy killing by another name.

There's a revisionist perspective of Brendan as someone who cutely courted fame by feigning drunkenness and going about the place in rags. This image of *negligentia diligens* conveniently ignores the fact that he died of alcoholism. If it was all a game, he played it to the last card, giving his final Oscar-winning performance in Glasnevin cemetery on 20 March 1964.

A first cousin of this revisionism is the theory that Brendan could have reached some kind of literary and psychological nirvana if he were taken away from the negative circumstances of his existence. Absolutely – but which of us could be afforded that luxury? John Jordan put it more eloquently than I can. "I have little patience," he said, "with the 'If' school of Behan criticism. If Brendan, the school says, had not been an alcoholic, if he had not been sexually bent, if he had not been a jail-bird, if he had not been a republican and so on...he would have been a great writer. A great writer of what? Indeed. The very things that warred against his longevity were the seeds of his inspiration."

Maybe it was giving up work that destroyed Brendan most of all. Even the heaviest drinkers can sweat it out of their system the next day when they have to work, but that's not the case if all you're carrying is a pen. I watched him in the house in Crumlin as he formally retired from the house-painting. He had a ceremonial burning of his brushes and whites, but Ma wasn't pleased by the spectacle. She rushed in shouting, "Waste not want not!" I agreed with her on that.

Most people's lives slow down when they get to 40, but Brendan couldn't accept that. He wanted the Behan Travelling Roadshow to go on, regardless of the consequences. He still wanted to be first into the bar and last out, regardless of how the barmen, or even the other patrons, might feel. There was always a story to be told or a song to be sung – even out of tune. Who cared about the consequences? We were only here for a short time. It was important to express yourself, to seize the day. We had but one life to live and he wanted to go at it full throttle.

In another age, his battle with the bottle could maybe have been treated, or stemmed, but he lived in an era when it wasn't kosher to admit to having a problem. Even at 40 he wanted to be the hare instead of the tortoise. His powers were dimming, but maybe The Great Irish Novel could come out of one of these nights, or the great Irish Play. And if it didn't, so what?

His liver was in bits, as was his cerebral cortex, but he was still at the helm, three wheels on his wagon, waving at people on the street who didn't want to know. He was trying to re-visit old pastures, imagining himself to be the man he was in New York when his plays were the property of the Sunday supplements. But life doesn't work like that. Things change. We grow old. Our bodies stop being able to cope with the abuses we unleash on them.

Brendan didn't understand that, or didn't want to. He acted as if things would always be the same as they had been, that he would still be able to out-drink everyone else at the bar and out-anecdote them with IRA yarns. But he was slowing down; he was starting to repeat himself. And people were noticing, people with long memories and short fuses. They weren't willing to suffer him any more, which meant he had to look farther afield for his fun.

There's nothing more pathetic than a man who has outlived his time and Brendan did that, even though he was only 41. He was an anachronism in a society that was becoming bland and sanitised. His bravado needed a new spin, but he was too spaced-out to give it that. He re-cycled the old stories, occasionally changing the details for effect, but nobody was fooled. We knew he was on his last legs, and his last reserves. He was still hungry for laughter, but that laughter wasn't forthcoming, either from himself or his company. The people who cared about him were dejected for one reason, and the people who didn't for another. Either way he was a lost cause.

His creative juices had stopped flowing, despite the better efforts of Rae Jeffs. He had started to repeat himself, the bane of the impoverished writer. It was getting harder to remember the good lines and the good times. All of which made him go for the soft option, the easy book, the quotable quote. When in doubt, lash out. So he started delivering all those post-Wildean oneliners to journalists who used and abused him for a catchy phrase, this senseless pubcrawler who provided quotable quotes when there was nothing else in the news to grab the popular, or populist, attention.

Brendan would have been content to oblige these crass journalists indefinitely, but eventually people stopped calling, deeming his quips to have passed their sell-by date. These were the hard rules of journalism. We weren't talking rehabilitation here, we were talking cannon fodder for The Great Unwashed. And when they stopped coming it was on to The Next Big Thing. For a time he had played the bowsie game, but now things were getting beyond a joke.

He couldn't hold his liquor, they said, the very people he had delighted so recently. He wasn't fit to be seen out with: he'd disgrace you in company, this two-bit playwright who had produced such a flimsy output to exaggerated acclaim. When you thought about it, what was really there? *The Hostage, The Borstal Boy, The Quare Fellow*. Books which were all semi-autobiographical, and with a distinctly limited view on life. So what was all the hullabaloo about? Was this all Ireland had to offer? It was time to call a time-out on this dangerous specimen known as Brendan Behan, who was as much a danger to the literary establishment as he was to himself. The honeymoon was over and it was only a matter of time before he himself collapsed with it. Let's hear it for the next phenomenon, because you just can't hack it any more. So die, Irish rebel, with *Richard's Cork Leg*, or whatever other white elephants you have up your sleeve.

In his last few books he was on auto-pilot, either rifling through

past works in search of inspiration or enunciating jaded witticisms into
the tape recorders hungry editors provided for him to advertise himself once again for a public that fed off his reputation like buzzards.
Like any showman worth his salt, Brendan could never stop trying to
provide what such a public would never stop clamouring for, but long
before the end the well was dry and he was merely going through the
motions.

Beatrice was at the film *Days of Wine and Roses* when the assassination of President Kennedy was announced in 1963. The film was interrupted for the tragic news bulletin. After Brendan heard the news he
went straight down to the American Embassy to sign the book of con-
dolence. Some people said he was doing this for some free publicity for
himself. I doubt it. He did it for two reasons: first because he liked and
admired Kennedy and was proud of a letter he had received from him
after his inauguration. Second, because it was an excuse for yet another binge.

Two days later, Beatrice gave birth to Blanaid. Brendan tried to act
enthusiastic, but he was on the way out now. It was his last winter, the
winter of his deepest discontent, but his fate remained an unspoken
fear.

Brendan loved children, but his own one arrived too late for him to
be a father to it. Children hung out of him everywhere he went, but
when Blanaid arrived she was no good to him. He hadn't it in him to
give the time to her he gave to other people's children in other years.
He was just going through the motions, like he was with the writing. If
she was born a few years before she was, who knows what might have
happened. He might have cut down on the gargle to be an old-fashioned daddy. We'll never know now. She could have been the making
of him.

He loved children just as he did old people. These two extremities
enabled him to escape the common generality of men who wanted to
tear the living flesh off his bones. I remember him sitting my own children on his knee when they were very young and making up stories
for them on the spot. Their favourite one concerned a travelling Scotch
mouse called Johnny McGrory. Johnny would be attacked from time-
to-time by a wicked witch of the north. As my kids sat spellbound at
his spirited delivery he would introduce a new character called Miss
Cool Wind who time and again saved the little mouse. He made up
many other stories for them and their eyes would light up with delight
as he came to the climax. At times like this I saw the best side of Brendan,
the one who needed neither drink nor hype nor adulation, who was
just a kindly uncle paying a social call: a kindly uncle would have dearly
loved kids of his own.

He wasn't at Anglesea Road now, or indeed anywhere permanent.
He drifted between houses and sometimes slept wherever he found

himself. There was even a belief round Dublin that he created storms in pubs with the express purpose of getting arrested so he'd have somewhere to sleep for the night.

The remainder of his time in bars is characterised by half-drunk pints, half-smoked cigarettes, half-told stories. In brief: a half-lived life. No longer buoyed up by the intoxicant of flattery, he retreated into the dark rooms of his pre-fame days...and the even darker room of his own mind.

Many of his old boozing friends had deserted him by now. The money had stopped flowing, as had that rapier wit. But his IRA buddies stood by him, even if he hadn't stood by them during the mad years of his literary success and theatrical openings. They had admired him for himself, not the hype, so whether he was lying at the side of the road or opening a new play, it was all the one. They might have said, as Ma often did, "God preserve us from geniuses."

They suffered his re-telling of stories they had heard perhaps a dozen times before in slightly varying form. One of his few pleasures in life now was re-hashing old 'Up the Republic' yarns.

"Guess how many bombs I planted?" he'd say, or "They'd never have taken me alive if I was armed." It reminded me of my grandfather down in the law courts in his top hat and white gloves imagining he was a High Court judge and saying, "Six months!" or "Twelve months!" or "Let him go free; he hasn't done much." It must have been something in our blood, this need to create imaginary worlds. He was like a scratchy old record, but his friends indulged him, suffering him or even goading him on. "He always loved to exaggerate," they'd say, "and what harm is there in that?" Like a man much older than his years, all he had were his memories to galvanise him into life. It was like Saki said, "The young have aspirations that never come to pass; the old have reminiscences of what never happened." And Brendan was old – make no mistake about it. But still dreaming the dreams of the sixteen-year-old borstal boy. He would play the patriot game to the last.

Eddie Whelan was his best friend now and he never went anywhere without him. Eddie came from a great republican family who lived in Benburb Street. He was famous for shooting a man in James Street, waiting until he passed under a lamp-post before popping him off. He went on trial for murder but all the witnesses vanished like snow on a hot tin roof. When push came to shove, Eddie was a great friend to Brendan, indulging his penchant for reminiscing as well as protecting him from the wrong kind of company. Paddy Kelly and Charlie Gorman were two others who performed similar functions.

Not long after Blanaid's christening, Brendan was back on the batter again. Coming up to Christmas, he was taken into hospital in a coma and given the Last Rites. Somehow he pulled through and discharged himself. On New Year's Eve, however, he was found on the road lying in a pool of his own blood and rushed to hospital. According to Ma, some of the "dirty gurriers" of Dublin had beaten him unconscious for money. He also had pneumonia. Beatrice felt the end was near but the doctors told her there was still a chance of prolonging his life if he agreed to some form of long-term treatment for his problem. Of course she knew he wouldn't. "I'm not putting myself in the hands of quacks," he insisted, as he had to me so many times before.

Personally I think Brendan preferred the idea of drinking himself to death than having to face the possible side-effects of his diabetes – liver failure, possible heart attack and amputation of the limbs and, worst of all, blindness.

He had also inherited a scepticism about the medical profession from our parents. Ma used to say, "Doctors practise on the children of the poor." Da had an even better one, "Doctors differ and patients die. Then they bury their mistakes." He also felt they were all messed up psychologically, citing the high suicide rate of the medical profession as evidence. Growing up in this environment, Brendan was never likely to put himself under the knife unless it was absolutely necessary. Even then he'd have to think about it.

Beatrice had lost almost complete control of him now. He was inclined to spend more time with Ma and Da than her, the salmon swimming upstream to die. Maybe he felt he would get nagged less in Kildare Road – or was he simply trying to remember the good old days, before it all went so horribly wrong for him?

He couldn't hold his liquor at all now – and I mean that literally. The glass would fall from his hands. He was sleeping rough, and staying away from Beatrice as much as he could. Even when he stayed overnight in Anglesea Road, he slept on the sofa instead of with her, leaving her to cry herself to sleep. He knew he was dying but he couldn't do anything about it.

Sometimes he brought people home with him and tried to act merry, but the harder he tried, the more pathetic he became. The people he drank with now were the people he knew when he was a nobody, people who couldn't have cared less if he was a Pulitzer Prize winner or the local bin-man. Those who had massaged his ego when he was the toast of London and New York had disappeared as suddenly as they had arrived. It was the old story all over again. He had gone from being a bull in a china shop to a bull in a bull-ring, but he looked as if he had had a *cornada*. He had no horns, and his feet were sinking deeper and deeper into the sand.

Around this time too he gave an interview in the street to RTÉ about an issue that had catapulted him to fame: capital punishment. It was a subject dear to his heart because he knew he could have been this soldier more than once. There but for the grace of God went he instead of Leslie. That was the only similarity to the Brendan of old, however. He looked grubby and unshaven, and had difficulty getting the words out. He was either drunk or hungover – or both. He could have been a hobo. Was it really only four years since the Eamonn Andrews interview? To look at him, it could have been fourteen.

The pretext of the interview was Caryl Chessman, who had been executed in the gas chamber in San Quentin in 1960. Like Brendan, Chessman spent much of his life behind bars. In 1941, at just twenty years of age, he was sentenced to sixteen years for robbery, assault and attempted murder. He escaped from prison in 1943 but was recaptured the next year. In 1947 – the very year after Brendan's amnesty – he was paroled but he was arrested again the following year for robbery, kidnapping and allegedly forcing women to commit sexually perverted acts. Chessman denied all the charges, conducting his own defence. But he was found guilty and sentenced to death: the norm at that time for these crimes. From 1948 until 1960 he malingered on Death Row, devoting himself to writing novels and treatises that garnered world attention. (It's not difficult to see how this would have fascinated Brendan.) His number came up in May 1960, however, and the ultimate penal sanction was finally delivered.

Brendan seemed deeply moved about the whole issue and talked about the barbarity of capital punishment. It was possible, he said, for a man to dangle at the end of a rope, still living long after he was supposed to be dead. It was an old obsession, but the difference between this interview and other ones he had conducted in the past was that it took him nearly five minutes to make a point he would once have made in as many seconds.

Watching it I was reminded of the words of Scott Fitzgerald, another unlikely depressive, "In a real dark night of the soul it is always three o'clock in the morning – all day, every day."

Listening to him was like listening to a computer somebody had short-circuited. He didn't stutter, but the words came out in fits and starts as if he was on tranquillisers. It was like watching him in slow motion, this man who used to be so good at pouncing on insights in nano-seconds. In the cold light of morning as life went on about him, he also seemed to have lost his humour. He was an old man in a young man's body, desperately trying to make sense of a world he had once loved so passionately, but which had betrayed him just as he betrayed it, burning himself out on the inglorious excesses of its harsh, malignant dawn.

He had always been fascinated by what he called *an scéal*, the story. In his letters or when he met you he would shout one out for all to hear, like one of the old bardic poets stravaging the boreens of Ireland in times past. But even that was gone now. Now that the furniture in the loft had woodworm he cut a sorry figure walking unsteadily round the backstreets of Dublin like an anachronism.

Anyone serving him a drink at this stage of his life, one commentator said, was a murderer in all but the name. And Brendan drinking one was equivalent to a hara-kiri merchant. Every year he made a pilgrimage to Gills pub in Russell Street to try and regain a past that had disappeared forever. His 1964 visit took place at the end of February and he had just one drink: a large brandy. Jimmy Burke saw him on March 9 and was shocked by the state of him. "You'll have to mind yourself, Brendan," he said, but he might as well have been talking to the cat. "Don't be lecturing me on my behaviour," Brendan snapped at him, "for the love and honour of Jaysus."

The last time Beatrice saw Brendan outside hospital was the very next night. His friend Paddy Kelly, with whom he had been drinking, became alarmed at his alternate sweats and shivers and had him driven by taxi to Anglesea Road. "Why did you bring him here, for God's sake?" she said. "Take him to hospital." She thought it was going to be just another brief stay, but the next day a doctor said to her, "Your husband has been in and out of hospital quite often, hasn't he, Mrs Behan?" "Too often," she replied. And then he said, "Well you mustn't expect to see him walking out this time."

The finality of the words hit her like a wet rag across the face. They were words she had expected to hear many other times from many other doctors, but when she didn't, she began to forget about the destructive things Brendan was doing to himself, or to blot them out. Just as Brendan was in what we call 'denial' today, Beatrice was a bit too. She had begun to be smug, to think maybe he was immortal after all. But not now.

The date was March 16, the eve of St Patrick's Day. But this was a Paddy's Day where he wouldn't be drowning the shamrock. One year he had been banned from the parade because of his wildness. This year his absence had a somewhat different cause.

Beatrice sat by his bed acting out her multiple role of nurse, wife, confidant and friend, playing out the inevitable last scene of their romance with fortitude and resignation. No priest he knew was ever in a hurry to get to the next life, and neither was he, but he had been living inside a clapped-out body for some years now and he knew that couldn't go on forever. By upping the ante in pubs, he was just bringing the date forward a bit.

Ma saw it happening and yet she couldn't believe it. In her mind's eye she had seen Brendan put up against a wall and shot a thousand and one times. Or dangling on the end of a rope. He could have stopped a bullet in Spain if she hadn't torn up that letter. He could have been picked off by a British Army sniper, or, like Collins, one of his enemies in the IRA. The slow erosion of the liver was different. It was a crucifixion for her to watch. Her darling boy with his mass of curls dwindling to nothing before her eyes. Was this justice? Was it fair? Her faith would

be tested severely in the coming days as he slipped in and out of co-
mas.

"Come on Brendan," she'd say, "rally for me." And then, when she
saw he was too far gone, "God love him, he's better out of it." She sat
by his bed with Beatrice and the rest of them, waiting for the announce-
ment that had been five years coming. A man could only push himself
so far, even a man like Brendan. But knowing that didn't make it easier
on anyone. Death could never be easy, even when it was courted.

John Ryan, who was smuggled into the ward to see him, didn't
think he looked too bad, but Ma knew better. She had seen him in all
his guises, from being fêted in the world's theatrical capitals to lying
on the roadside with blood spilling out of his mouth. She knew what
she was looking at. It didn't matter to her how famous he became, or
how infamous, to her he was always Brendan, the angel with the mop
of curls or the bold lump. Some mother's son. This mother's.

"His race is run," she said simply. No mother can have a more dev-
astating experience than to bury one of her own children, but there was
no self-pity in her voice and no drama. That wasn't the Behan way. She
had steeled herself for this moment many times in her mind and now it
had to be borne. Her Brendan was slipping away from her and no storied
urn or animated bust could call his fleeting breath back to the mansion
– or the tenement. The sting-a-ling of death was biting deep and all she
could do was witness it.

There was a tradition on our street whereby old women would shake
a baby round their heads to determine how long it would live. According to the folk wisdom, if the baby cried hard enough it would have a
long and healthy life. Well Granny English shook Brendan in that manner not long after he was born . . . and she said he never cried at all. Was
that an omen?

He died at 8.35 pm on March 20, 1964. Unlike his Welsh alter ego
Dylan Thomas, he went gently into the good night. Just this once, there
would be no Napper Tandy hangover, because there would be nobody
to have it. That big heart had taken its last, hoarse breath, and he was
gone from us. The Brendan storm was finally calmed in the only way it
ever could have been. In the way everyone expected it to be since his
first pugnacious gulp. Especially Beatrice.

"You made a big mistake in marrying me," he told her at the end,
but she didn't see it that way. She always knew what she was going
into and she accepted him warts and all. In the years following his
death, loneliness and pining for him would be far more painful than
the constant worry of whether she would get a phone call to say he was
in a hospital or prison. Such loneliness would affect others too, even
the ones who saw him but rarely in his last years, like myself.

Maybe it was good that he went when he did, because he crammed
too much into too short a space of time and his soul needed the release

of death to breathe freely again. He said to Dominic one time, with characteristic irony, "If I lived beyond 50 I'd die." So he knew it himself too, from long before when it happened. He may not have liked the dying lark, but everything about his actions had it plastered all over them.

Nature had smiled on him in looks and talent, but then played a cruel trick on him as if to compensate for being too bountiful in the first place. It was the old, old story: one drink was too many for him; a thousand not enough. James Jones, the author of *From Here to Eternity* put it pithily when he said, "Brendan was a sensitive person, perhaps too sensitive to live."

Anthony Cronin gave this memory in his book *Dead As Doornails*: "The last time that I saw him was at the counter of a bar. It was dark inside; you had to duck your head going through the door and come up two steps, so I didn't see Brendan until I was standing beside him, ordering myself a drink. He had the remnants of dried vomit still on his lapels and on his shoes. He made several attempts to say something to me, but I couldn't make out what it was. Sounds, evidently words, came out of his mouth, but they were incomprehensible. Since they were the last words Brendan Behan ever addressed to me, I would like to know what they were, but I don't. I finished my drink, said good-bye, and left."

Richard Fleischer said the last time he saw him was at a London theatre during a performance of *The Hostage*. "He was seated in a box just to the right of the stage and making a spectacle of himself. He was gloriously drunk and shouting a mixture of ribald advice and insulting criticism at the actors on the stage. The actors, being a spunky and spirited bunch, were, giving back as good as they got. It was hilarious. The audience loved it and got into the spirit of the thing, shouting abuse at both parties. Behan turned his attention to the audience, showering them with profanity. The place was in an uproar. Apparently, this was something that happened several times a week. It was one of the best nights I've ever experienced in the theatre."

Arthur Miller remembers him differently. "Brendan was on his last legs when I met him," he recalled. "He sat there, his wet hair haphazardly plastered down, his face blotched, lisping through broken teeth, laughing and eating sausages and eggs while black dancers moved in and out of the room, not knowing how to help him, or even whether to try. Brendan said with his fixed uneasy chuckle, 'I'm not really a playwright, you know, I'm a talker. I've a room upstairs where I'm talking a book to a secretary the publishers keep hounding me with. I've done a good bit of it in the hopes that it'll empty another purse over me head.' He would hold forth on the sidewalk outside, the vomit coming up and dripping on his tie as he joked and told his stories and sang a few ditties, rustling meanwhile through a newspaper to see if he was in it today, the columnists delighting in him now that he would soon be gallantly supplying them with the story of his rousing poet's death. There were so many ways you could help them kill you."

The last time I saw him myself, as I said in the Introduction, I knew he was dying, so when I heard he was gone on the radio a few weeks later – it was at the tail end of the news – I wasn't surprised. I remembered his last words to me as I hugged him, "See you in church." It was a con's slogan from the nick, but in this case I sensed it meant more. And it did.

His journalist friend Bill Kelly remembers seeing him in Tommy Moore's pub in Cathedral Street shortly before he died, standing up at the counter with his pants pulled up over his pyjamas, his eyes without their familiar glint. "I could see the death in him," Kelly said, "and him refusing to accept it, as if he believed that by standing in a bar as he had done so many times before, he could keep The Reaper at bay."

Brendan, oh Brendan, what were you trying to do: put out a fire with a blowtorch?

❖

When Brendan's doctor told him he would have to pick one day to stop drinking, he agreed entirely. "I'm thinking of the 24th of October 1967," he said, "it won't be too bad if I can start off again on the 25th."

❖   ❖   ❖

He appeared at the Hospice for the Dying in Harold's Cross one time with Granny English and a third party he wanted to have admitted there. All three of them were the worse for wear and were shown the door. Brendan commented afterwards, "I'd say it was the first time the Hospice had to throw out three people for being drunk: a grandmother, a prospective patient . . . and a child of six."

❖   ❖   ❖

Brendan is alleged to have said that he would like to have joined Alcoholics Anonymous, but held little hope he could be anonymous anywhere.

❖   ❖   ❖

Another anecdote, which could also be apocryphal, has him telling an auditor, "I drink to forget," and when the auditor enquires as to what he wants to forget, he thinks a moment before saying, "I can't remember."

❖   ❖   ❖

At the dress rehearsal of *The Quare Fellow* at The Pike Theatre he arrived drunk and promptly proceeded to fall asleep. He started to snore then, so loudly that he drowned out the actor's voices, before somebody was recruited to kick him awake every time he threatened to ruin the performance.

❖   ❖   ❖

Eamonn Andrews told Brendan that he never looked at his best on television when he had "one over the eight", but Brendan replied that it was necessary for a shy man like him to imbibe if he was going to be appearing in front of the nation. "I'm embarrassed now," he told Andrews, "and I haven't had one over the eight. In fact I haven't even had one over the seven."

❖   ❖   ❖

When Brendan was asked to come up with a new slogan for Guinness that would make it attractive for advertising purposes, he hit the nail on the head with a very sophisticated jingle: "It makes you drunk."

❖   ❖   ❖

Brendan knew an old man who drank a couple of pints of poteen a day for a fortnight. When he wasn't able to drink anymore, he took to the bed for a while and went off it – but not for long. Brendan (an ideal candidate for this question) asked him why he continued to drink so much when it made him so sick. "When I've been off it for a fortnight," the man replied, with eminent common sense, "I feel so good that I just have to go out and celebrate."

❖   ❖   ❖

When Brendan was about seven or eight, Granny English brought him in for a drink, which turned into more like a dozen. "I was twisted," he said in *Confessions of an Irish Rebel*, "as the saying has it, physically as well as the other way; my head was sunk on my left shoulder." As it started to lash rain, an old gentleman came over to Granny and said, "That's a beautiful boy, 'tis a pity he's deformed."

"The curse of Jaysus on you!" Granny shot back, "that child is not deformed. He's just got a couple of drinks taken."

❖   ❖   ❖

After a lengthy spell on the dry, he rationalised his decision to go back drinking with this elaborate statement, "If I drank milk, I'd be going against my doctor's orders, and I'd be going against my religion if I drank tea or coffee. I'm just about to have something to eat now, and I need something to drink with my food."

❖   ❖   ❖

He was the type of man to complain that his hangover was due to a bad pint he got . . . probably the 27th.

❖   ❖   ❖

As Brendan was on his way out of a pub one night, he asked the barman for twelve miniature bottles of Johnny Power. "That's an expensive way of drinking whiskey," his companion George Gale said to him, "half your money's going on the bottle and packing." Brendan agreed, but said he had his reasons. Exactly what those reasons were, Gale discovered the next morning when he saw Brendan's room. Two miniatures of whiskey lay on his coverlet, two more on a windowsill nearby, two more on a bedside table, and two more on a chair. Brendan opened his eyes slowly, picked up one of the remaining miniatures and after downing it in one gulp, explained, "Now you understand. If I'd had just one full bottle, I might have put it in all sorts of places. And just think of looking for it in the condition I was in."

❖   ❖   ❖

Brendan was thirsty one St Patrick's Day, so repaired to the Royal Dublin Society's Dog Show, which was the only place alcoholic beverages were being served on that day. Some hours later, one of his friends said to him, listening to the canine racket, "Hell, what a place to bring dogs." He'd forgotten where he was.

Brendan altered the circumstances of this anecdote in a piece he later wrote for the *Evening Press* which concerned a man who, somewhat the worse for wear with drink, trips over a pup at that show and exclaims angrily as he falls, "What a stupid effing place to bring a dog."

❖   ❖   ❖

He was presented with marijuana only once in his life, and the experience was hardly memorable to him. "It had to struggle against a couple of bottles of bourbon," he explained, "so I cannot tell much about it."

❖   ❖   ❖

On another occasion Brendan claimed he drank to forget. When he was asked what he was trying to forget, he said, "That I'm a bleedin' alcoholic!"

❖   ❖   ❖

The following remark has also been attributed to him, "No, me old segotia, you don't necessarily live longer if you're a pioneer: it just seems that way."

❖   ❖   ❖

John Ryan said he was on a plane to America with him one time when no drink was available. "Have you any after-shave with you?" he asked Ryan. He asked him to produce it and downed it on the spot.

❖   ❖   ❖

"I hate camels," he proclaimed, "or any other man or beast that can go for a week without a drink."

❖   ❖   ❖

A familiar New York newspaper headline during Brendan's heady forays into the Big Apple – there are those who would say he swallowed it whole – was: 'When Irish Eyes are Bloodshot.'

❖   ❖   ❖

"It only takes me one drink to get drunk," he said once. "The only problem is, I don't know if it's the 16th or the 17th!"

❖   ❖   ❖

When an acquaintance enquired what made him drink as much as he did, he replied, "Nuthin' – I'm a volunteer." Pressed on the issue of exactly how often he drank on a daily basis, he said, "Only twice: when I'm thirsty and when I'm not." He then elaborated, "I drink when I'm thirsty and I drink when I'm not thirsty and when I can't make up my mind if I'm thirsty or not, I drink to find out!"

❖   ❖   ❖

John B Keane's son Billy was once sitting on Brendan's knee, and implored him not to have another drink after seeing his condition. "Whatever you say, Bill," Brendan agreed, "whatever you say. But I'll just have one more to wash down the last one."

❖   ❖   ❖

C A Joyce, the Governor of Hollesley Bay Borstal, got a call from him once at 1 am. "Go back to bed, Brendan," Joyce advised, "and phone me in the morning."

"Sure that's drinking time in Ireland," Brendan replied. Remember we're talking about a man who often used to order shorts while the head on his pint was settling, so as not to waste precious drinking time.

❖   ❖   ❖

Brendan's thirst for alcohol was well-nigh unquenchable. Maybe that's why, when he saw a sign in a bar saying, 'Happy Hour – all you can drink for £1' he went in and said, "Two nicker's worth of that – and make it snappy."

❖   ❖   ❖

An Englishman came to Ireland and decided he'd like to sample some of the hallowed watering-holes he had heard so much about. He stopped Brendan on the street and said, "Excuse me, could you show me the way to the nearest boozer?" Brendan hiccuped and replied, "You're lookin' at him, mate."

❖   ❖   ❖

Brendan knew a man called Michael Meagher who was asked to deliver a speech on temperance. He was nervous before speaking in public. When Brendan asked him how he coped with the jitters, he replied, "I bought a half bottle of poteen with me. Before I got up onto the stage, I went into the lavatory and had a good slug of it and it gave me the courage to go on."

❖   ❖   ❖

When Brendan was told that sobriety would prolong his life, he said, "It's true. I spent a day sober last week and it was the longest day of my fuckin' life."

❖   ❖   ❖

Brendan once said he had devised a way of getting from Rathmines to Donnycarney without passing a pub – go into them all!

❖   ❖   ❖

Beatrice was sitting at home alone one night in Anglesea Road, the story goes, when a knock came to the door. When she answered it, a woman said to her, "I'm collecting for the new home for alcoholics."

"Come back in a few hours after the pubs close," Beatrice said to her, "and you can bring him with you then."

❖   ❖   ❖

In London in 1961, he was looking for a hotel where a friend of his was staying when he accidentally knocked on the door of a nursing home. He was a little the worse for wear at the time and was admitted by the doctor in attendance and given a bed. A few days later, he learned it was a place that specialised in dealing with recovering alcoholics. He remained here for over a week, but made himself scarce when surgery for his condition was discussed. Thereafter, he always looked twice before ringing uncertain doorbells.

Samuel Beckett visited him while he was here and was shocked by the decline in his health since he had last seen him in Paris, a decline of which Brendan himself seemed blithely unaware. "Did you bring any drink?" was the first thing Brendan said to him. Beckett said he hadn't, which lost him a few brownie points straight away. Then Brendan looked at him and said, "You know you're far too happy being miserable. Your kind of living will be the death of us all." Beckett was amused, but he could only take Brendan in small doses. It was easier visiting him in hospital where he didn't have to fear an interminable session of singing and story-telling, which was the way it was in Paris.

❖   ❖   ❖

One time he was made foreman of some painters who were doing up a hospital. Instead of getting down to the job in hand, however, he sat on a laundry basket between two char ladies singing, drunk as a skunk. The rules of the job, as one of his colleagues put it, were, "Seven hours for drinking and one for the work – and if that interferes with the drink we'll get rid of it."

❖   ❖   ❖

Dublin journalist Alec Newman put it to him that he was never sober after 10 am. "Don't believe a word of it," said Brendan, outraged at the insult *mar dhea*, "the operative time is the holy hour. Two and a half hours to go yet."

❖   ❖   ❖

John Ryan describes him towards the end of his life, tottering from one end of a bar to the other under the influence of treble brandies, occasionally throwing up onto the floor but not letting that mere detail stop him from continuing whatever yarn he was telling . . . and then mauling your wife or girlfriend to the accompaniment of a generous stream of expletives.

Bill Kelly remembers him in similar mode, telling fellow drinkers, "I'm Brendan effin' Behan, or if yis want to be nice, effin' Brending Behing. Me and me pal Kelly here are goin' to drink. Any of yis that wants a drink, effin get it yourself." John Hume once said that Ian Paisley would be struck dumb if the word "No" was obliterated from the English language. Maybe Brendan would have suffered the same fate if cursing was done away with.

❖   ❖   ❖

Brendan claimed he ruined his health by drinking to everyone else's.

❖   ❖   ❖

He was drinking in a pub in London one night with the writer Donal Foley, and, suffering from one of his familiar cash flow problems, sought to borrow money from him by talking in Irish so the rest of the company wouldn't be aware of his situation. This entailed raising his voice above the surrounding din. The barman wasn't impressed by the cacophany, imagining it to be the result of the pair's drunkenness. He finally removed both of their pints from the counter and asked them to leave the pub. Behan was flabbergasted and said, "I've been barred from pubs for many things, but I've never had the distinction of being kicked out for talking Irish."

❖   ❖   ❖

"I can't ever remember *not* drinking," he told Eamonn Andrews merrily in his much-publicised 1960 interview, "I didn't turn to drink; it seemed to turn to me."

❖   ❖   ❖

On his way to England to be put into prison in Liverpool, he got so drunk in Holyhead that he wasn't allowed go any further. "That's the first time I've ever been refused admittance to the wick," he remarked wryly, "for being sloshed."

❖   ❖   ❖

The following quips have all been associated with Brendan, for obviously reasons:

> "*I don't drink much – I spill most of it.*"
> "*I'm not a steady drinker; my hands shake too much.*"
> "*Yes, I have a drink problem – I can't get enough of it.*"
> "*I was breastfed on an optic.*"

❖   ❖   ❖

He showed an unusual sense of priorities when he said about a barman's strike in Dublin, "Not if I was to die of thirst would I pass a union picket."

❖   ❖   ❖

Brendan's long-time friend Bill Kelly said boozing with Brendan called for "the thirst of a camel, the stamina of an ox, the stomach of an ostrich and a neck like a jockey's buttocks".

❖   ❖   ❖

"Brendan never entered a pub," Kelly claimed, "he burst in behind a belly and a blast of noise. Barmen shuddered, journalists sweated and the cash-strapped beat a hasty retreat for fear they would be touched for a loan. Brendan remained blissfully unaware of all of this, hobnobbing with all the old dears in the snug as he broke into song and poured the drink into himself. If he was broke he looked for benefactors, and if he was flush he would buy drinks on the house, but one thing seemed to be constant: the fact that, before the end of the night, he would be asked to leave before he wanted to. And that request was often followed by another one importuning him not to return."

❖   ❖   ❖

Asked if he regretted his drink-sodden past, he replied, "If I could remember it, maybe I could answer that question."

❖   ❖   ❖

When *The Quare Fellow* opened in Wyndham's Lane in 1959, Brendan couldn't make it over because he was hospitalised in Dublin. He sent a postcard to the theatre, though, to tell them he was with them in spirit.

❖   ❖   ❖

When I asked Ma how Brendan became so fond of the hard stuff, she laid all the blame at Granny English's door, as I half-expected. He could do no wrong in her eyes, she said. "They used to go off to wakes and weddings, the pair of them, her an old woman and him just a little chislers. A fine pair of drunkards! She used to send him out for her beer: that's how he got to like it. She would send him for a pint in a jug – at that time you could take a jug to the pub and they'd fill it for you – but on the way back he'd drink half of it and then fill it up with water. She never even noticed. Blinded with adoration, I suppose."

It was Granny English who planted the seeds of destruction in him. Granny felt she was doing the Lord's work in this, as I said before, with her theory that early exposure to drink might quell the fascination or it later on. But as Brendan commented, "Sometimes, *mo bhrón*, these theories have little or no scientific basis." Whatever her logic, more than one local remembers Brendan as a 'regular' in pubs from the age of ten onwards, sticking his head round the doors of snugs asking people for the froth off their pints. And, unfortunately, he still wanted for it 30 years later.

Brendan gave many reasons for why he drank, none of which were consistent with the one given above, as you'll have noticed by now. Maybe his most ingenious was, "I drink alcohol because a pint of orange juice is twice the price of a pint of stout. Putting it plainly, I can't bloody afford to go off the stuff."

❖   ❖   ❖

A journalist with the *Hot Press* magazine once asked me whether I could ever see myself coming back from London to the "land of my fathers". I told him I couldn't because I was a workaholic. When the article appeared, the reason given wasn't that I was a workaholic, but an alcoholic. That's Irish journalism for you. Freudian slip, or what? Brendan, me oul flower, you have a lot to answer for.

❖   ❖   ❖

The final yarn I heard about Brendan concerns a night he was turfed out of a pub for general disorderly conduct. He found himself sprawled on the ground when he suddenly felt a trickle of liquid down his leg. Remembering the hip flask of brandy he had stored away for later usage, he said, "Fuck it" but then he saw the liquid pouring out of him is a deep red. "Thanks be to Jaysus," he muttered, "it's only bleedin' blood."

Chapter 15

After the Wake

More legends have grown up about him since he died than about
Finn McCool.

Bill Kelly

Brendan's funeral has often been compared with that of Michael
Collins or Charles Stewart Parnell. Such was the turn-out, one
could have been forgiven for imagining a state dignitary had died.
And such was the shock on the faces of the mourners – comprising all
elements of the socio-economic divide – that it was hard to realise his
early death was blindingly inevitable. He himself must have known he
was living on borrowed time for the last few years of his life, but whether
he did or not, he was powerless to prevent the descent of the final curtain.

Some trick-cycling psychologists have suggested that he had a death
wish, but this is surely a facile diagnosis. Brendan loved life as much as
he did drinking, but unfortunately the two were almost mutually exclusive to an addictive personality such as his.

He never wanted to die even in his darkest moments, but he probably knew the kind of life he was living was leading inexorably towards that impasse, and he didn't have the willpower to change it. To
this extent, I suppose he pushed the self-destruct button by default. A
moment ago I quoted him saying he didn't turn to drink, but drink
turned to him. In a different sense I could argue that he didn't turn to
destruction either but that it turned to him.

But such destruction was a long time coming. When he finally died,
he was 41 going on 70, a man finally released from his demons, and the
poisoned goldfish bowl of his insane existence. Death is always a shock,
no matter how many times a man has been on the brink of it before.
Maybe even more so on that account, because he cheated it on so many
other occasions after getting the Last Rites. But on March 20, 1964 his
luck finally ran out. Maybe it was a release for him, for life hadn't been
too much fun in the sixties by and large.

The drinking bouts became shorter and less enjoyable, and the
hangovers harder to bear. He always seemed to be pushing his life towards this conclusion, as if it was his only way out, the only decent
exit, a logical end to the identity he had carved out for himself and

then tarnished beyond recognition.

Sean O'Casey put it like this, "There is something peculiar in the Gael or Celt when he decides to go along the Primrose Path – he runs too quickly. That is what Brendan did." O'Casey, Brendan's old mentor and guiding light (remember he said on the Eamonn Andrews interview that praising him would be about as nonsensical as trying to praise the Lakes of Killarney?) would die himself later in the same year. It seemed somehow fitting. Kenneth Allsop described him more profoundly when he said, "He always had to push the boat out to avert being stranded alone on the bleak island of his memories and fears."

The funeral turn-out was massive. The cynics said people were just there to make sure he was dead. Maybe these accounted for about 1 per cent. There were also many 'mourners' who would have jumped under a bus to avoid him when he was alive. But the majority were genuine: his own people, literary and unliterary, the political and unpolitical, the rich and poor, the alcoholic and pioneer, the highbrow, lowbrow and middlebrow. They came to see the laying low of a mini-legend, and not, as Dominic said, "a brain hit by a bottle".

The city of Dublin wept like one large mourner as his body was taken from the Meath Hospital to the Church of the Sacred Heart in Donnybrook, stopping for a few seconds outside his house in Anglesea Road. Heads of state joined little old ladies with shopping bags to commemorate a man who spent time like he did money and words – as if there was no tomorrow. And suddenly, there wasn't.

The *Evening Herald* captured the irony of the occasion in a picture of a Garda saluting the cortège. God knows, he hadn't got many of those in life – nor wanted them either. It was like a State funeral, with people from all walks of life coming together to reminisce about perhaps the only thing they would ever have in common: a merry little man they might never have met but still felt they knew. He was like everyone's brother, everyone's buddy, every mother's son.

But why hadn't these same people come to him before to stop him destroying himself? Or would they have been able to? Would anyone? He had brutalised his body in a way that would have killed him five years before if he hadn't been such a horse of a man. Only the Behan durability had delayed the inevitable. If he stayed off the drink he could have lived to be 75 philosophising about Gerry Adams or the McCracken Tribunal or Roddy Doyle or whatever. But such was not to be.

John Osborne, another angry young man who reached the apex of his artistic powers in the seminal year of 1956, gave him a fitting tribute, and one that came from the heart. "Dear Brendan is dead," he said, "we will never again hear him hammering on our door at the Algonquin Hotel and shouting, 'Is there anyone at home in this fucking cat house?'"

He was strangely uncruel for an Irishman – and an IRA one at that. He once told me you could tell the wealth of a country by its bread and

its whores. That was our Brendan all right. The really sad thing, as Ted
Boyle pointed out, was that by the time of his death, Behan the writer
was "completely overshadowed by Behan the brawling drunkard". His
reputation was much like that of the dog whose master had taught him
to play checkers: the dog didn't win many games, but the fact that he
could play at all was amazing.

When Brendan died, people didn't generally remark about the passing of a great writer, but about the death of a famous drunk who also
wrote a bit. Bill Kelly gave this bitter evaluation of the mourners, "They
boasted about their times with him, the Peters who didn't want to know
him before he became famous, and who avoided him when he was
drunk, which was often, or when he was broke, which was often too.
They were safe now: Brending Behing was dead. . . . We Irish are good
at the *nil nisi bonum* trick. Our cemeteries are crowded with "horrible
dacent fellas who'd give you the shirt off their backs". (But) when they
were alive they were boozers, bowsies or bums to be avoided by all
right-thinking people. The ineffectual intellectuals could boast about
knowing the Borstal Boy because no longer need they fear that Brending
effing Behing would burst into a pub behind his belly and his stream of
profanities to upset their cosy abstractions."

Dominic said it was the first time in his life that Brendan didn't
monopolise the conversation. And yet in another way he did, because
everybody was still talking about him. A good percentage of the mourners would have shared a pint with him at some stage of their lives –
and another good percentage would pretend they had. They swapped
yarns about him as he was laid to rest, their faces creased with a mixture of grief and relief as they reminisced about Ireland's most unlikely
candidate for literary grandeur since the year dot.

But where were all these people a week ago when we drank our
sup in O'Looneys? Where were they when Brendan cried out in a
drunken stupor for understanding? Where were they when the little
boy in him grew afraid at the dead of night, or when he woke up at the
side of the road in the middle of nowhere, not knowing how he got
there? It seemed to be in the nature of humanity to turn out in force to
commemorate a legend, but legends have to live too, and surely that's
the time they need the endorsement. What good were the accolades
now, when he wasn't there to hear them? What good were the pints
when he couldn't partake? In life he had been ignored and in death
championed: it would always be the Irish way.

As his coffin was being driven to Glasnevin cemetery, an old man
shouted at the cortège from the side of the road, "May you never get
there." That man spoke for many of us. There was even a joke at the
graveside. One of his eulogists said he had been proud to have been
'interred' with Brendan instead of interned with him. I could imagine
Benjy enjoying that one all right – and rocking the heavens with his

belly laughs.

Another twist Brendan would have enjoyed was the fact that Carmel was stopped going to the funeral by a flock of sheep blocking the road to Holyhead, which caused her to miss the boat. His friend Mattie O'Neill gave an oration in which he said, "We shall never see his like again." As he finished speaking, he told me he heard Paddy Kavanagh muttering out of the side of his mouth, "Thank God for small mercies!"

The day would have been complete if he had leapt up out of the coffin brandishing a bottle of stout. Well he had his first drink at a funeral: why shouldn't he have his last one there as well? He expressed disgust at a funeral he was at as a boy because it didn't have a large turn-out. He insisted people would come from far and wide for his own one – it was one of his many prophecies about himself that came true.

One wouldn't have been surprised if he had left a few thousand pounds in his will for them all to go on a bender, but of course he had been too busy spending his money, and his life, on that very activity himself. The great thing about the funeral, Colbert Kearney wrote, was that it showed Brendan to be "like a younger Northside Falstaff, not only good company himself, but the inspiration of good company in others too".

There was a kind of consensus among the mourners, Kearney said, that it was all for the best, that Brendan was as well off out of life, which made it as much an occasion for mirth as misery. Kearney kept to himself at the funeral. He didn't want to sit in a big black car, he said, or be part of anything official. He had simply come to mourn. "But," as he put it, "when I saw the traffic stopping to allow the cortège through, when I saw bus drivers pull over and stare silently at the coffin, when I saw hundreds of women interrupt their shopping to line the route, shaking their beads and blessing themselves and muttering about poor oul' Brendan, when I saw the dealers and delivery men, artists and bookies, publicans and republicans, upper class and working class rich and poor, media men and messenger boys, religious and irreligious, young and old, when I saw all Dublin turning out to say goodbye to their favourite quare fella, their one and only prodigal son, I couldn't be anything but glad and I wanted to enjoy the occasion. It was the ultimate award for Brendan, and one he would have appreciated a million times more than any Nobel Prize or any Prix des Nations."

"I'm deeply touched by all the love shown to Brendan today," Da said, "but isn't it a pity this show couldn't have waited another 40 years."

John B Keane etched in a bigger picture of the event, "The IRA, like characters out of his plays, marched at either side of the coffin. Two nuns from his kindergarten days followed close behind. The gurriers, the bowsies, the ould wans and the chislers were all there. Respected publicans, wealthy businessmen, lawmen and wanted men, all walked side-by-side in that last trip to Glasnevin. The Dublin pubs did a roaring trade. Television cameras whirred and a Frenchman spoke over his grave. He would have enjoyed it all but he would have preferred if the ould wans with the shawls and the down-and-outs with the caps on the sides of their heads were up in front where they belonged, because the Dublin poor were closest to his heart and he never forgot that he was one of them. Never were so many characters gathered together in one place. It was a scene that only Brendan Behan could create."

"All over Ireland," wrote W R Rodgers, "from Donegal to Kerry out to the Atlantic Islands and east to Dublin, every publican and gypsy's child will be reminiscing about Brendan."

Joan Littlewood added, "He squandered his life and his genius, but he took the world on a spree." And David Nathan said, "He was a man capable of inspiring as much love in his friends as disgust in those who only read about him." It was refreshing to see such tributes delivered without any trace of the old small-mindedness that was so ubiquitous when he was alive. And yet in another way it buttressed the pain.

Rae Jeffs, as one might have expected, added a personal touch, "While Brendan would have loved the marvellous theatre of the spectacle, he would have enjoyed particularly the sight of the old ladies with their shopping baskets standing by the graveside, the children squabbling amongst themselves for a better position, the gravedigger waving his spade in the air to make sure that his one chance of appearing on television did not go unobserved by his friends, and a colleague speaking over his grave in sonorous tones of the privilege of being *interred* in The Curragh camp with Brendan. At once, the verbal slip echoed in our minds with Brendan's unheard laughter."

On the evening after the funeral, Niall Toibin went to the house of Joe Dwyer, the then-proprietor of Dwyer's pub. He was a man who had had a difficult relationship with Brendan, as any pub proprietor would have had. One night Brendan had arrived drunk into Dwyer's with a cooked chicken under his arm wrapped in tin foil. When he went up to the counter, Dwyer said to him, "I'm not serving you. You've had enough. Go home." Brendan, as one might have expected, took the chicken from under his arm and flung it at Dwyer saying, "Fuck you and your chicken!" Toibin asked Dwyer what he thought of Brendan generally. "Ah sure the poor old divil," Dwyer said, "He was an awful fucking nuisance." Toibin claimed this was one of the most honest epitaphs he had ever heard.

If there's a God in heaven, Brendan is there with Ma, Da, Rory and Dominic. If not, he's safe in our hearts till we too go to our final resting place. Either way, he left us an estimable legacy of memories.

Cyril Connolly said he had "a demonic energy that notoriety has not entirely dimmed". Meanwhile, Proinsias Mac Aonghusa asked a question that was on many people's lips, "Is it better to die young, having lived a full life and left behind a handful of good books, a couple of first class plays and a half dozen poems, than to die quietly at four score, leaving behind only a handful of dust?" It is, of course, a question that answers itself.

Brendan was too big for his own skin. A lesser man might have peeped out at the world and made notes. Brendan jumped into it instead – and gave that old triangle a mighty swipe. He may not have lived to see a man on the moon, but neither did he have to endure the McDonaldisation of art, the demise of the 'character' in Irish society, the violence in the North, the spluttering out of communism . . . and an era where every second gobdaw is penning 'The Great Irish Novel'.

Greater writers have graced the literary canvas than Brendan in Ireland's history, but not greater *characters* – before or since. We're living in an age, as Norman Mailer says, in which personalities have begun to disappear and everybody is becoming like everybody else. "In this special triumph of the age of plastic," Mailer commented, "rock-ribbed characters give us nourishment. They're like a great reef in the sea that, in the fog, is terribly feared. In a bad storm, however, that same reef gives you something to hold onto and protects you."

I like to think of Brendan in that light: as more a creature of the elements than a human being. Maybe he's the closest Ireland will ever come to producing a living, breathing Heathcliff. I see him as a cross between Christ and Faust, a man who suffered the little children to come unto him and then used a short spoon to sup with the devil. A man who might have agreed with Lord Byron, "Let us have wine and women, mirth and laughter, sermons and soda the day after."

So where is he now? It's anybody's guess. As he told Eamonn Andrews with a glint in his eye in that famous interview, "We know where we are, but we don't know where we're goin'." Maybe he's that head of cabbage Ma talked about.

There aren't many of us left to mourn him. Dominic is gone, as are Rory and Beatrice. Seamus, Carmel and myself live in England, occasionally going home, if Ireland is home, for funerals. It's a different age now, one which probably wouldn't have vilified Brendan in the same way his own did, and which may have prolonged his life by giving it stability. On the other hand, how could he have lived in the Ireland of the present when all the characters are gone and the old haunts he held so dear have been prettified beyond belief? Neither could he have lived in a country where every Tom, Dick and Harry was writing a book, as seems to be the case now. God knows, he couldn't even live with the idea of his two brothers having a go at the writing game, never mind the other 99 per cent of the population as well. If not the cat in Number

70. . .

Brendan came, saw and conquered. And then life conquered him.
Hype catapulted him to fame and the same hype caused his early demise. There are certain tribes in Australia that believe that when you
take a photograph of a person, you suck their soul out of them. Such a
notion might well serve as a metaphor for his life. Brendan the showman hid Brendan the nervous child, Brendan the aggressive hid the
gentle soul beneath. Brendan the vocal hid Brendan the stutterer. His
whole life was a gigantic attempt at over-compensation. You don't have
to be Freud – or Einstein – to see that.

"Everyone should be famous for a day," he said "and then allowed
get on with their lives." But Brendan wasn't, which meant his own one
stopped early.

A lot of this was down to the fact that he couldn't bring himself to
leave Beatrice and stay in New York. She took him from a woman he
said he loved more than her, dragging him back to a city that was destined to kill him as it killed Paddy Kavanagh and Flann O'Brien and
Sean O'Sullivan. If he had stayed in America with a new partner I feel
sure he would have recharged his batteries.

I suggested in an earlier chapter that Beatrice may have done herself in. I know for a fact that her last years were very miserable. Like
Brendan, she let herself go, feeling she had outlived her relevance. She
put up a good front, but she was hurting inside. She always looked
tired and worn in her last years, hiding herself away from the public.
The kitchen in Anglesea Road was piled high with dirt, and the garden
like the Malayan jungle. When Brendan died, the buzz went from her
life along with the pressure. People stopped calling after she took off
her widow's weeds. She became just another woman. There was no
more glory in which to reflect, no more illustrious parties to attend.
Maybe she even missed the worry about Brendan – as they say some
prisoners fall in love with their chains.

Just as Brendan had to acclimatise himself to the calm after the storm
of fame, so did she. Sadly, neither of them did this very well. It's also
possible that she had herself driven demented with guilt over an affair
she had, which resulted in a child. My own view is that she started this
affair when Brendan was alive. She was a lovely lady, but when God
made herself and Brendan he certainly didn't match them.

In some ways it was a bit like our own parents. Ma told me one
time that she would have left Da every day for 30 years if she had
anywhere else to go. She and Beatrice bit their lips and stayed the course
because that was the way things were done then. You took your man
for better or worse, for richer or poorer, in sickness and in health. When
the going got tough, the tough didn't get going. This was divorce, Irish
style: grinning and baring it.

If Brendan and Beatrice had split up, I firmly believe it would have done them both good. But maybe Brendan's Catholic conscience wouldn't allow him make that last decisive move. As Shakespeare said, "Conscience makes cowards of us all." Even fearless freedom fighters like Brendan.

I don't want to sound like I'm blaming Beatrice, but if he could have been allowed to end his days in America – where the mantra of 'doing your own thing' always held sway – he could have turned out plays like Niagara Falls. Even if the well of inspiration ran dry he could have become a 'talking head' on television (the medium that, after all, made him famous) or turned his hand to writing film scripts. Such an activity would have meant big bucks for relatively little work. Let's not forget that *The Quare Fellow* was turned into a film with Patrick McGoohan. *Borstal Boy*, *Richard's Cork Leg* and *The Hostage* could well have followed suit – if not the short stories. There might even have been a biopic: he was, after all, a living legend by then.

Brendan told me in the utmost confidence that all sexual activity had ended with Beatrice years before, and with it his creative flow. For this we cannot blame her. But there's a time in the affairs of men and women when it's necessary to move on. If a relationship is dead, people have a right – even a duty – to let go. If he was fulfilled in a new relationship – he had already fathered two Yankee children – he might even have gone off the bottle. We've seen before how he could remain as dry as the Sahara when things were going well with his work. And America might have embraced him to its heart if he had put down roots there.

Beatrice claimed she had first preference on the simple grounds that it was she who had mopped up after him during the bad years. Fair enough, but what she couldn't see was that their claustrophobic relationship was, in its way, actually driving him to drink. Like Da, he sought refuge from the turmoil of marital strife in the pub. No barman could nag him there like an over-protective wife. It might have been the story of a whole generation of Irish men who weren't cut out for a life sitting at home with a blanket over their knees doing crosswords.

When Beatrice came to Brendan with her ultimatum, he became the victim of an eternal dilemma. He was caught by the hasps of the arse between the twin pincers of freedom and duty. He chose duty, of course and then he died. Neither him nor Beatrice gained from this scenario. As I say, the last time I visited her I found her kitchen to be like a rubbish tip. It was as if she had a kind of twisted nostalgia for Brendan's lack of hygiene. As I looked at her I saw a sad and lonely woman sinking fast, with neither chick nor child there to ease the pain of her last days. I couldn't rightly put my finger on the reason for it all. My guess is that she would have been far better off flying her kite than becoming yet another one of Ireland's sad literary widows.

Nevertheless, this is all water under the bridge and I must stress that it's just my own viewpoint of Beatrice and her strife-torn relation-ship with Brendan, which has of course been coloured by time.

Hardly a day goes by but I don't think of him. Hardly a month goes by but people confuse me with him. Brendan, Brian – some peo-ple don't even notice. All they care about is the surname. A surname Brendan has bequeathed to the world. I have both gained and suffered from the fall-out of that.

Let me give you an example of each experience. In a Bronx pub in the eighties a drunk Mayo architect came over to me and asked me who I was. "Brian Behan," I told him, adding that I was Brendan's brother. (There was a picture of Brendan on the wall.) He exploded with rage at this. "Brendan Behan had no brothers!" he fumed. "You're a lying bastard! You should be shot, using the memory of a dead man to get yourself noticed." I wondered if he knew something I didn't. Maybe the old bugger was right, I thought. I didn't, after all, have any pictures of myself with Brendan when we were growing up, or a cer-tificate of my identity signed by Brendan in his blood. He broadly an-nounced to all the other drunks in the pub that I was a fraud and an imposter and I sunk lower and lower in my seat trying to pretend I didn't exist. In the end, fearing the man's friends would descend me on me, I ran for my life. I was jogging down the street like a marathon runner when I heard these footsteps behind me. "Stop!" shouted a voice, and I thought my end was near. When I turned around, however, who was it but the barman. "You didn't pay your tab," he announced. I can tell you, I was never happier to part with a few dollars, whatever my true genealogy.

Another time a man congratulated me for being Brendan's brother. "Why," I asked, "do you remember him?"

"Who," he declared, "can ever forget *Under Milk Wood*." Sadly, that's what you're up against in this crazy world of ours. I was tempted to reply, "Brendan didn't write that – Bob Dylan did."

The Irish-American satirist P J O'Rourke said, regarding nepotism, "A very quiet and tasteful way to be famous is to have a famous rela-tion. Then you can not only *be* nothing, you can *do* nothing too." I'm sure there are people who saw myself and Dominic in that light in the early years of Brendan's fame, but I think we've done enough since to disabuse cynics of the notion that we were content to bask in his glory. Dominic always claimed he got on fine with Brendan in private, even though he argued with him publicly. I dispute that, like I dispute most of Dominic's expostulations.

Dominic's attitude to Brendan was very different when Brendan was alive than it was when he was dead. After March 1964 he gilded the lily when Brendan wasn't there to set the record straight. I can im-agine the two of them up in heaven now, banging harps over each oth-er's heads about who's the better writer. If they're down in the other place, they're most likely breathing fire at one another, with Nick proving himself a most unsatisfactory referee.

I wasn't the only member of the family with whom Dominic fell out. Apart from Brendan, he annoyed Seamus when he pissed in his backyard. He seemed to delight in making himself unpopular. I met Edna O'Brien at a party in the Irish Embassy in the early sixties and she told me Dominic was a right little shit. He had struck her one night, she said, as well as shouting insults at her, saying she had slept her way around Fleet Street in order to make a name for herself. I told her I would have tried to get him to apologise to her but I couldn't as we weren't on speaking terms.

Having said all that, I still have regrets about Dominic. I sometimes think that if I put more thought into our relationship he might have come round. Considering he resented everything I represented, however, that's dubious. To me he was like a microcosm of the type of writer I have come to hate since he died: those who strut around like eminences, deeming themselves infinitely superior to the rest of us.

Brendan wasn't like that, contrary to what you might imagine from some of his more acerbic outpourings in the book you're now holding. He had bile to be sure, but it was always leavened with wit. He also had great respect for his peers – all the way from Joyce to Beckett to Sean O'Casey, manfully acknowledging his debt to all three. He even confided to me one night that he held Paddy Kavanagh, God love him, in great store, but he asked me not to publicise this seeing as he enjoyed raising his dander so much.

We hear a lot about the people Brendan hurt and abjured, but not so much about those he held dear, and who were held dear by him. This is particularly so in the context of family relations. Rumours of rifts in the Behan family still grab headlines. This is fair enough, and I can put my hand up and say I've been just as guilty of fanning the flames as any tabloid journalist. But if I got even an ounce of compromise from Dominic, I would have walked the extra mile for (and even with) him.

Brendan got along brilliantly with Rory, as is evidenced by the number of letters he sent him from America. In a sense he regarded him as the head of the family – the best at coping, the best all-round man, the best peacemaker. He also used to say that Rory's spirited renditions of American tunes like *Buddy Can You Spare A Dime* made Broadway instantly familiar to him when he got there.

His relationship with Sean was as untroubled as that with Rory. Da used to say that was because neither Sean nor Rory wrote, which meant that they were no threat to him. If this is true, it wouldn't be the first time a writer neglected his own and sought out the company of nonwriters. We all love our opposites. E E Cummings used to say his favourite people were ice cream salesmen. And by now you must know that I myself would prefer to bungi-jump over the Golden Gate Bridge than have to endure an evening with the breed. Brendan enjoyed the craft of writing, but not all the bullshit that came with it. When he talked about it, it was in the same unpretentious tones he would use to talk about how he planned to paint a wall. I also have that attitude. I see it as a job like any other. I do it because I think I have a flair for it, and because I think that putting words together on a page is an activity at least as laudable as building a house with bricks. But maybe not any better either. It's also a bit less laborious than the latter activity – at least when it's going well. But God preserve me from the breed that prune their syllables like prize gardenias, the people who put in a semi-colon before lunch and replace it with a comma after much soul-searching. Life is far too short for crap like that.

Writing should be just like anything else in life. When it takes over completely and there's nothing else, look out for misery, whinging and an early death. Writers can only write out of experience and when that dries up they go round in ever-decreasing circles. When the creative urge has nothing to feed on it becomes sour, and in the end a deadly poison. Not only do fallen legends have nothing more to say, but the parts of their lives they've used up on paper have now become public property. They have, in effect, abolished their own identities.

This didn't only happen to Brendan, but, as I've mentioned, to people like Paddy Kavanagh and Flann O'Brien as well – and rumour has it that Joyce went crackers writing *Finnegans Wake* too. The point is, these men were all used up. If Brendan lived, I feel confident he would have been chuffed about the fact that Dominic and myself attained some degree of literary success. When he passed those comments about genius not coming in litters or the cat in Number 70 writing next, there was always more humour than venom in evidence. He knew me too well to think that I'd take anything like this to heart. Far from upsetting me, all I could conjure up was a vision of a cat with a scribble-pad in her paws, busily jotting down notes under the table. Even the fact of him using an image like that showed he wasn't as upset as some people would like to believe.

I've always felt that once the immediate shock of Dominic and myself getting some of the Behan publicity died down and as he himself became bored with adulation – both were beginning to happen almost simultaneously – he would have adopted a live-and-let-live attitude to the pair of us.

He's over 30 years dead now, but in many ways more alive than when he was with us. Some days I wake up and think of growing up with him and it seems like yesterday, then other times it seems like an eternity away.

So here I am, an old man in a dry month mixing memory and desire. Trying to make sense of life in a way he never could, from the

inside out. If I popped my clogs tomorrow I would be worth nearly
£200,000, but I still feel poor inside. You can never forget that gnawing
ache, no matter where you go or what you do.

I'm a bricklayer who's been to university. How many people can
say that? I've been in prison and I've written hit plays. I've been a trade
union organiser, a hod-carrier, an actor, a lecturer, a memoirist and many
other things besides. But I doubt if I'll ever shake off the lanky lad who
laughed and cried in Russell Street, and cried and cried in the approved
school at Artane, under Christian Brothers who had no Christianity.

I haven't married Baroness Thatcher yet, or fought any more Bat-
tles of Waterloo, or even buried characters up to their necks in sand
like Sam 'house-of-pain' Beckett, but people are still going to my plays
despite (or maybe even because of) the charges critics have levelled
against them. I will continue to wage my war against such critics and
against the navel-gazing, self-regarding elitists that pass for intellectuals in Ireland's new-found cafe society.

Beckett once wrote a play called *Breath* that consists of about twenty
seconds of silence followed by a huge breath. Apparently this went
down a bomb with some of our resident theatrical pseudos. Myself,
I'm thinking of doing a similar one entitled *Fart*. I'm very hopeful of
getting rich on the proceeds.

Sam, you see, was in the happy position of being both rich and a
groaner. He got both the crown of thorns *and* the 30 pieces of silver. I
see him as little more than a creeping Jesus for the middle classes.
Whenever I think of Beckett I remember Samuel Johnson's comment
on Thomas Gray, "He was dull in a new way, and that made many
people think him great." And when I think of Brendan, on the other
hand, I remember that great line out of *A Catcher in the Rye* where Holden
Caufield says, "What really knocks me out is a book that, when you're
all done reading it, you wish the author that wrote it was a terrific
friend of yours and you could call him up on the phone whenever you
felt like it."

I know Brendan's books had that effect on people because they told
me so. No doubt the many tales told about him nourished that desire. I
would be the first to point out that a prolonged stay in his presence,
particularly on the wrong side of a bar counter when he'd had one over
the eight, would drive you barmy, but when he was on song in his
salad days, and when the drink went down the right way, there was no
better company of an evening. And he was lucky enough to be able to
make that presence resonate off the page.

His infectious personality caused him to be embraced by everyone
from Granny English to the Guinness family and the American press,
but all these people were bad for him. They moved him in a direction
that carried him away from the work in hand. Seduced by the mythic
dollar and the glass-bottomed sewer that was Hollywood he tried to

raise the bar, to climb the wall of risk, but he didn't quite make it. His art was great but limited – like his life.

He strove after perfection but maybe he drove himself too hard. It was like pushing a car into a gear it doesn't have and the moment you realise that you just drive it into a ditch or over a cliff – with yourself in it. There was always a rage for perfection in him, coupled with the realisation that he was travelling farther and farther away from that perfection as he became a prisoner of creature comforts. *La dolce vita* and the *via dolorosa* finally became one for Brendan. That was both his irony and his tragedy.

His art became little more than craft, his inspiration bowdlerised into tabloid soundbites. Freed from the pressure of editorial deadlines, he settled instead for the quick payback of media repartee. It was like trading in architecture for model toys. Right from the moment he took Malcolm Muggeridge's cigarette from his mouth moments before going on television in 1956 his future was mapped out for him.

If he'd lived he would probably have done much more television. We may be thankful he was spared this temptation. Can you imagine Brendan Behan advertising hair restorer or after-shave for a four figure sum to feed his drinking habit? Or becoming a fixture on some programme like *The Late Late Show* as his biographer Ulick O'Connor did? It might have made good television, but it would have made bad Brendan. When all the usual suspects were rounded up week in and week out for yet another 'talking heads' interlude, he might well have been reduced to saying, like his alter ego Dylan Thomas, "Somebody's boring me – and I think it's me."

Under the microscope, as Paul Durcan, said, each of us is unique, and we broke for cover crazily breasting the barbed wire. Some of us made it to the forest edge, and some of us didn't. Brendan left us prematurely because he believed his own publicity. He had lost his ability to stand outside it. He died of an overdose of self. He has been all too frequently misunderstood, all too frequently his life, in a kind of photomontage, has been used as the key to his books rather than the other way round.

Such a tabloid appraisal – the laziest form of litcrit I can imagine – has proliferated since he died. The image of the pugilistic drunkard, as I have been at pains to point out in this book, wasn't one he chose but one that was delivered upon him. Once it became nailed down, however, he was content to run with it, and by the time he realised the danger it was doing both to his reputation and his ability to work it was too late to do anything about it. He might as well have tried to fight the waves.

Lord Halifax once said that the world would have been much easier to manage if Herr Hitler and Signor Mussolini had been at Oxford. Perhaps, or maybe it might even have been more chaotic. I stepped over a class barrier in the sixties just as Brendan did a decade earlier, but was this liberation for us? Or for the world? Not really, because the same sins keep on happening in every generation, even if sociological details change.

This is why I sometimes despair of my own 'leftie' involvements. But I will continue to tilt at windmills instead of tugging at forelocks, regardless of the outcome. As the aforementioned Mr Dylan has put it, I will keep on keeping on. In much the same way as Brendan would have, if he had been able to share my longevity.

Osbert Sitwell said that it's fatal to be appreciated in one's own time. Agreed, but is the alternative any more desirable? Would it be better to be a Van Gogh than a Behan? Both of them died young, one from lack of recognition and the other from an excess of it. The ideal is obviously somewhere in the middle, but not many achieve this. When one struggles to be appreciated and then the appreciation comes, it's difficult not to play the success game, even to the extent of forgetting exactly what put you at the top of the tree. There's also a temptation to freewheel, and to put more energy into the marketing of your talent than its inner development. Brendan never thought he would become half as big as he did – in every sense – and therefore there was that much more to gain and to lose.

Like most writers, he tasted failure before success. For some people that fact works as a kind of protection from the seductions of fame, but for him it only resulted in a kind of desperate clinging to the masthead. He saw it disappearing before it did, and when it finally became a mirage, all he could do was gaze forlornly at its after-image. By now he was only a supporting player in the story of his own life, surveying its booms and slumps.

His life went all the way from the era of the Civil War to that of the Beatles. In those four decades, Ireland's image of itself was changed and changed utterly. A love child of republicanism first and then the box, he saw much more than the two days. He died at a time when things were going to get much worse for him and I doubt he would have written much more of note considering the state of his health if nothing else. My tears were chastened with this knowledge as I tried to tell myself he was gone to a better place. God knows, it could hardly have been worse.

The Ireland of today is beset with crime and drugs and whatnot but as least Dáil Éireann isn't run from the Archbishop's Palace any more. And no longer can somebody like Noel Browne be informed by a man in purple garb that his Mother and Child Scheme has no place in holy Ireland. Brendan fought hard to achieve all this. He hated the Church idea that this world was simply a vale of tears, with paradise in the next. The Church told us that the needs of an individual were to be subjected to saving sinners with collective prayer, and the greater the suffering, the greater the rewards in the hereafter. Brendan's paganism warred against this because he wanted his paradise now, but his devotion to all the liturgical rituals of his youth created a conflict in him. He wanted the trappings of religion, and its sanctuary in times of trouble, but he rebelled against its ideology. Even at the end of his life he hadn't resolved this contradiction. When you think of it, which Irishman has? I heard of a priest recently who didn't believe in God but he still said mass fervently. Only in Ireland could such schizophrenia take root. Such is the pull of the institution.

The journalist Joe O'Connor put it well. "The Irish dream," he said, "used to be of a post-revolutionary Celtic Erin where we would all without exception be rural, Catholic, heterosexual, conservative and in a family as nuclear as the Waltons. It would be an Ireland where we would all know our places, respect our elders and betters, wear bawneen jumpers and Aran knickers, smoke pipes and write turgid poetry in Irish about fishermen." This was the Ireland Brendan was born into: it wasn't the one he died in. I'm not saying he effected that change single-handedly (he was shaped by his time as much as he shaped it) but he did as much as any of his contemporaries to eradicate shoneenism and crawthumperism.

The year after Brendan died, John Charles McQuaid was instrumental in getting the author John McGahern sacked from his teaching post. McGahern was a fine teacher, respected by colleagues, pupils and parents alike, but McQuaid told the parish priest of Clontarf (the area in which McGahern was teaching) to get rid of him. McGahern's problem was twofold. He had married a Finnish woman in a registry office and had also written what McQuaid deemed to be a 'dirty' book *The Dark*. (Posterity has rightly reclaimed it as a minor masterpiece.)

McGahern wasn't told directly that he was sacked, merely suspended. But he refused to go until he faced the business end of the establishment upfront. This was when the wagons began to circle. His colleagues weren't able to help him, and the parish priest, who had liked and admired him, wasn't available – he had conveniently gone 'on holidays'. The union rep said to McGahern (in a story he still dines out on), "I could have done something about the book, but why did you have to go and marry a foreign woman when there are hundreds of Irish ones with their tongues hanging out for a man?" McGahern was amused by this. If there were, he said, he certainly didn't see these desirable tongues pointed in his direction.

The upshot, in any case, was that he lost his job and *The Dark* was banned. The publishers, Faber & Faber, were outraged, having recognised the book for the prose poem that it was. Nothing really had changed since Brendan's years of glory in the fifties, once again Britain had seen art where Ireland could only see filth. And it's still going on today to an extent. If you look at the series *Father Ted*, which wasn't art but was still savagely funny, it's not hard to see why RTÉ, a fiercely conservative institution at base, rejected it, thus making Ireland's loss England's huge gain. The fact that it changed its mind on this, as I said, directly mirrors Brendan's experience.

McGahern, like Brendan, became one of "the leaders of the banned" when *The Dark* was banned, something which mystified him. Being banned is something you always expect to happen to others rather than yourself. It hurt him for a while, and of course being unemployable in Ireland in his chosen trade didn't help. The parish priest, when he returned from his 'holidays', told McGahern he would give him a good reference so as he could get a job in England, which caused the author to reflect wryly, "He didn't mind the dirty writer corrupting English children so long as he didn't stay in Ireland and corrupt native ones. Or maybe he felt the English ones were corrupted already."

This action, however, was really the Catholic Church's last death rattle. McGahern's fate was like a wake-up call to the generation that was to come. A decade later McQuaid would be gone and de Valera's comely maidens turned into pillars of salt. The times they were a-changing, even if Brendan wasn't around to see it.

The sexual revolution, the Beatles, experimental literature: all this would happen while he was under the sod, but he helped bring it about with his irrepressible exuberance and irreverence. We don't have so many valleys of squinting windows in Ireland any more, nor books banned for "bad" language or ribaldry. The roar of the Celtic Tiger has meant our literature has become more cosmopolitan, more suited to a global village than a paralysed one. And neither do Irish writers have to hawk their wares like the poor relations of their neighbours across the water. No, to be a writer in Ireland today is sexy. It's hip. Today's writers are being fêted at book fairs and spoken of in hushed syllables at fashionable cocktail parties. And they'll probably be forgotten about within a year. That's publishing. But it's a type of publishing Brendan and his contemporaries missed out on. He had to push the boat out for his own maiden voyage to foreign soils, but many of his successors have become rich on the fall-out.

Brendan's characters were real, his whores and hostages and crippled IRA men sing and dance because they're bone of our bone, flesh of our flesh. This is why his plays will live on, and why the works of playwrights who prey on humanity's failings will vanish like last year's snow. Brendan is firmly in the camp of the hopeful. In *The Quare Fellow* we laugh with the cons. We know that on the hour of the execution the most hardened one of them will rattle his mug on the door to show a feeling of love towards his doomed colleague. His plays tackle deep issues using comedy as a guide.

And so the questions go on. Who was Brendan Behan? Where did he go astray? Why did he drink himself to death when he had so much to live for? Why did he fight for a country's freedom when he couldn't even free himself? Who were his friends? Could they have stopped his decline? Could Beatrice, a woman who said she couldn't leave him when he was down but refused to when he was up? And why was he devoured by the Old Hag Ireland, a country that doesn't eat her young any more?

If you ask why he turned out as he did, my answer is that it was inevitable. Slum kids like us became IRA men just as toffs went to the high-priced schools and played rugby. Brendan used to throw rocks at the lads from Belvedere when he was young, just as he later abused those who passed port under the high tables of Trinity College. But in borstal he played rugby himself, and when he came out of it he mixed with the high and mighty, so he crossed a line there. Then he plied his trade in the sanctuary of a foreign land, thereby breaking another taboo. And even though he died in Ireland, his heart was gone from it almost right through the sixties. Is there any lesson we can learn from this? Does it tell us anything about either Brendan or life, or that bastard beast called Anglo-Irish literature – which, more often than not, is neither Anglo nor Irish nor even literature?

The modern Irish writer doesn't tend to drink like Brendan did. He doesn't tend to hold contentious opinions, or voice them in crowded pubs with the foam of a pint visible on his lips. He doesn't cause commotion on the street. He doesn't bring his typewriter to McDaids, or scribble mnemonics on soggy beer-mats. No, he's got his modem and his PC and his mouse and his laptop and his fax and his trendy agent and his possible movie tie-in and maybe even a video too, with Boyzone and/or Van the Man doing the auditory honours. Because literature today is more an industry than a labour of love. And many of the people running it have the moral fibre of alley cats.

Brendan was lucky that he died before he was swallowed up in that synthetic vortex. The book trade today is largely built on hype. We give authors publicity that seems almost to vary inversely with their talent. The medium is the message, and that nebulous element called 'quality' seems to have somehow gone missing in the process. The advertising campaigns which books have mean that writers are in danger of being lumped in with toothpaste commercials in the long term – which on second thoughts mightn't necessarily be a bad thing considering the amount of cotton candy they churn out.

Then again there's all that incestuousness. You know the kind of thing I mean: Writer A reviews the book of Writer B who lives up the road, so he does a puff job on it as a favour – or if they don't get on, a hatchet job. This is like two sides of the one coin. Either way there's a kickback. Ranging from palm-greasing to score-settling. The chances of getting an objective review are about as good as the chance of getting a straight answer from a Tory about what he earned on his last

Euro-stint. Of course this kind of thing goes on in every country, but I think it's more pronounced in Ireland. Brendan said if you get six out of six good review, you should ask the President of the United States to sell you the White House, whereas if you got none you should take a pill to put you out of your misery. I don't agree with either of these stratagems. Brendan overlooked the fact of prejudice in reviewers, though God knows he had enough experience of it to know.

My personal belief is that nobody should be allowed to review a book – good, bad or indifferent – unless they've had a stab at writing one themselves. That's the only way they'd know how difficult it is. You get whippersnappers coming out of schools of journalism today who think contemporary literature began with somebody like Hunter S Thompson.

There's also the fact that the modern generation, with its CD ROMs and its camcorders and its computer software, seems to have forgotten the art of page-turning. Did you hear about the little girl who received a book from her Daddy one Christmas morning and didn't know what to do with it because there was no place to put the batteries? Maybe we're approaching such a *Fahrenheit 451* society as I write: a society that seems to pride itself on the transience of its vision.

I hate the way writing has been turned into an industry today, almost like show business. I hate literary workshops and creative-writing courses and fiction seminars and bursaries and scholarships and fellowships and summer schools and things like Bloomsday where a lot of posers who haven't the foggiest what *Ulysses* is about (did even Joyce himself?) go about the place making total eejits of themselves in funny get-ups as they munch gorgonzola cheese and spout mouth-jaded witticisms. I also hate the way anthologists use shorthand terms like "earthy freedom fighter" to pigeonhole Brendan, but that's a subject for another day.

I think Brendan owes much of his importance to the size of the themes he tackled: nationalism, capital punishment, incarceration, forbidden love. I notice the modern writers now boast that they don't need the big themes. They prefer to search for the emotional effect people have on each other. This is fine in its place but I don't think it will wash in the long haul. These people have a niche appeal, but they lack universality or longevity.

The talent he expended telling yarns in pubs would have been better employed working on his plays, but what good is it saying that now? Cyril Connolly said of good talkers, "When they run down they're very miserable. They know that they've betrayed themselves. They've taken material which should have had a life of its own and tossed it away on the empty air." That's what happened to Brendan. He gave his plays to all the loveable old biddies in pub snugs with shawls wrapped around them and a ready quip on their lips. In an age before video and camcorders, it's all lost except to the folk memory, surviving only by word of mouth. Which is why no university scholar will ever succeed in putting an endline to Brendan's output, it's too open-ended for that. In fact this very page may trigger a memory in some reader.

What did Brendan achieve? Well he made a hero of a British soldier in *The Hostage* and a *Romeo and Juliet* out of a relationship between a squaddie and a Dublin peasant. This was his way of mooting a love affair between England and Ireland rather than a killing match. As we have said already, "He was born an Irishman and remained an Englishman all his life."

The Irish invasion of the London stage is very strong today. Brendan was largely responsible for that. We send England our plays, our actors and our dreams. Two million of us have sought work with oul Britannia to date. That can't be bad. And the world would be a poorer place without Anglo-Irish literature, whatever its faults. Brendan said an Anglo-Irishman was a Protestant on a horse, but I would beg to disagree. Any Irishman who speaks English is an Anglo-Irishman. It's as simple as that. There's no exclusivity.

The legacy he left seems confined to his art rather than his life. You won't see many contemporary playwrights with their arse hanging out of their trousers – or a safety pin holding them up. Nor will you see many with their hair tousled, their shirt buttons undone and a mouth missing half a set of teeth. No, the modern playwrights do all the 'politically correct' things: arriving on time for their premieres, chewing the fat with 'People Who Matter', not getting squiffy when there's business to be done . . . and definitely not throwing pebbles at editors' windows when they're short of a few bob to pay the rent. That age is gone just as sure as God made little green apples. What has replaced it is a generation of cute Ballygowan hoors who are short on inspiration, big on perspiration, and very good at hammering out high quality deals with their agents. Literature has gone from being a cottage industry to a kind of cartel, and very often the writer is little more than a bit player in the proceedings.

I find that sad. And I also find it sad that there are still people, Hugh Leonard being the most vociferous, who continue to decry Brendan's originality. It's true that Joan Littlewood was a midwife to his work, but she wasn't the mother. Brendan was a creative artist in search of an editor, and he was lucky enough to find some excellent ones, but don't try to tell me these people, or even the lags, wrote his plays for him. What they did was adapt them. They created order out of chaos. But it's from the chaos that art springs, and these people wouldn't have been able to manufacture that without Brendan. When you've got genius you attract talent, and when you're Brendan Behan you attract people like Alan Simpson, Carolyn Swift and Joan Littlewood.

People like Hugh speak of Brendan as, at best, a footnote to Ireland's literary history, and at worse a curse upon Ireland as well as its cultural back pages. Such people don't bother me any more. They don't make me laugh and they don't make me cry. In fact I have no reaction to them at all, save to ask: If what you're claiming is true, why are the punters still voting with their feet to attend revivals of Brendan's plays? And why are those who knew him much better still speaking of him with love and affection?

The author Nigel Nicholson wrote in *The Spectator* in 1992, "One last tip to rebels: always have a second profession in reserve." These are words Brendan might have benefited from if he had heard them in time. I mean that when the IRA guns were silent and he underwent writer's block from his hard drinking, he needed to tap into something deeper in himself to tide him over the vacuum.

Afterthought

Through Brendan, I have learnt to accept myself as I am – good or ill, changing the things about myself I feel able to, accepting the things I can't change, and praying to Christ that one day I will finally learn the difference between the two. I never want to be anything but myself, whatever metamorphoses that entails. To be perfect is to have changed often.

If my inspiration dries up, or if some mad Tory finally succeeds in getting me silenced for good, I might have to go back to McAlpine's again – though at 72 I can't rightly see myself carrying a hod with any degree of confidence.

I live primarily for my family now. My wonderful wife Sally keeps the ship afloat and is the centre of my life. We enjoy a relationship that is frank, open and upfront. My last secret from her was blown wide open at a party I attended for contributors to *The Daily Telegraph* in the Mall Galleries some time ago. I met a fellow contributor who asked me how I was. "I'm beginning to get delusions of grandeur," I told him. "I have two books coming out, and two plays being staged and I'm frightened of all the success because that's what killed my brother."

"Do you think it will kill you too?" he asked me.

"Oh yes," I replied, "but since I'm already 72, it really doesn't matter."

It was at this point that Sally gave me a funny look. "72, are you?" she droned. "Now he tells me."

My children keep me sane as well – a luxury Brendan never experienced, as Blanaid arrived too late. One of my daughters, Janet, is an actress and another, Lindsay, a magistrate's clerk at Bexley. Rosemary is a trainee journalist for *The Daily Telegraph* and Dan, a lad of six foot four, is at university. My other daughter, Ruth, plays the fiddle and sings and dances in a band.

Dominic took a shine to Ruth and once asked her to accompany him to Paris. Her reply was classic. "You're so tiny," she said, "where would I find you?" She then started to chant the feminist song *I Am A Woman Giving Birth To Myself*. That was enough for Dom, who made his excuses and left soon afterwards.

Hearing this made me feel rather sorry for him. A little man with big ideas, in the end he realised he couldn't be another Brendan and he couldn't live with that fact. Meanwhile yours truly, the so-called Mad

Mick, started to make some running in the writing game as well, which caused him even more concern about his place in the pecking order. Can venom like this eat into a person so much that it even gives them cancer? I'm not sure. But you can see what a Pandora's Box Brendan opened by having the ill-fortune to put his name and ours on the unforgiving printing presses of the Western world. If he hadn't, I doubt if Dominic and myself would have fallen out. We would have been the same as all other brothers, going about our daily work without fuss, selling our souls on hard-hat sites or dead-end, white collar jobs, making other people rich as we ourselves propped up the bottom of the crude capitalistic ladder.

Writing this book has been an exorcism of sorts for me, in that it has dredged up some memories I thought I had forgotten, and put others into the kind of shape our lives only have in retrospect. Reading it you may labour under the misapprehension that I am a sorted-out individual, but this is far from the truth. I am gloriously confused by life and all its vicissitudes. And long may things continue that way.

All too often I've been regarded as an outrageous spokesman of the 'Looney Left'. Usually by people who are too lazy to hear me elaborate on some of my more eccentric ideas.

My flag will always stay red, but I don't want it stained with the blood of honest working men who are being exploited every which way by the state, women their own myopia. Not too long ago the Labour movement looked forward to a leisure society. They saw the march of the machine forever ending drudgery. The romantic view of labour is an infantile disorder, the right to work is a slogan fit only for slaves – the pitprop of capitalism. We must always remember that the great only appear great because we're lying down looking up. My vision is of a society where everybody is equal without some being more equal than others: the great post-Orwellian dream.

People accuse me of trying to be controversial for the sake of it, but that's not true. It just so happens that I hold strong views on many issues that seem to go against the grain of the majority. I don't see myself as left-wing or right-wing, as many have tried to label me. If you're looking for a way to describe me, perhaps 'evolutionary democrat' would do. It's certainly better than a revolutionary one. Too many people, I've noticed, get killed in revolutions.

I hold a dream of becoming Prime Minister. If I did, I would pay parents to stop their children becoming delinquents. Isn't this a more practical way to stem the crime epidemic than locking people up in buildings where they have little or no hope of rehabilitation – again at huge expense to the taxpayer? Brendan noted that on one wing of a prison he stayed in, 90 per cent of the inmates were illiterate. He was convinced an educational programme could help solve many of society's problems. When you consider that it costs as much to lock up a con as it does to stay in the Dorchester Hotel it doesn't make much sense to have nicks as human warehouses where people are turned out one door and in another.

Another matter I feel very strongly about is prostitution. I would take steps to legalise it, thus taking it out of the hands of pimps and middlemen and letting it be a contract between just two people, which is all it is anyway.

Last but not least, I would make sea-bathing compulsory. I say this because of the healing benefits of water, which I have been more than a witness to in my 72 years on the planet. Put me in Number 10 and I'll have my constituents drag all the whingers I can find out of every hospital ward and doctor's waiting room I can find. I would then plonk them on the nearest strand and await developments.

Having said all that, I feel that the gentleman currently occupying Downing Street is doing a marvellous job. I salute Tony Blair for brokering the Stormont Agreement, particularly when we still have people like Ian Paisley running round the place like a headless chicken screaming "No!" to every attempt at reconciling different traditions – and I know Brendan would share my opinions on this matter. If he were alive today he would be singing the praises of Bertie Ahern and Gerry Adams the way he once did Michael Collins. After the Good Friday Agreement was signed, Bertie told me he was glad to have the opportunity to let the IRA prisoners out of Portlaoise. I know what he meant. How many IRA men did I see coming back from England having served 20 to 30 years, and unable to adapt to civilian life? Burnt-out men like Ned Stapleton, who spent the rest of his life staring into an empty grate. As was the case with Brendan, Ned learned to his chagrin that not all imprisonment takes place within the walls of a cell.

Now as the Northern Assembly begins, Brendan's old heart will rejoice wherever it is. He once told me that he asked the Belfast brigade of the IRA to consider entering the House of Commons if they got an MP elected. He said it was the last place on earth the Unionists wanted to see them so it must be the first place they should seek to go. He called it "taking the war into the heart of the enemy". He was told that they had long passed such efforts, but look what the future turned up. He would he happy to see his prophecy fulfilled. In England he was asked about a united Ireland. "It was all the one country when I left," he declared.

So that's all I have to say to you. I hope you understand my family a little better for having read this. We've owned theatres, dressed them and acted in them. We have kept printers and reporters happy. Like the character in Joyce "we have lived so long and did so little harm". And perhaps a little good, though some would quibble with that. We have also, through Brendan, put our stamp on the oral tradition of dear, dirty Dublin – a city that still breathes with the ghosts he left wafting through its portals.

But we'll leave the last word to Beatrice, who had been with him through the whole pantomime that his life had been. "Years after his death," she said, "one almost expected him to step out of a taxi shouting, 'What's all this about? I'm not dead!'"

In later times, though, she contented herself in imagining him in some heavenly bar, chewing the fat with the likes of Shakespeare and Jonson and Marlowe. If not Joyce, Kavanagh and Flann O'Brien. Such an image gave her succour and helped her deal better with the fact that, after the mourners dispersed from Glasnevin cemetery on that overcast day in March 1964, our 'laughing boy' hadn't, like his young hero in *The Hostage*, leap out of his coffin to give us all a last bittersweet rendition of *The Bells of Hell*.

Index